THE
IDENTITY
OF
JESUS CHRIST

*The Hermeneutical Bases
of Dogmatic Theology*

BY

HANS W. FREI

Wipf and Stock Publishers
150 West Broadway • Eugene OR 97401

For
William A. Clebsch and David H. Kelsey

The Identity of Jesus Christ
by Hans W. Frei
Copyright©1997 by Geraldine Frei

ISBN: 1-57910-057-0

Reprinted by *Wipf and Stock Publishers*
150 West Broadway • Eugene OR 97401

CONTENTS

THE IDENTITY OF JESUS CHRIST

Part I
THE PROBLEM OF PRESENCE

Part 11
THE PROBLEM OF IDENTITY

Part 111
DISTORTIONS OF CHRIST'S IDENTITY

Part IV
THE NEW TESTAMENT DEPICTION OF JESUS CHRIST

Part V
THE PRESENCE OF CHRIST

EPILOGUE

INTRODUCTION

Hans Frei was not the most prolific of theological authors, his output pales in comparison to that of Barth, Tillich, or Rahner. Nevertheless, his impact on theology in the last half of the twentieth century is substantial, far our of proportion to the number of books that he published. Most are familiar with his influence on the Postliberal and Narrative theological movements. Frei's impact goes further than these two schools of thought. His particular theological challenges have forced sensitive thinkers to reconsider their appeals to universal religious experience. We can also thank Dr. Frei for much of the renewal in the study of Karl Barth's thought. Additionally, Frei's insistence on the priority of biblical narratives for Christian Theology is, ultimately, a gift that will serve well the Church that continues to look to be shaped by a faithful reading of scripture. We can think of no better gift than this.

As Publishers we feel very privileged to make available Hans Frei's *Identity of Jesus Christ* to the Christian and Academic communities.We are in debt to many people, first and foremost Geraldine Frei who has assisted in every step of this project. Our thanks also go to John Woolverton, Stanley Hauerwas, and George Hunsinger for their input and support.

We have decided to include Dr. Frei's essay *Theological Reflections on the Accounts of Jesus' Death and Resurrection* because it was Frei's own opinion that the essay went together with *Identity of Jesus Christ*; he felt that they were parallel books. It is our hope that the essay will fill out and compliment the rest of the book, providing insight into the intellectual history of Frei's project and clarity into the concept of identity.

Wipf and Stock Publishers

THEOLOGICAL REFLECTIONS ON THE ACCOUNTS
OF JESUS' DEATH AND RESURRECTION

The story told in the Gospels, which became the cornerstone of the Christian tradition of belief, is distinguished from other, parallel accounts by its urgent insistence that the story of salvation is completely and exclusively that of the savior Jesus from Nazareth in Galilee. This exclusiveness distinguishes the story both from ancient dying and rising savior myths and from a kind of story to which it is formally much closer: that of the Christ figures of some modern novels. The form of the Gospel story is sufficiently novel-like that we have to say that the pattern of redemptive action exhibited in Jesus is so identical with his personal story that he preempts the pattern. It is *his* story and cannot be reiterated in full by the story of anybody else—just as any particular person's story, whether fictional or real, is exclusively his own and not also that of somebody else.

The inextricable, mutual involvement of specific, unsubstitutable chains of events with equally specific individuals is a common feature of historical description and the narrative of the classical novel. (Beyond it there are of course great differences between the two.) However, in both instances, history as well as fiction, we meet with a problem of interpretation. Without some perspective of our own the story has no discernibly significant shape for us; but on the other hand we must not imprint either our own life problems or our own ideological analyses on it. The proper approach is to keep the tools of interpretive analysis as minimal and formal as possible, so that the character(s) and the narrative of events may emerge in their own right.

The significantly unique identity of an individual, in this instance Jesus of Nazareth, is to be discerned by asking (1) where the bond between intention and action in his story is most clearly evident; and (2) where the direct bond between himself as individual subject and his outward self-manifestation is strongest and most clearly unitary in character. The answer to both questions is in the crucifixion-resurrection

1

sequence. Here he is most of all himself in his unique and specific human identity as Jesus from Nazareth in Galilee. In this sense the story, whether fictional or historical, is quite clearly nonmythological. (Myths are stories in which character and action are not irreducibly themselves. Instead they are representative of broader and not directly representable psychic or cosmic states, states in some sense "transcending" the scene of finite, particular occurrences.)

The obvious implication of this claim is that if one is to make the mysterious and always problematical transition from literary description to judgments both of historical fact and of faith concerning this particular story and its significance, it is at this climactic point of Jesus' resurrection that one must do so. Similarly, the point of transition and connection between the person and teaching of Jesus in the Gospels and the "kerygma" concerning Jesus Christ and true life through him in the early church's faith, mirrored in the New Testament writings, can be none other than the story of the resurrection. A further implication— which I do not develop in argument—is that the resurrection must, in the eyes of those who believe, be a factual occurrence of a wholly unique kind, the conceptual content of which is the climactic establishment of Jesus' identity. This means that the resurrection events are not, in the first place, reducible to an ontological status allowing us to call them peculiarly "verbal" in contrast to "objective" or "factual" events (the position of Gerhard Ebeling).

Secondly, it goes almost without saying that the conceptual content of the resurrection, whether fictional or real, cannot be reduced to the faith of the disciples (the position of Rudolf Bultmann). Finally the resurrection cannot be reduced to a kind of occurrence, for the credibility of which historical evidence from the New Testament and from the experience of historical life in general would be pertinent. And, therefore, the character of the resurrection appearances cannot be compared and contrasted speculatively to that of other occurrences; e.g., we cannot say that they are more like visions than like experiences of a physical miracle, or vice versa (the position of Wolfhart Pannenberg).

I. THE DISTINCTIVE PATTERNS OF THE STORY OF JESUS

Gods were raised from the dead in liberal numbers in the ancient world, especially at the time of the birth of the Christian community. We ought to make clear to ourselves at the outset that the claim of the early Christians was in one sense, therefore, not all unique. Historians of religion often point out this fact, and its implication is obvious. If you have a very large number of candidates for the same unproved miraculous occurrence, the likelihood is that the claim of one is as good as that of the others, that it is none too good for any of them, and that for the *real* explanation of resurrection you had best look elsewhere—to the myth-forming, poetic, and religious yearning and imagination of ancient peoples.

Against this sort of argument Christian believers, searching their Bibles, find that they have no ace up their sleeve. Even the form of the particular resurrection story which lies at the heart of the New Testament Gospel may have certain parallels outside the Scripture, reducing its uniqueness even as a literary account, to say nothing of its unique factual claim. Yet we would be remiss if we did not also recognize that there are tenacious and often haunting qualities about the New Testament death and resurrection story concerning Jesus Christ which do not easily fit the patterns of other ancient accounts of dying and rising gods. The precise literary parallels would have to be demonstrated by those looking for them.

Caution in generalizing on this matter becomes the layman. However, it appears that there are at least two types of the "redeemed redeemer" motif in the religious syncretism of the era of late antiquity. There is the ritualistic, ecstatic participation in the dying and rising god of mystery religion. There is also the Gnostics' reflective, depth-introspective insight into the identity of the mythical, fallen archetypal man with the ascending mythical divine savior figure. I take it that the debate about the extent to which the Gnostic version of the redeemed redeemer motif is either typical of or original with the Gnostic is so far inconclusive. I assume further that there is some real question concerning the parallel between the phenomenon in both forms and the thoroughgoing, on the surface at least much more radical, application of the same or a similar motif to Jesus in the Gospels. I should want to raise the question at least if, for example, in the case of both Gnostic and mystery savior the relation between his fallen (dying) and his redeemed (rising) states is not much more natural and organic than it is when the motif is applied to Jesus Christ in the Gospels.

The Unique Descriptive Identity of Jesus

One thing is sure. The early Christians identified the mysterious, to most minds no more than halfway personal savior figure *exclusively* with Jesus of Nazareth, allowing no other name to be substituted. In two ways this claim was quite uncanny in their religious surroundings. First, as we have said, in this association of cosmic redeemer and human person they would allow no *human* substitute for Jesus. Secondly, they tended strongly to have the human person, Jesus, bestow identity upon the savior figure rather than the other way round (although we have to note that while the testimony of the New Testament is unanimous on the first point, it is not nearly so unambiguous on the second). The emphasis was on the confession that *Jesus is* the mysterious Lord of the cosmos. They emphasized this rather than the reverse, i.e., that everyone believes in the hope and reality of a cosmic redeemer and Jesus happens somehow to fit him or remind us of him.

People have often been converted against their own wills and most strenuous inclinations. Many of the New Testament writers had been either pagans or paganized, Hellenized Jews in origin. At times—I am thinking of Mark as well as the Pauline and Johannine writings—it seems almost as if the pagan cosmic savior figure or the Jewish Son of Man figure is still very vivid and real to the New Testament writers, and that they are still astounded by the fact that to think of him at all they now have to think of him as Jesus of Nazareth; yet so think of him they must. It was this exclusive identification that made Christianity more clearly than most others the religion of the "redeemed redeemer." In other religions the savior's having to be redeemed (he undergoes death) and himself doing the redeeming (we rise with him) easily merged into one process. Likewise it seems that the line which separated his bestowal of immortal divine salvation upon men from their achievement of it by their own insight—knowing him through a kind of mystical inward penetration rather than by meeting him in the occurrences of the world—was often very thin and blurred. A good many paths to salvation seem to have depended on first making and then overcoming such distinctions as these.

But in the case of the Gospels the figure of the cosmic redeemer was indeed so completely identified with the human being Jesus of Nazareth, and he in turn was so completely at one with his human brethren, that *he* the *savior* became just as helpless as they (a statement that must, however, be modified drastically in the case of the Gospel of John). There is no natural, organic transition from his need for redemption to his being redeemed. The divine figure suddenly stands before us without his divine power, especially as that power would affect himself. Indeed, there was truth in the sarcastic remark that he could bring salvation to others but not to himself.

The theme on which we are touching now is dangerous and has sometimes been driven to the point of a literalistic, simple-minded, speculative, and rather incredible heresy (i.e., that in the incarnation the Word of God divested himself deliberately and self-consciously of omnipotence over the world). But a heresy is often the sign that orthodoxy has sacrified the elements of mystery, and along with it tentativeness or open-endedness, to an oversimplified consistency. Jesus' followers in the early church did not doubt that the work of saving men was the work of omnipotence. But it is equally true and far more easily forgotten that they believed this power to be mysteriously congruent with Jesus' all too human helplessness and lack of power in the face of the terrible chain of events leading to his death, once that chain had begun to be wound around him. We find these two apparently contradictory tendencies converging in the gospel narrative. To make them harmonious by means of an explanation or theory of Jesus' passion would be very difficult indeed; but in the story—the descriptive and interpretive retelling of the events—they fit together naturally and easily. We are given hints of his abiding power, of the abiding initiative that remains in his hands even at the moments when he is most evidently helpless, when acted upon rather than agent. But his helplessness is at least equally manifest and genuine. The two are never merged; one may say both that they coexist as well as that there is a transition through circumstances from one to the other.

However, it is easy to exaggerate the contrast between Jesus' power and his powerlessness, so that before long he appears to be nothing more than the human point of coordination where these two contrasting qualities (and any two others for that matter, e.g., love and wrath) come together. He is then seen as the embodiment of paradox—an affirmation which has often been made by theologians and in a different way by modern novelists who have been preoccupied with this figure. But that way lie lifelessness and the dehydration of any man's humanity. For a man's being is not the juxtaposition of characteristics or sets of qualities, contrasted or otherwise, that become embodied in him. A man's being is the unique and peculiar way in which he himself holds together the qualities which he embodies—or rather, the qualities which he is.

Modern scholars have told us rather convincingly that we do not know much about the "historical Jesus" who stands behind the gospel portraits of him. Nevertheless, the descriptions themselves as descriptions, whatever we may or may not be able to conclude about the "real" man in back of them, surely portray something profoundly human in at least one respect. They are the portrait of a person and not of a series of characteristics or changing circumstances, paradoxically or otherwise related and held together in one (of necessity) by a person-figure. If there is the paradoxical embodiment of contrasted qualities about him and his experience in the portrait, they are held together because they are *his*. As he is sketched out in the gospel accounts, he holds these contrasts together, not they him. That is why the word "paradox" ought at least to be used with caution in reference to the personal being of Jesus of Nazareth, and why this warning was necessary even with regard to our own description, seeing that we had drawn attention to one such basic "paradoxical" contrast between power and powerlessness.

When we speak of the contrast of power and powerlessness in Jesus as he is depicted in the Gospels, we have in mind then no mere paradox, tension or transition between two states, qualities, or elements in a cosmic, spiritual power struggle. Rather, we have in mind the mystery and the changing situation of a human being whose consistent intention is also portrayed as that of his and the universe's God: the accomplishment of men's salvation. For that reason the contrast and its holding together are best expressed in terms of the quality of love in his relation to his fellow men. But we must stress that the quality is not simply and directly predominant over all other characteristics that we may see together with it.

The unity of his personal being depicted in the Gospels, we are saying, is not to be seen directly, by adumbrating the personal excellences discernible in him and then choosing that most noticeable in comparison to the others as the first. That unity is seen more nearly indirectly as the shaping of all his personal qualities in conformation to his mission or aspiration in obedience to God. In this sense love to men governed his life. In this respect his intention was, as far as the portraits show him to us, wholly assimilated to the intention of his heavenly Father who, in the words of the fourth Gospel's commentary on the story of Jesus, "so loved the world that he gave his only son" (John 3: 16). It may not be too bold to say, though we have no warrant for it by direct instance from the gospel stories, that in the service of this love Jesus was willing to govern and exercise the power appropriate to it, just as he was willing for its sake to be governed and suffer helplessly when the occasion demanded.

In other words, the coexistence as well as the transition between power and powerlessness, of which we have spoken, are ordered by the single-minded intention of Jesus to enact the good of men on their behalf in obedience to God. It is he who holds and orders all his qualities, and he, insofar as his single-minded intention is his being or his identity, who orders the situation about him as it affects him. In short, he makes his power and his powerlessness congruent to each other.

The Failure of the "Christ Figure"

There has been one particularly interesting result of the modern and direct (in contrast to the Gospels' more nearly indirect) identification of the mission or intention with the personal character of Jesus as love, an identification that has resulted in the elevation of love over every other personal virtue in him as *the* single excellence of his character. The result has been a simplistic overdrawing, frequently pressing all too close upon the mysteriousness of the figure of Jesus who, after all, does not, in the portraiture of the Gospels, come provided with a single clue to unlock his character, not even with a clear-cut predominance of love deportment.

The resultant direct characterization distorts and exaggerates the modern writer's refracted picture. It is often quite right—yet it is simplistic and doctrinaire. Modern writers, especially novelists, have often discerned the well-nigh modern personal and historical vividness of the original man in his portrait (in contrast to so much unhistorical, not genuinely personal ancient writing).[1] Hence, writers of this century have taken Jesus to be the paradigm of humanity more than other ancient fictional figures except perhaps Odysseus or Oedipus and more than other ancient historical personages.

But they tend to forget that love as mission and as sole personal deportment or virtue is not identically and without differentiation the same thing. They forget, furthermore (or wish they could forget), that there are stylized elements in the original accounts that cannot be ignored. The conceptions of the savior figure, eternal life, sacrifice, God, miracle, and salvation are intrinsic to the original accounts. Modern writers by contrast (and perfectly correctly) take only the historical, personal, and not the stylized elements of the story. That is, after all, what the character of a novel demands. They see the intention and the personal character of a wholly personal love, and they make these the clue to a character-in-action description. The result is often ironic. For now we get, in the name of flesh-and-blood life and in protest against conceptual stylization, a stylized and stereotyped figure whom critics can then label with the rather awful and by now tired term, "Christ figure." It is sufficiently stereotyped and artificial that it often comes to life only if, in addition to its obvious mirroring of Jesus, there are some important details in which the figure comes into its own, either in contrast to or at least in deviation from the portrait of Jesus.

Many times, however, there is something artificial and predictable about the prefashioned qualities or states of potential conflict in character and historical circumstances, both within the savior figure and between him and his environment, which are put together in order

---

1. On this point as it affects style of presentation, see Erich Auerbach, *Mimesis* (Princeton: Princeton University Press, 1953), ch. 2.

compositely to produce a saving man—in the literature from Victor Hugo's *Les Misérables* and Dostoievsky's *The Idiot* to the defeated yet conquering, shameful yet pure heroes of Graham Greene's and François Mauriac's novels. The savior figure here becomes unwittingly and ironically stylized, even though the intention is evidently just the opposite— to rescue him as far as possible from ancient stylization and to invest him with a fully personal dimension. In the wake of this stylization of a human, personal figure (rather than an ancient savior figure) there seems often to be an empty place—a purely passive, *vague lacuna* exactly at the point where (in a genuine human being) one expects to find the focus, centeredness, and capacity both for initiative and receptivity which breathe life into the virtues and qualities of his humanity.

While theologians were engaged in trying to restate the uniqueness of the New Testament savior in terms other than the "mythological" ones of the original sources, novelists were doing the same. Writers of fiction have attempted to find a modern and personal equivalent to ancient stylization and miracle about Jesus. They have done this by trying to show that utterly contrasted qualities, situations, and perspectives come to focus on this figure, whether in conflict or in harmony. *Here,* they have suggested, such conflicts and contrasts (e.g., murder and innocence or purity) which usually remain unresolved, can be shown to cohere in poignantly, indeed exemplarily lifelike fashion. This coherence of clashing elements in or about the personal being and/or fate of the savior figure has been the modern substitute for the ancient concept of miracle and for that contrast between the ordinary and the unique which miracle implies.

Thus modern novelists indicate the veiled coherence of his authority with his helplessness as these are manifest especially in his stance in the presence of religious (and other) viciousness, power, and hypocrisy. The savior figure mysteriously combines rebellion against constituted authority (showing it up for a brutal fraud and along with it a good many ordinarily decent standards) with great and selfless goodness, the prime quality of all self-sacrificing, absolute love.

The combination of rebellion with pure selflessness usually means some routs of opposition to prevalent authority and evil other than that of violence, even though there are times when the latter is involved. But even then there is about this violence often a kind of primordial innocence, so that the basic purity of the figure remains untouched by it. (Yet even this must be modified. At times he combines utter goodness with full guilt—an especially appealing way of portraying miracle or the paradox which the savior unites.) Ordinarily, however, he combines innocence, even ignorance, with wisdom and sensitivity. He manifests and embodies sheer purity in such a way that, paradoxically, it is of greater comfort to those who are themselves soiled than to those who are or at any rate seek to be too much like him. (Thus he is, as the church's Lord, taken to be among those outside rather than with those inside the fold.) So he is invariably more nearly at home in soiled, broken, and vitiated rather than conventional communities; he is almost invariably anti-bourgeois; he is in the demi-monde rather than in the family (which, together with constituted authority, is one of the savior's most persistent, evil, and hypocritical opponents—most often in the form of marriage partner or parent). Additionally, however, one often finds that he is present in all communities, good or evil, ordinary or extraordinary, as a visitor and stranger from elsewhere.

The refracted portrait usually draws attention to his hidden intention to manifest and embody love, utterly without obsessive possessiveness and therefore usually willing to suffer painfully and passively in the face of rejection. It is an intention that is never self-advertised and yet steadily seeks the good of the other person; but—and the point is important—the intention is content to remain consistently veiled, or at least half veiled, ambiguous, and defeated in the man's lifetime, never quite discernible though always nearly so. Hints of the mystery break through, but they are clearly apprehended (with pain and sometimes with healing, sorrowing relief) only after his apparently futile death. Indeed all that he is and does come to focus in this final denouement and in our retrospective glance from and toward it.

After that climatic event, which he must risk totally without comfort not only in its terror but also in its possible futility, the waters of the tide of events close once again over the whole episode, as they do over all things historical—leaving the situation at one and the same time just as it was before, ambiguous and with evil to the fore, and yet wholly different, with a moment of truth now unveiled and with meaning newly enhanced in the consciousness of some participant character(s) and/or the reader. It is always too late and yet not too late in the world of time, so that futility and victory now join together in this transition from the figure's denouement to the new consciousness within and beyond the confines of the fictional world. He conquers, yet he does not conquer because he is defeated. But if he conquers it is by virtue of the fact that his victory is veiledly identical with his defeat. It is the victory and defeat of love.

It is not only the heroes of modern fiction, in their veiled, unadvertised, and unadvertising intention to seek the good of others (often looking like its very opposite), who correspond to this refracted portrait. In their very anonymity, serving Christ secretly or as outsiders because that is the only way to serve him with passionate disinterest in the distorted yet pitiable world, some recent historical figures have echoed and embodied that same portrait in the eyes of many people: for example, Søren Kierkegaard (in at least one stage of his life) in the last century; Simone Weil and Dag Hammarskjöld, in this.

Who would not be able to hear the echo of the original story in these elements of its reiteration? To many a convinced Christian this reiteration is indeed by far the most convincing argument for Christianity—far greater than theoretical argument, sacrament, and proclamation (granted that these various things may "convince" concerning different matters). Yet the portrayal of this intention, the mysterious and self-sacrificing enactment of men's good on their behalf, is bound to depart from the New Testament story in various ways. The main clue to that fact lies in the reversal to which I have already pointed. There are elements in the New Testament which are cast into ancient, stylized thought patterns (Jesus as the fulfillment of the figure of the cosmic savior, the redeemer of Israel, miracles, etc.) and are therefore bound to look mythological to the modern reader. Jesus does indeed, in the New Testament, bestow in a most startling manner a human, personal identity upon the stylized savior notion. But the latter element does and must remain part of the original; otherwise we simply do not have the New Testament portrait of Jesus as the Christ (to borrow Paul Tillich's phrase).

To try to historicize these stylized concepts is obviously impossible for the modern fiction writer. But his own consequent reversal is equally unfortunate. He transfers the intent of the stylized element to the personal, historical description and tries to indicate by means of the mysterious coincidence of clashing elements in personal encounters (victory with defeat, purity vicariously present to impurity, guilt with goodness, etc.) the miraculous ingredient at the heart of the figure, corresponding to the stylized element in the original account. The result is the predictable pattern of a savior figure whose person and history are the embodiment of pre-established opposite human or personal qualities. The result in other words is a stylization of the humanity of Jesus through the juxtaposition of predictably contrasting predicates (contrasting either within himself, or between himself and his context). They have, at their juncture or point of coordination, a subject who is hardly a subject in his own right and therefore cannot hold the predicates as his own. In short we have a modern equivalent of the ancient denial of Jesus' humanity in the Christ-figure motif.

In the Gospels, on the other hand, the stylized elements are there, but they do not overcome the concreteness of the man portrayed. He is, as we have suggested, not simply the coincidence of those opposites that come together in and about him, nor is his saving activity a function of their coincidence. His saving activity, though nothing without his enactment of it in his and his people's circumstances, is in one sense prior to these circumstances and even to the qualities which he comes to embody. He *intends* the enactment of his saving love, and he consents to its defeat. And in harmony with his intention, his power as well as his helplessness take shape in appropriate response to varying circumstance. It is *he* who holds the pattern, including that of opposite, together, not they him—not even love as the most dominant quality, which would tie itself and its opposite into one.

The point is to be made, then, that if one identifies the savior figure with a fully human being, the story cannot be retold by substituting somebody else as its hero who is then made to be fully identical with that original person. No matter who the savior may be, if he is a person, once the identification is made he is *that* person and no one else.

This must be especially true for that type of fiction which owes so much to the gospel stories in the first place—the novel and the short story—for which a personal figure is unique, particular, and unsubstitutable within his equally unique and unsubstitutable circumstances. If such fiction is to remind us of Jesus and tell us his story over again, it must remind us by some other unique, particular person's or people's identity and story. And to do that means that in the very likeness of the mirrored story to the original, the concrete, specifying *difference* will have to stand out as clearly as the similarity, so that that other person will have his own individuality and not simply echo Jesus. But when I say "difference" I do not mean "absolute contrast"; for the story and its refractions being what they are in their mysterious combination of opposites, the absolute contrast to Jesus very often comes, in the hands of modern writers, to look suspiciously like total identity (e.g., in the recurrent modern celebration of the coincidence or paradoxical identity of total sinfulness and total loving goodness).

The particular story of Jesus, then, is pre-empted by him and him alone. Only those refractions of it will be credible and concrete that do not seek to reiterate it completely but only in part, not from too close by but at a distance, in the figure of a disciple rather than in the cosmic, miraculous, and abysmal destiny of the original. Such stories may be more ordinary and less profound, but on the other hand they may have a credibility and authenticity of their own which may well be deeply convincing aesthetically as well as religiously. (One thinks of a book like Alan Paton's *Cry The Beloved Country.*)

The Central Enactment of Jesus' Identity

In the story of Jesus we recall his transition from initiative to increasing passivity in the face of circumstances, beginning with the scene in the garden of Gethsemane. It may be fruitful to add to this an instance (recorded as taking place immediately afterwards) that not only points in a like direction but actually perfects the previous instance. In the Matthean version of the passion story Jesus reminds an ardent partisan, who would defend him, that he himself could pray to his Father, and more than twelve legions of angels would come to his aid: "But how then should the scriptures be fulfilled, that it must be so?" (Mt. 26: 54). There was indeed the envisagement of a possibility of his own salvation. But it was envisaged only to be rejected decisively, in this transition from power to powerlessness. What we have in the story of Jesus' arrest is the external parallel, or more correctly the enactment of the same transition which had taken place, just before this, on the inner plane, in Jesus' prayers in the Garden of Gethsemane. Both of these instances in their very unity point up the fact that there is an inner and outer, yet unitary, fine point of transition when an intention is being carried into action—a point where a free resolve initiates and at the same time meshes into a chain of circumstances which, once started, cannot then be reversed. Jesus is the unity of this intention-action pattern which is particularly and uniquely his own.

What is a man? What we learn from the New Testament about this question is in part gained from its portrayal of the man Jesus of Nazareth. A man—in this instance the fully human savior who, by his action peculiar to himself, bestows a particular human identity upon the mythological savior figure—is what he *does* uniquely, the way no one else does it. It may be that this is action over a lifetime, or at some climactic moment, or both. When we see something of that sort, especially if we see it at some climactic stage which recapitulates a long span in a man's life—when we see the loyalty of a lifetime consummated at one particular point, but even if we see several hitherto ambiguous strands in his character pruned and ordered in a clear and decisive way at that point—then we are apt to say: "Here he was most of all himself."

In that kind of passage from free intention into action, ordering the two (intention and act) into one harmony, a free man gains his being. He becomes what he is; he gains his identity. Something like this seems also to be the portrayal of Jesus in the Gospels. Jesus, in this portrayal, was most of all himself in the short and climactic sequence of his public ministry, rising to this resolve and this entry into the situation of helplessness. We must, above all, not abstract one from the other: as if, in the

New Testament, the event of the crucifixion were anything without Jesus' resolve, or the resolve anything without the event in which it took concrete shape! In his general intention to enact, in obedience to God, the good of men on their behalf, and at the crucial juncture in his specific resolve to do so if necessary in this terrifying way—and in the event in which this intention and resolve were enacted—Jesus was most of all himself in the description of the Gospels. This was his identity. He was what he did and underwent: the crucified human savior.

We now enter into the most puzzling portion of the New Testament report concerning Jesus Christ. He was raised, it is said, from the dead. We have noted the theme of tension between the power and helplessness of Jesus in the testimony of the synoptic Gospels. Obviously the theme rises to a climax now. The redeemer himself, we have said, stands in need of redemption. Indeed it is by his fitting his intention to such radical participation in this our need that he is said to save us. But is he himself redeemed? If the answer has to be that he is not, then how is his failure of redemption to avail as salvation for us? The question has been raised, implicitly and explicitly, by modern writers, theological as well as fictional. The answer often seems to be that the sacrifice of the Messiah is in itself sufficient for us. In his very failure of redemption, voluntarily assumed, he saves us. The crucifixion in that case is the *event* of which the resurrection is the *meaning*

Whatever may be the case in the independent or refracted modern stories of Christ figures, the story of Jesus is that of the redeemer both in need of redemption and yet also in fact redeemed from death and the power of evil. No matter, then, how much the ancient authors may share our own modern difficulty in making the transition from death to resurrection, they do trace it perfectly naturally under the conviction that this transition is not one from a personal account of a man's death to its stylized or mythical religious application (the naming of an immortal savior figure), but rather that the one who died is the same one who is risen. *The identity of the crucified Jesus and that of the risen Lord are one and the same in the accounts.* This is the important theme that we must now pursue.

Apart from our long inherited and incredibly yet so casually anthropocentric outlook, it is indeed an astonishing thing that the cosmic, immortal redeemer figure should be not mirrored by but identified completely with a human being of particular historical identity. Quite likely it was as astounding to the original authors and the little community from which they emerged as it is to any of us —if not more so.

II. FORMAL ELEMENTS OF IDENTITY DESCRIPTION

But what is the import of speaking of the "identity" of the crucified Jesus with the risen Lord? And what is it to have or to be an "unsubstitutable identity"? It is certainly not a self-evident notion. We face a dilemma as we now raise the question of its nature. On the one hand we ought not to apply a modern notion too precisely, for fear of pressing foreign thoughts onto what we find in the Gospels. On the other hand we must approach the Gospels with some conceptual tool in hand, otherwise we understand nothing at all. To say that this dilemma presents a "small" problem may seem to be a gross understatement. It has, in fact, become the topic of one of the most persistent discussions among Biblical exegetes and theologians in our day. But in a certain sense theologians have to proceed in piecemeal fashion, confronting one problem or question at a time. In doing so they must be careful not to foreclose other issues which are not at that point up for consideration. This seems a better procedure than the endeavor to reduce all questions in theology to a basic systematic position which can then be applied ready-made to any and all problems that come along. For that reason the dilemma just mentioned, the necessity and yet the distortion of approaching the interpretation of the Bible with conceptual tools in hand, while it may in itself be an important one, does not loom large in our present context.[2] We are concerned with other matters. Let us simply try to leave our description of "identity" sufficiently loose and minimal, so that the conceptual device may not overwhelm the subject matter to which it is to be applied, understanding the account of the resurrected Jesus Christ.

My thesis, already touched upon, will be that the development of the gospel story is such that Jesus' identity as the singular, unsubstitutable human individual that he is comes to its sharpest focus in the death-and-resurrection sequence taken as one unbroken sequence. Therefore, no matter what one may believe about the possibility or impossibility, factuality or nonfactuality of his resurrection, the story of that resurrection is literarily not of the type of a mythological tale. For surely in such tales, unsubstitutable personal identity developed in interaction with equally unsubstitutable transpiring does not constitute a significant theme. Comparison of the Gospels with various types of literary forms, ancient and modern, is always a problematical business. But if one is to do it, it seems that this drastic focusing of Jesus' unsubstitutable identity in the crucifixion-resurrection sequence makes this part of the story not

---

2. See the excursus on hermeneutics, etc., at the end of this essay for some remarks on the issue.

a mythological tale but something much more like the realistic novel (despite certain problems in this parallel which we have already discussed). For this type of literature depicts the plausibility of character and situation in their interaction precisely by means of the singularity or unsubstitutability of both. I do not mean to imply that the Gospels are throughout more nearly like the novel than any other form of ancient or modern literature. I am speaking only of an aspect of the passion-resurrection sequence. Obviously there are also other elements, e.g., tragic and epic motifs, about the Gospel story as a whole and the passion narrative in particular. I assume there is general agreement that it is difficult and even undesirable to reduce the Gospel story by formal analysis to any one type of literature, even if it should be that of a divine comedy.

Obviously my analysis of identity will be shaped toward the claim that Jesus' identity is most sharply focused in the passion-resurrection narrative sequence. I may hope that the concept of identity can be significantly and appropriately applied to the contents of that claim, without being narrowly dictated by it. Respect for the integrity of the New Testament text and for the conceptual tools of interpretation as well as their mutual appropriateness is the obvious aim in such a conceptual analysis and its application to the text. The concept of identity will involve, both in general and in regard to the Gospels in particular, an affirmation that the singular and true identity of a person is mysteriously and yet significantly manifest and therefore accessible, rather than being a remote and ineffable, unknown quantity. I shall affirm that this significant, singular human identity is, in the case of the gospel narrative about Jesus, both most fully focused and therefore most fully accessible to the reader in the passion-resurrection sequence. As a character in a story we know him far better here than in the earlier parts of the story. Whatever judgments one may wish to make about the veracity and significance of this sequence in the accounts, beyond such strictly literary judgments concerning Jesus' place and accessibility within the narrative, constitute a wholly different problem on which I shall touch briefly in conclusion.

"Identity" is obviously a highly personal term, applied to non-personal beings, alive or unalive, only by transfer. Identity is essentially the action and testimony of a personal being by which he lays true claim to being himself and the same at an important point as well as over a length of time. It is personal in the sense that it involves, in order to be at its most typical, the recollection or memory of one's intercourse with others as well as oneself and the willingness to accept responsibility for actions in which one's own intentions have played a prime part.

There is something essentially circular about such terms as "identity." Whenever we try to describe them we find, as Augustine did about time, that they are elusive, known, and yet not easily describable, because their use seems to involve constant reference to themselves as already in use, rather than to something else in terms of which they may be described. Expressive of this situation is the habit from which we all find it so difficult to depart, even though most of us admit its wrongheadedness. The self, we say, is not a thing among other things, a second substantial but not physical existent together with the body and causally related to it. We have been taught this negative conclusion firmly by modern philosophers all the way from the post-Kantian idealists to Gilbert Ryle. Still, the old doctrine, the "official doctrine" Ryle calls it, is tempting. For it refers the self to a larger class of knowables ("substances"), i.e., to a genus inclusive of specific differences. As a result it seems to avoid (whether it does so in fact is another matter) that hidden or open circularity which so often makes the upshot of modern philosophical reflection about the self look either banal or else esoteric to the point of unintelligibility.

In this awkward situation, and before we go on, I should like to offer four brief methodological comments.

1. It may well be that self description necessarily involves the use of analogies, one analogy always qualifying another. The traditional dualism of body and soul, particularly the concept of a soul, probably involves such an analogical situation; so may a certain social view of the self, in terms of which the unity of the self is a complex one, at least articulated if not actually conceived after the fashion of an absolutely irreducible "other" who becomes my listener or judge standing over against me, but from within. But the usefulness at least of the first pair hinges on the meaning of the term "substance," the traditional common term applicable to both "soul" and "body." Whatever is meant by it, it cannot have a purely univocal meaning derived by inference from sense experience. (I should add that in what follows, analogy is once or twice drawn upon, but I shall not use it as a systematic instrument or particular type of self description.)

2. The use of polar or dialectical description may be useful in self description. That is to say, circularity may at least be postponed, though perhaps not at last avoided, by describing the central term, the self, by means of an unabstractable relation between two different terms, in fact by referring each term finally to the other. Thus, as we shall reiterate in a few moments, an action is an explicit intention, an intention an implicit action, and the self is to be described as each and yet one and the same in the unity of the two.

3. Most important in the present context is the fact that we shall confine ourselves to self *description*. This is different from a metaphysical explanation. Confinement to description allows for possible alternative descriptions of the same data (rather than the claim that these are additional data not accounted for in the first description), without covering all of the *descriptions* under an inclusive superdescription. Metaphysical explanation, I take it, must account not only for all the data but must also include all the descriptions in one scheme. Without wishing to prejudice the latter possibility, I would want to say that the substitution of self-description for self-explanation, which really had its philosophical beginnings with Kant's distinction between the noumenal and phenomenal perspectives upon the self, is extremely helpful to the theologian who wants to use philosophical concepts for relatively modest, descriptive purposes, and for whom a certain degree of flexibility in regard to self description is about all he asks of philosophers.

4. The enterprise of description instead of explanation does not, it seems to me, preclude the possibility of some weak, systematic connection or even a variety of possible connections, *between* descriptions. "Weak" means simply that the connective principle cannot serve as a central clue for the construction of the type of supertheory to which reference was just made. Moreover, the presence or absence of such a link is not sufficient either to establish or damage the possibility of the simultaneous or rather alternating use of the several descriptions. I believe that a polar or dialectical relation between descriptive terms may obtain not only within one description but among descriptions. However, I am not at all sure that the point is of great importance. As long as two alternative descriptions do not conflict, there is really no need that one maintain a connection between them.

Intention-Action Description

One characteristic of self descriptions under the consensus that the self is not a private mental thing inside the body, a "ghost in the machine," that the "paramechanical" like the "pare-political" myth of the self ought to be abandoned,[3] is the one just referred to—their polarity. It is also a feature of the first of our descriptions, intention-action description of the self's identity. We referred to this earlier when we said

---

3. Gilbert Ryle, *The Concept of Mind* (New York: Barnes & Noble, 1962), p. 23.

that one way to know a person's identity is to know his typical action. So when we say of him in a certain situation, doing and undergoing certain specific things, "Here he was most of all himself," we identify him by these occurrences. To know a person's identity in this specific context involves the total coincidence, nay unity, of abstract defining virtues or qualities with the specific way they are being held together in and by an individual and enacted by him. His style of action and expression is himself. To say of an individual that the relation between his *ousia* (the "what" of him) and his *hypostasis (that* he is) is accidental for purposes of formal description, that one (at least the first) may be describable without the other, and that the second adds nothing to the defining knowledge of the first—to say all this is not only existentially but analytically unenlightening in the context of this description. The strong link between a person's continuing centeredness in himself on the one hand and his personal qualities, changing bodily structure, and overt activity in both physical and social contexts on the other is so tough and organic that it is perfectly proper to describe *what* a person is by what he *does,* and *who* he is by what he is and does.

A description of a human act may be exhaustive in each of two ways, psychophysical and intentional. However, the intentional description does not have either antiphysical or antisocial bias. Indeed, the matter must be put more strongly. Such description must be bodily and social description from an intentional perspective. As some of the phenomenologists have reminded us, the body is at once—and under different descriptions—the link *between* the self and the public world and the intentional self in, or enacted in, the public world. Knowledge of my own intention and its transition into action is immediate rather than inferential, and the description I give of it seeks to be a description of that passage. Knowledge of another's action is less immediate. But even it cannot be said to be simply inferential or analogical (I don't want to linger long in the large arena of arguments about the knowledge of one's own and others' intentions), if the connection between intention and action is strong and direct rather than inferential and remote. The kind of knowledge we have of the intention of an agent with whose activity we actually have to deal is often as much like the knowledge one has of a character in a story as it is like the inferential and analogical understanding by which the historian reconstructs persons' intentions from their public actions and sayings.

The *desideratum* of self description, certainly not always possible to reach, is the description of intention-with-action-in-public. But where it is incomplete we still describe it by this norm. And the relation between the two terms in such description is inescapably polar. To describe an occurrence as an action I must describe it as explicit intention; to describe an intention as just that and not as a putative mental "thing," I must describe it as an implicit action. In this description it is a distortion to treat the "act" of intending as having a separable, self-sufficient mental location ("to perform intelligently is to do one thing and not two things"),[4] but it is equally incorrect to eliminate intention by reducing it to a function(or even no function) of physical behavior.

In a limited sense the latter reduction is indeed more viable than the former. For it may well be possible to give an exhaustive behavioral description of any and all acts, including intentional ones, while it is impossible to describe all physical or social behavior exhaustively as intentional action. But this does not alter the fact that some occurrences may be given exhaustive description under either perspective, so that in such cases the claim that one kind of description is improper is simply inaccurate.

Who a person is, is first of all given in the development of a consistent set of intentions embodied in corporeal and social activity within the public world in which one functions. When a person's intentions and actions are most nearly conformed to each other—and further when an intention-action combination in which he plays a part is not merely peripheral to him but is of crucial importance, involving his full power in a task—then a person gains his identity. A person's identity is constituted (not simply illustrated) by that intention which he carries into action. If we look for the kind of description to do justice to this perspective, we must look to self-knowledge (perhaps simultaneously also to knowledge of others, but I am not at all certain of the degree to which this is true) and to the kind of illumination on the passage of intention into action and the interrelation of character with circumstances that we get in a novel or a short story. Henry James wrote, "What is character but the determination of incident? What is incident but the illustration of character?"[5] As for the historian, he does many things. Whether and to what extent, when he deals with the person of a given individual who is known only from a given set of peculiarly slanted documents, he deals with him in the same way as the self (and perhaps other-self) describing agent and the novelist or dramatist, I want to leave as an open question in this context.[6]

4.*Ibid. p.* 40.
5.Quoted in S. Garnet, M. Berman, and W. Burto, eds., *Aspects of the Drama* (Boston: Little, Brown and Company, 1962), p. 242.

Description of the Ascriptive Subject

But now what of that "I," the "index word" Ryle calls it,[7] which serves to indicate that *to which* both states of consciousness and physical characteristics are ascribed,[8] the *ascriptive* center or focus of intentional activity? No doubt it was this, whatever it is or whatever we may hope to say of it, which was the metaphysician's hoped for "subsistent substance" and the ontologist's hoped for "subject."

The fascination of it lies in its *ultimacy,* its *elusiveness,* and its *persistence.*

1. It is ultimate, for states and qualities are predicated of it; but it is itself unpredicable of anything else. But it is not ultimate in the sense that reference to it involves a self-description more basic and inclusive than intention-action description. To say that one is engaged in describing the self under a subject-predicate scheme obviously forces one to go on to say that the subject is "ultimate" in relation to its predicate. But it does not of itself support the claim that the subject-predicate scheme gets at something more "basic" about the self than does a description of the self under an intention-action scheme.

2. The "I" is elusive and elusively "now," for—to put it with Ryle—"a higher order action (i.e., concerning oneself about oneself as one would with another, an action analogous to that of a reviewer who reviews book reviews instead of books) cannot be the action upon which it is performed. So my commentary on my performances must always be silent about one performance, namely itself, and this performance can be the target only of another commentary."[9] This is obviously another way of stating Kant's distinction between noumenal (subject) and phenomenal (object) self description, except that it does not involve Kant's judgment that the subject is the reality of which the object is the appearance.

6.In these reflections, constituting section I of this larger section on "Identity," I have been helped by the analysis of Robert H. King in his unpublished doctoral dissertation, "The Concept of Personal Agency as a Theological Model" (Yale University, 1965), ch. I, and (in the last paragraph) by a formulation of my own suggestions by John C. Robertson, Jr. See also R. H. King, "The Concept of the Person," *The Journal of Religion,* XLVI (January 1966), pp. 37, 44.

7.Ryle, p. 188.
8.Cf. P. F. Strawson, *Individuals* (New York: Doubleday, 1963), p. 84.
9.Ryle, p. 195.

3. It is persistent, though the way this persistence is rightly to be claimed has always been a matter of great difficulty. It has often seemed that one could elucidate it only by sacrificing the articulation of the reality of change in the self, i.e., the reality of those specific qualities, states and actions of its own which modify the self itself and by means of which it is directly immanent in the public domain. Conversely, it was often assumed that insistence on such concrete and specific predicates and acts loosened our grasp on the subject's persistence to the point of its disappearance.

In respect of persistence (and probably of elusiveness also), self-description as the description of the unity of intention and action is notably weak. For if intention-action is one and the intention is the action-as-purposed and not an inferred, independent, mental action, it is hard to see how intending in a given case can be understood to be any more perduring than action, which, ideally speaking (if we take Aristotle's description of the drama as a model or heuristic ideal), has a beginning, a middle, and an end. Indeed, intention-action description is usually description of the self's enactment in a completed act. But the intenderactor knows perfectly well—whatever the conceptual difficulties—that he is anterior to that beginning and subsequent to that end, that the action is his qua enduring subject. If the description cannot take that persistence into account, we do not say, "so much the worse for the idea of persistence," but, "so much the worse for the description." Despite the obloquy positivists heap upon anything savoring of introspection, it seems safe to go further yet and say that the intender-actor knows himself to be anterior and subsequent to each intention-action in a way that he does not know that he is anterior and subsequent to himself. There is indeed such a thing, in part through self-ascription and in part through other-ascription (at least for some modern philosophers the two seem to go together without reducing either or both to behavior description),[10] as knowledge of the self as at least a limited persistent. Surely nobody would want to adopt a position that denies the possibility of biography or autobiography, or that makes accounting for them a strenuously complex business. I have argued in this paragraph that even though intention-action description may describe the identity of a person exhaustively, it is in a sense open-ended, for it points to the possibility or need of another (though perhaps more difficult) description of the same identity or the same basic data. It is this open-endedness which involves the possibility of a weak, systematic connection between them of which I spoke earlier. I stress, however, that neither

---

10.Strawson, p. 96.

description depends for its validity on this weak systematic connection with the other. Description of the ascriptive subject (if it can be undertaken) is not that of his completed action but of his ongoing, open-ended persistence in continuity with himself.

We have claimed that the self may be known as limited persistent but have said nothing so far about the description under which it is so known, if such is to be a knowing at all. "Knowledge" would be largely though perhaps not wholly empty if it did not involve describability. But is there in fact a description of the subject of ascription in its ultimacy, elusiveness, and persistence? Or does its elusiveness, its subjectivity, which defies "objectification" of itself, deny such an ambition? It is useful to stress again that description is a modest endeavor, involving no supertheory of what is "most real" about the self, or what description is most inclusive. For the temptation to do these things is obviously greatest when we speak of the self as subject of ascription. It must further be reaffirmed that (equally obviously) the description of the self as ascriptive subject must indeed be more elusive and indirect than that of intention-action description which holds firmly to the self as publicly enacted. The description of the ascriptive subject cannot do this in a simple, straightforward manner. But on the other hand ascriptive subject description is not merely description by inference from public to purely private data, nor ought we to suppose that there is a total lack of resemblance between the specific data of the two types of description.

Congruence between the two kinds of description means not only a parallel in descriptive method but a cross reference between their descriptive contents. But this cross reference is based on the unitariness of the self and is not simply descriptively locatable. We do not have the superdescription which would integrate the contents and descriptions. Some sort of analogical scheme of concepts seems inevitable here. There is then a certain justification for using expressions like "verbal occurrence," "performatory utterance," or "verbal action" and (conversely) "bodily speech." But such phrases get their meaning from that complex unity of data and descriptions which, in the absence of a metaphysical theory, I want to leave alone. That only would be the final justification (if one is needed) for the conditional use of such a transfer or *communicatio idiomatum*. But these expressions and others like them, precisely because they involve analogical predication, cannot serve as primary or exhaustive descriptions of the self's identity in being what it does and who it is. To make such expressions do the work of proper description results in a mixture of descriptions in which (frequently without one's knowing it) the contents of one kind of description are often reduced to illegitimate contents of the other. Thus (in present-day theology) "verbal event" may in fact mean the reduction of "event" to the verbal manifestation of a thought, and that surely is not the genuine meaning of "event."

The description of the ascriptive subject in its persistence is an indirect matter, but it is not impossible if the elusive subject is not ineffable. It is indeed elusive and its location is therefore correspondingly fugitive. How is one to answer properly such questions as "Who am I?" or "Who is he?" Ryle has pointed out that any higher order commentary cannot be commentary on itself; only the next comment can be that commentary on what is to it now a previous performance. Retrospectively—a point at which Ryle is perfectly content to leave the matter—no thought of the I is a mystery. But as to its present thinking, Ryle puts the matter very nicely: "Even if the person is, for speculative purposes, momentarily concentrating on the Problem of the Self, he has failed to catch more than the flying coat-tails of that which he was pursuing. His quarry was the hunter!"[11] (He then proceeds to take away most of what he has just given because he apparently does not understand the uniquely nonobservational and anticipatory nature of the knowledge which an agent has of his own intentional activities.) It is the hunter with whom indirect description of the ascriptive subject is concerned. As far as possible such description—in obvious contrast to Ryle's "higher order description"—must at least mirror the prospective direction of the self, its unending forward movement rather than its specific and completed act.

We have repeatedly emphasized that ascriptive subject description must be indirect. The instrument for this indirect portrayal is the scheme of polarity. Now there are two different polar schemes available for subject description.

Subject Manifest in Difference

The first is that of describing identity by means of self-differentiation in self-manifestation. A word, for example, is taken to be nothing other than the verbal self-manifestation of the speaker. One must be cautious not to reduce all meaning to personal, and in that sense nonpublic, meaning not to cut the nerve of connection between the two. Nor must one reduce the speaker to a function or the sum total of his words. Nonetheless it makes sense to say in some contexts that a person is wholly present in the words with which he identifies himself. Performatory utterances and some kinds of rhetoric are of this sort. The person himself stands surety for his utterance. Verbal manifestation then is

---

11.Ryle, pp. 197 f.

identity with oneself in a medium different from himself. Identification with one's name is undoubtedly the paradigmatic instance of identity-in-difference. The classical document of the modern theological use of this kind of ascriptive subject description is Karl Barth's phenomenology of revelation in *The Doctrine of the Word of God, Church Dogmatics, I:1.* In patristic theology Augustine's *De Trinitate* bears resemblance to this method. The medium of differentiation from the ascriptive subject is, in this description, neither a basic distortion of it, nor an accidental accretion to it. In addition to the word, this sort of description uses the unique location or perspective of the body that is at once mine and myself as a paradigmatic instance of the identity-in-difference of the elusive subject. There is, by virtue of the polarity between identity and difference, between subject that both *has* and yet also is a body, no fear of rending the unitary self into mental and physical components. In philosophy, Merleau-Ponty and some Dutch phenomenologists are proponents of this position; in theology, Austin Farrer and once again Karl Barth.

Subject-Alienation Description

The other form that ascriptive subject description has taken is the polarity of identity and *contrast* rather than *difference*. The self in the public world is understood to find its identity there, but as though in a distorting mirror violently caricatured. The subject qua subject is frozen or "objectified" in the public world Because for both forms of subject description the medium of manifestation is not in any simple or univocal way "other" from the subject, neither the identity difference nor the identity-alienation or contrast scheme presents the I as the ghost in the machine, though I believe there is an inescapable tendency in the latter to do so, unless checked by a counterdescription. In the subject alienation description the medium of manifestation hovers between absolute continuity with and total alienation from the subject. It is rare that the body plays a significant part in this scheme. The assumption of the dialectic of total opposition to and total identity with the subject is not designed to relate the body to it. In his scheme the world which is both the mirror and the distortion of the self is much more often the social and historical than the natural world. The significance of temporal, social events is then said to be their subject reference rather than their public character. They are, in objectified form, the crucial stages in the transition of the subject toward full self-penetration or reconciled selfhood. The subject here is usually, especially for existentialistic phenomenologists and theologians, the individual self. For some thinkers it is the social consciousness or spirit of an epoch which then passes over into the next. History thus becomes its own inward or subjective bond, the dialectical transition of the I toward itself through the stages of its own alienation, its journey into a far country and its return home to itself. Where the emphasis of a commentator is more nearly on the moral side of this transition than on the transition as insight or self-recognition, it is apt to be represented as one crucial transition rather than an indefinite series. Yet even then that one decision has to be reiterated constantly at the level of temporal existence. In either case, the crucial transitions take place not precisely privately but certainly subjectively rather than in their character as public transpirings.

In the subject-alienation form of ascriptive subject description, the identity question may be most troublingly raised. This is especially true of that form of the question involved in the process of naming. "Who is he?" or "Who am I?" (the latter is unfortunately an often rhetorical and overdramatized remark) is a question that may involve a number of issues. It may be a formal inquiry, trying to solve the difficult problem of locating the logical status of the ascriptive subject. It may involve inquiry concerning the specific self-referral of a unitary focus of personality characteristics, conscious and physical states. It may also point to the focus of individual coordination of a number of overlapping human communities, from a family to ethnic and professional groups. The highly diverse problems which concrete specifications of identity pose for individuals are often covered under the general name of "identity crisis." This large term covers a broad penumbra of issues, of which we may distinguish two. At the very least it may mean the individual's sense of isolation from any and all communities which alone could serve to identify him to himself as well as to others. Beyond this, it may also signify a disruption in the sense of temporal self-continuity which the subject ordinarily has in the process of integrating his own changes as well as those within the communities which should help him maintain that self-continuity. "Who am I?" may only symbolize such questions of identity, or it may be a direct and concrete expression of them. In either case, the process of naming, which is presumably the most concentrated answer to the "who" question, illustrates most acutely the issue of ascriptive subject description in such situations. It also illustrates in sharpest fashion the difference between the two forms of this description.

In the first form of subject description, that of the subject manifest in differentiation from himself, the naming question points to an illuminating mystery rather than a haunting problem. Who I am is answered by my presence in and to my verbal expression, most perfectly in my being named and naming myself that same name, thereby accepting and standing for the identity between myself and my name.

In the second form of subject description, on the contrary—that of the subject-alienation scheme—naming and being named constitute not an illuminating mystery but a haunting problem. Who am I? The name a community bestows upon me is precisely not identical with me, though I cannot say that I have an identity safely hidden somewhere else which escapes unscathed from this intrusion. My name now is not the perfect expression of the subject in the medium of self-differentiation; nor on the other hand is it a thing-in-itself isolated from that manifestation. On the contrary, the world is also a distorted mirror or even form of the self. My name in the world presents myself as subject, but in alienated, distorted, "objectified" form. In this world my identity is itself alienated; in this world I am without true identity. "X" is what I should be named or rather what I should name myself in the world of historical communities. My journey through that world is a journey in search of myself, constantly mirrored though not truly present to myself nor self-reconciled in the world. What would constitute such reconciliation, or the achievement of true subjecthood, is answered variously and does not here concern us.[12]

---

12. In literary art Kafka is, I take it, the great representative of this perspective. In philosophy its proponents are Schelling, Hegel, Marx, and the existential phenomenologists. In psychology their name is legion. In theology Tillich, Bultmann, and some of Bultmann's students represent it in different ways. The affinity of this outlook with the subtle movement of late antiquity called Gnosticism has often and rightly been noted (though, of course, there are differences, especially in the tendency of Gnostics to become pure escapists from the world). The parallel was first noted by Ferdinand Christian Baur in *Die christliche Gnosis* (Tübingen: C. F. Osiander, 1835). In our day it has been pointed out again in Gilles Quispel's brilliant interpretation of *Gnosis als Weltreligion* (Zürich: Orego, 1951). Cf. also the illuminating descriptions of Gnosticism by Hans Jonas, including especially his methodological or hermeneutical suggestions in *Gnosis und spätantiker Geist*, II, I (Göttingen: Vandenhoeck & Ruprecht, 1954), pp. 1-23. In describing the journey of the subject away from and toward identity through the historical world of alienation, several alternative forms of the subject-alienation scheme may be developed. The world is said by some commentators to be the medium by which the self is alienated from itself. Others suggest that the self is alienated not from itself but from the world. Hannah Arendt's profound criticism of Marx's typically modern one sidedness in this respect is instructive because her critique involves, among other things, a view of the world as both historical and yet also material in a strictly nonhistorical sense. For that among other reasons she can say: "World alienation and not self-alienation as Marx thought, has been the hallmark of the modern age." *The Human Condition* (Chicago: University of Chicago Press, 1958), pp. 231, 364 f. The evident parallel of the sense of alienation of perceptive folk in an advanced capitalist and a relatively advanced socialist society where, at least according to some interpretations of the rules of the dialectic of self-alienation, the phenomenon should not exist might well be evidence in favor of her thesis.

A Biblical Application of Identity Description

In the Old Testament, Exodus 3:13-15 is the classic example of naming as the first form of ascriptive subject description—description through identity in the medium of self-differentiation. (Cf. the cumulative impact of the "I am" passages in Deutero-Isaiah.) In the New Testament the fourth Gospel in particular illustrates the same sort of subject description in its repeated ἐγώ εἴμι passages. These sayings are especially instructive, for they are obviously written by an author who is intimately and not only as it were externally acquainted with gnostic wisdom and therefore with something like the other form of identity description, that of subject-in-self-alienation.

At least some of the ἐγώ εἴμι passages in the fourth Gospel, as well as its prologue's proclamation that the Word was made flesh (1: 14), clearly seem to express the immanence of the subject in a medium different from himself yet fit to receive him. As a result they express the accessibility of the mysterious ascriptive subject center for and to those who will believe. There are certain expanded ἐγώ εἴμι passages (especially Jn. 14:6: "I am the way, and the truth, and the life") in which the "I am" is analytically, not synthetically, related to—or as it were made transitive in—its own predicates. In all of these, who or what he is is not primarily a matter of certain acts or *transpirings*. In this respect such theological exegesis of these passages as Karl Barth's[13] seems to me mistaken. Rather the relation is that between the subject who is the same in himself and in his manifestation. Neither is he a static substance accidentally connected with what is externally manifested of him so that he does not himself appear in it, nor is he an identity distortedly manifest so that he does indeed appear in his manifestation but only in alienation or *Entäusserung*. Rather, once again, he is the same subject in the medium of external appearance that he is in himself (here Barth's exegesis[14] seems to me perfectly correct), truly manifested in his identity. Hence predicative description is a description of the subject himself in his transitivity.

I do not mean to imply that the ἐγώ εἴμι sayings are antagonistic to identification through action or eventfulness—not at all. I do, however, think that that scheme is simply not applicable to this approach to identity, captioned by so weighty a pronunciation of "I AM...." There certainly is no bias in the Gospel against the cruciality of identification of a person with his significant events. Nonetheless, it is by and large true—

13.Karl Barth, *Church Dogmatics,* III, 2 (Edinburgh: T. & T. Clark, 1960), p. 56.
14.Idem.

especially in 14: 6 which is not (as some other ἐγώ εἴμι sayings are) commentary on a preceding public act—that knowledge of Jesus as the truth and liberation by that knowledge are matters of crucial insight rather than results of crucial changes accomplished through public events within a temporally connected and significantly developing series.

But if the identity of Jesus is here described, in terms of our analysis, most nearly under an ascriptive subject manifestation scheme, it is important to remember once again that with regard to Jesus the manifestation is one of difference rather than alienation from his subject center. The point is that the identity-alienation scheme is, in the fourth Gospel, not even formally applicable to the knowledge of Jesus. That is to say, one cannot even contrast him with others by saying that like others he is also manifested in distorted "objectification," but that unlike them he does own a true subjecthood in himself beyond this distorted external manifestation. The identity-alienation scheme is not applicable to him even to this extent.

On the other hand, such a Gnostic scheme would be applicable, formally and materially, to the nonbeliever if he could come within the author's purview as a person having some sort of integrity of his own being. But one must hastily add that this is, of course, impossible, precisely because Jesus does have an identity, and we have our identities in him, so that the nonbeliever's very conception of himself and man's situation is sinful and unintelligible. The nonbeliever is alienated at the same time from Jesus and from his own true self, so that if *per impossibile* one were to adopt his own perspective, one would have to say that as long as he does not believe his only "truth" is to grasp his nonidentity in the world as being mysteriously one and the same as his identity in himself. That is to say, the "truth" for the nonbeliever would indeed be that in a hidden way his supposed insight that he has no final, true identity is one and the same with his true identity. For him, in the end, silence and negativity would be all. But this is, of course, his sinful error. For Jesus is he who is the way, the truth, and the life for men because he is these things in being the true Son of the Father, and thereby we also have identities.

All in all, one may say that Gnostic thought schemes (identity-alienation polarity) are very much within the horizon of the fourth Gospel's author; but it needs to be added that he is so keenly aware of their implications that he rejects them not only materially but formally. He claims not only that true man does have an unequivocal identity, but that even posing the question of identity in terms of the polarity of identity-alienation is already part of the very problem it would overcome.

To make a wholesale judgment regarding the sense of identity in

Old and New Testaments and what description would be appropriate to them would at least lack proper caution. However, it is evident that the subject-alienation description of identity will at the very least have to be balanced by the other subject description scheme. In all likelihood both kinds of subject description will have to be balanced by intention-action description.[15] All this becomes especially clear when we reflect on the fact that so much of the sense of divine agency in both Testaments is attached to public events that can be narrated in their important temporal transitions.

Ascriptive subject description is deeply concerned with the continuity or persistence of the subject, which intention-action description cannot well show forth. But the opposite difficulty plagues subject description, especially in the form of the subject-alienation scheme. What is the link between stages of temporal, public human events? For subject description the answer has to be, in large part, the subject itself. This bid for the description of subject continuity can produce startling results. In the case of Hegel it led to the rejection of any and all links between subjectivity and the passage from event to event which were not amenable to description in terms of the development of communal subjectivity. Others (e.g., some existentialists) are not so radical, but even for them the extent to which events in their transition from stage to stage resist a description which links them through a subject's activity or awareness represents the threat of absurdity to a self's continuity and its continuity with the rest of the world. Every endeavor to articulate a way to transcend the awkward choice between the absurdity for the subject of non-subjective events on the one hand and an all-devouring subjectivity on the other has proved to be most difficult and problematical (e.g., for the later Heidegger). The danger, certainly in subject-alienation description, is that the very success of its analysis of the subject may have to be measured by the loss of any and all significant external connectedness between the subject and the material and social world in which he is set. The danger obviously does not plague intention-action description, nor indeed indentity-difference description. In the alienation scheme that danger becomes obvious at two points. In the first

---

15.It is evident that I regard intention-action description and subject-self-differentiation description closer to the kind of procedure we find in the New Testament than subject-alienation description. This is especially true of the synoptic Gospels, in which something like the first two kinds of description prevail (as we shall see). I have noted the applicability of the second, the subject-self-differentiation scheme, to the fourth Gospel. Whether or not the third, subject-alienation scheme, is at all applicable to the New Testament is a matter I cannot here try to determine. It would depend largely on an exegesis of Romans 7, and on an examination of the complex history of the exegesis of this chapter. Limitations both of space and technical knowledge prevent my undertaking such a task here.

place, the body obviously cannot mirror the self either in its persisting subjectivity or in the radical distortion of true subjectivity to nearly the same extent as can the social or historical world. In this view, the body and in fact the physical world tend to be foreign and disjunctive entities to the self. Secondly, as we have already discussed, even the social world is in one sense only the estranged manifestation of the self, and therefore, qua manifestation, absolutely continuous with the subject. But in its estrangement, in the "objectified" public transpirings of historical events, the world is alien; the "I" becomes posited at an infinite distance from its own public world. It is, in short, difficult for this view, at least in isolation from other identity descriptions, to escape the "ghost in the machine" position.

Here then we have two (or three, depending on the arrangements) descriptions of the self, each containing a polar relation within itself (intention-action, identity-manifestation in difference, and subject-alienation). In addition, however, there is the possibility of a polar relation between them, either by necessity because of the open-endedness of each, or more loosely because each is an exhaustive description of the self within one situation or schematism—but in that case the other situation remains outside as an awkward appendix. Ascriptive subject description is a significant description of the experience of the question "Who am I?" in the context of social-historical and personal, verbal experience; but in one form at least (not in the other) it tends to treat the body as an appendage or instrument simply of subject or intersubject relatedness. Intention-action description is more successful in describing the unity of thinking and acting, a bodied self not only being but doing directly in the public world. It can describe how a person is what he does and undergoes; but the elusive I with its mysterious search for self-identification through historical experience and naming escapes this description altogether.

What then do we mean by a man's identity? Until a supertheory comes along, we will be content to say that we know him when we can say of him over a period of time or in a crucial occurrence, "when he did and underwent this, he was most of all himself," and when we can say of him, "his self-manifestation was a rightful expression of who he was." A person's identity is known to us in the inseparability of who he was and what he did.

III. IDENTITY DESCRIPTION AND THE STORY OF JESUS IN THE GOSPELS

We return to the synoptic Gospel accounts. We have already said that in the story itself, especially from the arrest to the crucifixion, the identity of Jesus is focused in the circumstances of the action and not in back of them. He is what he does and undergoes. It is an intention-action sequence. Indeed, in and by these transpirings he becomes what he is. But in the synoptic Gospel accounts there is a profound ambiguity about him up to this point in terms of subject description. It is important to say that it is not that he stands mysteriously or ineffably in back of his manifestation. Rather, in terms of the story (though, undoubtedly, not in the authors' conviction) there is an ambiguity about *who* Jesus is. It is this ambiguity that is resolved in the resurrection account, especially that of Luke.

About this resolution, four things are to be said.

1. It is indeed a matter of ascriptive subject description.

2. Even though this description is to the fore in the resurrection account, it is not done in abstraction from action. The resurrection is not simply the manifestation of the meaning of that event which is his death. But the action recedes into the background. It becomes as ambiguous as its line had been clear before this. In the description of Jesus in the gospel accounts, then, his identity is describable (a) through intention-action description, clearly in the passion narrative but ambiguously in the resurrection story; (b) through ascriptive subject description, ambiguously in the passion narrative but clearly in the resurrection story.

3. The subject description delineates the identity of the human individual, Jesus, at once as the manifestation of the presence of God acting and as the one who, having a true identity of his own, can bestow it without distortion on the community of Israel in which he is a member.

4. The shape of the story is such that in the resurrection Jesus is declared to manifest himself as who he is, the one who as the unsubstitutable human being, Jesus of Nazareth, is not a myth but the presence of God and savior of men.

All this is right in the marrow of the story. As a literary account, the gospel story makes Jesus accessible to us. The question is, does it open up the possibility of a more than literary accessibility of Jesus to us? If so, at what point? Where could one make the transition from literary description to historical and faith judgments?

The implication of what I want to suggest is that those who endeavor on old and new "quests for the historical Jesus as well as their opponents have looked for Jesus' identity with a faulty, one-sided under-standing of identity.[16] They end with abstractions of their own making, in which the being of Jesus finally is not intrinsically connected with nar-ratable occurrences, and such events therefore have no genuine signifi-cance. Moreover, both have looked for Jesus' identity with a faulty, one-sided view of the New Testament narrative as *purely* historical and/or kerygmatic—never literary. In contrast to both, I believe one may affirm (a) that in the narrative the person of Jesus is available to us descrip-tively; (b) that there is identity between Jesus so described and the sav-ior's description, and hence (c) there is continuity between Jesus and the proclamation of his name in the early community. I believe further that this descriptive availability, identity, and continuity represent not a trans-formation of Jesus into a myth but the demythologization of the savior myth in the person of Jesus. If this is true of the descriptive narrative, that narrative has met one criterion for allowing us to say that at the cru-cial juncture (death-resurrection) it may—though it *need not*—be true in fact.

According to the gospel accounts Jesus is not simply in need of redemption; he is in fact redeemed, though the story of the connection between his death and resurrection is not an organic but a dramatic transition. Just as his power and powerlessness were not merged but coexisted or were present still in and after the transition from one to the other, so the vindication of his intentional action does not mean that there is a simple mergence or supersession of his need of redemption by the fact that he was redeemed. The point is that the accounts tell us that the one who is the risen Lord is also the crucified savior, and that the abiding identity of each is held in one by the unity of him who is both in the transition of the circumstances. The resurrection is not the stylized ending to a realistic tale, the naming of a mythical figure. Nor, on the other hand, is the crucifixion the shadowy death stage of a rising savior. The crucifixion remains an indelible part of Jesus' identity.

Manifestation and action are ultimately inseparable in the under-standing of identity, and our careful methodological distinctions are undoubtedly too refined and neat to do justice to the synoptic narrative. Yet there are different stresses concerning identity in differing personal situations. It would not do to say that the Gospels bespeak the identity of the resurrected Jesus simply as the manifestation of who he is. No; they still portray him as embodied in a range of events or actions. But whereas in the crucifixion the stress is on identity in event or action, and

---

16.Consult the excursus on hermeneutics, etc.

the identity of manifestation, while present, is ambiguous and not sharply focused on him, the reverse is true in the resurrection. The distribution of the formal elements of identification now is different. Action is indeed present. It is the action of God who began to supersede Jesus' initiative beginning with the arrest and now is climactically the agent here. But the divine action remains in the background, dark and veiled. Something does indeed take place in the resurrection, but it is not described and doubtless cannot be described. And even its effects in further act and event (the resurrection appearances as transpirings) are swathed in confusion and contradiction (the place of the empty tomb in the chronology of the accounts; the order of appearances in Galilee or Jerusalem). The foreground and the stress in the resurrection belong not to the action of God but to its confirmation of Jesus' identity. It is he who is present and none other when God is active. Jesus alone is manifested.

Indeed his identity as God's presence which is singularly he himself, Jesus of Nazareth as that one and unsubstitutable individual, is climactically manifested in the resurrection. In the story up to his death it was right and proper to say of Jesus that his identity was embodied in the activity of his passion, his own activity as well as its gradual supersession, as it were through identification, by that of God. Here he was most of all himself. He *was* this transpiring of circumstances in action. It is equally right to say of his resurrection that here his identity is most fully *manifest*. In the resurrection he is most sharply revealed and attested not as a mythological figure but as the human Jesus; nor is this manifestation a semblance for something more "real" underneath. In one sense then his full identity was established on the cross; in another sense, in the resurrection. The two forms, in their dramatic transition, constitute a unity. In both one may say, "here he was most of all himself" and mean by this expression not a mythological figure but the specific man named Jesus of Nazareth. That seems to be the import of the accounts in the synoptic Gospels.

In view of this assertion of the unity of the crucified and risen savior as one and the same Jesus of Nazareth, it is all the more important to stress the directness of the connection between the two events. The accounts are terse and tense in their rendition of this transition. One might almost speak of dramaturgic unity in the sequence. Christ resurrected is far from being a mythological figure in the accounts. He is most fully historical at this point in the narrative, if by "historical" we mean that he is regarded as an unsubstitutable individual in his own right. His actions and manifestations do not have a symbolic or purely representative character; they do not gain significance through being in an exalted or elevated sense typical of human or divine activity *par excel-lence.* They fit, at this point, neither the classical tragic nor the mystery account. They are more nearly like a novel or a short story. They are, whether fictional or real. a specific set of particular actions and reactions for which no other could plausibly or fittingly be substituted—just as in a novel the actions of the principals upon each other gain their peculiar and significant character by being these particular and no other actions, wrought by these and no other interactions of events and persons. That is why and how they are the embodiment of his unsubstitutable identity. And similarly, all the acts and sufferings are to be ascribed to him. No one else than he, Jesus, is manifest as the central agent or patient of them. In these actions he emerges as who he is.

Stages of the Identification of Jesus

Let us put the assertion of the unity of cross and resurrection in the accounts into the broader context of the identification of Jesus as the unsubstitutable subject that he is. It is doubtless true that the task of writing a life of Jesus, especially one including as its pivotal point his "inner" life, is difficult if not impossible—whether it is undertaken as a reconstruction from the recorded data or by entering by imaginative reiteration into his self-understanding, or both. But if the Gospels do not lend themselves easily to this sort of enterprise, they do manifest another kind of structure, indeed perhaps a series of (not mutually exclusive) patterns, as literary works often do. And these, in turn, lend themselves to interpretive ordering or to a series of such orderings.

If we may take the liberty of treating the synoptic Gospels as one composite account (with individual variations), at least one possible sequential arrangement or three-part pattern seems to emerge.[17]

1. There are in the first place the pre-birth, birth, and infancy sto-ries—including, we ought not forget, the genealogies. In Matthew and Luke this first phase comes to an end with the transition to the next, Jesus' baptism at the hands of John (which begins the whole story in Mark). The striking fact about this first stage is that both in the story (or stories) and its liturgical or poetic decorative material the person of Jesus

---

17.The outline to be followed is largely, though not exclusively, that of Luke. The same type of analysis could have been applied if Mark had been used as the focal narrative though the formal structure of the story is obviously somewhat different. The resurrection is just as indispensable in Mark as in Luke. But whereas it is the climax of the Lukan account and the preparation for Acts, in Mark it is the veiled center toward which the action moves, the open mystery not actually included in the narrative, which nonetheless serves as the narra-tive's mainspring.

is identified wholly in terms of the identity of a community, the people of Israel. He is not the individual person, Jesus, certainly not "of Nazareth." He is not even an individual Israelite, but Israel under the representative form of an infant king figure. He is a representative person in barely individuated form. In his being and in the events surrounding him and focusing on him, we get a cross section, a summing up through miniature reiteration of that whole history of events which in its total transpiring makes up the people of Israel. The crucial events that happened to the people happen symbolically and in miniature to and about him, but in such a way that in connection with him there is a symbolic completion of what was originally left unfinished. In Matthew his identity is determined by cumulative reference to Abraham, Israel's single progenitor; to Jacob, the eponymous figure first called Israel; to Judah, the father of his tribe; to David, the great representative King. In Luke his identity is located by means of Adam in whom Israel, mankind, and God are all directly connected. (Luke's procedure is reminiscent of Paul's juxtaposition of the first with the second Adam who is Christ, a theme in turn reminiscent of some of the Gnostic religions as well as of some Jewish themes.) This is who Jesus is: not an individual in his own right, but Israel—even (to some extent) mankind. They lend their identity to, they bestow it upon him.

2. With the account of Jesus' baptism, the story undergoes a break, or rather a decisive transition to a second stage. Far more than in the first part he appears as an agent, an individual in his own right. Yet this is correct only to a limited extent. Certainly he is no longer in representative form the people as a whole and its history. He now performs mighty deeds, the signs of the kingdom of God. He proclaims its advent and teaches its marks and those of life in it. Nonetheless he retains something of the symbolical or representative quality that he had in the first part of the accounts. But now it is not the past of which he is representative.

Instead it is the immediately pending rule of God. In short, he does indeed begin to emerge as an individual in his own right, and yet it is as witness to and embodiment of the kingdom of God that he does so. It is perhaps precarious to make the claim, but it does seem that at this stage he is identified by the kingdom, rather than the kingdom by him. Even the titles—Son of Man, Son of God, Christ, King, etc.—serve to represent him as the representative of that kingdom and his identification by means of it.

In the earlier stage we find so obvious a proliferation of legends, symbolic events, and myths that history, understood either as lifelike representation or as events that actually took place, can hardly arise as a pertinent idea to be applied to the understanding of the reports. In the second stage, on the other hand, the lifelike representation of the specific individual in specific situations raises the question of historical veracity in acute fashion, since the individual here represented is generally agreed to have lived. We are bound to ask at certain points, "Did this actually take place?" "Was this actually his teaching?" Nonetheless, the specific individual's identity and the situations in which it is enacted are at this stage so often tied to a more ultimate referent, the kingdom of God, that it is frequently (probably in the majority of instances) at least a matter of great ambiguity, if not useless, to try to sort out what is actual happening and what serves stylized depiction, illustrating his representational character.[18]

3. It is worth emphasizing these matters in order to stress the contrasting situation when we turn to the next transition and the third stage in the story. It is in the first place the part generally taken most nearly to reflect actual events—at least in part. But even more important from our present perspective, it is the part of the story most clearly historical in our narrower use of the term. It clearly describes an individual in his own right and in connection with him as central character a series of events which, whether fictional or real, are what they are in their own right. Neither person nor circumstances can be abstracted from each other. They are not symbolic but unsubstitutably what they are and gain all their significance from being this specific set and no other, and from the interconnection between this unsubstitutable person with these circumstances. He alone is at their center and lends them their character,

---

18.In all that I have said here I do not mean to prejudge the relative success (or lack of it) attending specific historical endeavors to reconstruct the setting of Jesus' preaching and acts in his own life and in the cultural matrix of his time. Nor do I wish to make *a priori* pronouncements concerning the significance of some such specific historical endeavors for judgments of faith and theological truth claims. On both matters I find myself sympathetic to the position adumbrated by Nils A. Dahl, "Der historische Jesus als geschichtswissenschaftliches und theologisches Problem," *Kerygma und Dogma,* I (1955), 104-32; translated in C. E. Braaten and R. A. Harrisville, eds., *Kerygma and History* (Nashville: Abingdon Press, 1962), pp. 138-71. I agree with Dahl's remark, *Ibid., p.* 161, "That faith is *relatively* uninterested in the historical Jesus research does not mean that it is *absolutely* uninterested in it. To draw this conclusion would be a kerygma-theological Docetism." On the other hand such a cautiously affirmative position obviously does not entail any one particular argument for tracing the identity of Jesus proclaimed Messiah with Jesus of Nazareth who preached and was crucified, certainly not an argument from the historical evidence concerning Jesus' "self-understanding."

With respect to this particular problem, viz., the identity of Jesus as both crucified and Messiah, as it is presented in the particular shading of the New Testament sources, the position set forth in this paper again bears resemblance to that of Nils Dahl in his essay, "Der gekreuzigte Messias," in Helmut Ristow and Karl Matthiae, eds., *Der historische Jesus und der kerygmatische Christus (Berlin:* Evangelische Verlagsanstalt, 1960), pp. 149-69.

so that they can focus neither on any other hero, human or divine, nor on that "everyman" for whom he might mistakenly be thought to be a symbol.

The transition to the third stage comes with Jesus' brief announcement to his disciples that he and they would now go to Jerusalem, and his prediction concerning the Son of Man's fate. (As a possible alternative place of transition I would suggest the events connected with the Last Supper and immediately subsequent to it.) The atmosphere becomes heavy and fraught with a troubled anticipation which is all the more effectively conveyed for its cryptic description, ". . . and they were amazed, and those who followed were afraid" (Mark 10: 32). We are still at a point where the stylized characterization of Jesus in terms of his mission (i.e., his identification by means of the enactment in him of the Kingdom of God) holds good. Nonetheless, that very identification from now on becomes increasingly problematical and tenuous. Especially beginning with the arrest, or just before it, the connection with the Kingdom of God becomes loose. The figure of Jesus emerges more and more as one whose mission it is to enact and suffer his singular destiny, while the Kingdom of God and the Son of Man who embodies it with its authority fade into the background. There is an increasing tendency to use the titles of that authority (Christ, Son of God, King, etc.) with an ironic and pathetic twist, when they are applied to Jesus. It indicates the apparent incongruity between them as well as the kingdom they represent and the figure supposedly embodying them. By means of this ironic or pathetic detachment or ambiguity (in the midst of which, however, we remember the traces of his yet abiding power!) between the figure of Jesus and the kingdom, the focus of the last part of the story falls more and more on him in his unadorned singularity. He is simply himself in his circumstances, truly a person in his own right. Everything else about him which has hitherto served to identify him and make him a representative figure or symbol of something more than himself now becomes ambiguous.

What is important for us now is not the question, did Jesus apply messianic titles to himself or was it the early church that did so? What is important instead is to understand that the ambiguity of the relation between Jesus and these titles is foursquare in the account of Jesus and of the relation between him and those who had followed him up to this point, and that the ambiguity is one that stretches beyond the printed page and is bound to raise a question concerning this man in the reader's mind. No doubt, indeed quite obviously, the writers themselves had no question concerning the identity of Jesus and the complete coincidence between him and the kingdom with its titles. But as an account or integral part of the story the ambiguity presented is real and remains at this point to be resolved. Its resolution, when it comes, must also be presented as *enacted* in the course of genuine transpirings, though at the same time, of course, it must be the enactment of the *true manifestation* of Jesus, telling us decisively who he is. Jesus must become who he is. He must gain, in enacting it, his own identity in which he is truly manifested as the one who is in some specific way related to the Kingdom and the messianic titles.

Now the story gradually begins to accelerate into an increasingly terse and spare climactic telling, virtually unimpeded in its final stages (beginning with Jesus' arrest) by any and all didactic material (until the resurrection appearances). Such material had hitherto been strongly to the fore, assuming some very somber hues after the entry into Jerusalem. But now it would be an encumbrance. The story's focus remains on the action by which the destiny of Jesus is accomplished. It remains on Jesus as the unsubstitutable person he is his own right through passion as well as resurrection. In terms of the movement that we have traced, from a symbolic or representative person to an individual in his own right, we have reached the last stage of the story. There is no further focusing of his identity. In this respect the passion and resurrection represent, in the very transition from one to the other, not two stages but one. In both, he is equally himself, none other than Jesus of Nazareth. In the unity of this particular transition, passion to resurrection, he is most of all himself, most historical (in our narrower sense of the term) as an individual in his own right. The difference is that whereas in passion and death this identity is *enacted* in the particular circumstances in which he is most of all himself, in the resurrection his identity is presented to us as that same one now ambiguously and rightfully *manifested* as who he is. Yet the difference is not absolute. For, as we have seen, the very question of who he is is ambiguously present and unavoidable in the very midst of the action beginning with his arrest. Conversely, the resurrection is not simply the true manifestation of the crucified Jesus but also the veiled action of God. The identity through act and subject manifestation of Jesus becomes, through distinction as well as identification, closely linked with the veiled activity and subjectivity of God.

In the descriptive account the matter is perfectly natural and in that sense not difficult. For any conceptual ordering it is mysterious indeed, and such ordering is at its best if it does not take us beyond the narrative description to an independent explanation of its own. The rising curve of God's activity increasingly supersedes Jesus' self-enactment in the passion story. But just at the point where the divine activity reaches its climax in God's resurrecting action, it is Jesus and not God who is manifest as the presence of God. It is a complex sequence, but nonetheless a sequence in unity. The unity is the sequence of Jesus' identification. In the resurrection he is most nearly himself as a person who is an individual in his own right. He above all others is totally at one between manifestation and the identity manifested. And if, the writers seem to tell us, this one has a genuine identity so that we know who he is, how can we possibly say that human destiny is loss of identity or alienation, or even that alienation and identity are mysteriously and finally identical in the mythical savior-man figure? For it is he and none other, Jesus the Son of God, who is the representative man, the second Adam, representative of human identity and not alienated in his very singularity. Because he has an identity, mankind has identity, each man in his particularity as the adopted brother of Jesus.

Clearly the story of this redeemer is no ordinary dying and rising god story, no matter what the facts were and how deeply dyed the story was in the vat of syncretism. Its climax is that now, for the first time, Jesus is manifested as the true ascriptive subject of the hitherto ambiguously ascribed descriptions and prophecies concerning the Son of Man. The ambiguity is resolved, and furthermore it is Jesus who manifests himself in the resolution. He imposes his identity on the mythical figure as well as on that history which is the substance of the community of Israel. It is, therefore, fitting that for Luke the climax of those steadily repeated predictions of the Son of Man's sufferings (which at the time of their pronouncement referred only veiledly or at best ambiguously to Jesus; cf. Lk. 9: 22, 9; 44-45; 17: 25; 18: 31-34) should *now* and only now receive their proper ascriptive reference and that at this crucial juncture they should receive it from Jesus himself, who alone is capable of manifesting his identity rightfully and securely. Walking with two of his disciples toward Emmaus, he asks them, "Was it not necessary that the Christ should suffer these things and enter into his glory?" (Lk. 24: 26). Now that the ambiguity, which had appeared at the outset of this stage, is resolved, the author is in a position to say for the first time that "beginning with Moses and all the prophets, he interpreted to them in all the scriptures the things *concerning himself*" (Lk. 24: 27). Here then the elusive ascriptive subject is identical with his manifestation; the ambiguity is resolved. And not only his own history but all of the past of Israel receives its ordering by reference to his manifestation. The wheel has, in one sense, come full circle. Now that he is fully manifest in the absolute coincidence of his manifestation with his unsubstitutable individuality, the identity between him and the community is also restored. But whereas at the beginning, in the first stage of the account, it was the community which served to identify him, the reverse is now true. He, Jesus, provides the community and its whole history with his identity, just as he imposes it on the mythical savior figure.

IV. MYTH, GOSPEL STORY, AND FACT CLAIM

Myths are convincing or true by virtue of their embodiment or echo of universal experience. "Universal" may be too strong a term. But myth surely is the external, expressed mirroring of internal experience which is both elemental and, at the same time, a common possession of a whole group, possibly a whole culture. New Testament students, echoing a gradually growing trend in Romantic philology, learned from D. F. Strauss that where myth appears to be the key to the meaning of an account, no question concerning the factuality of the story need arise. Myth as the unconscious poetizing of a folk consciousness is a sufficient explanation. I do not wish in this context to call into question this claim. But in view of its prevalence, it seemed well to examine the gospel account of the resurrection, to see if its structure is that of myth. At the very least, a positive answer to that question would have to be heavily qualified. In point of fact, the evidence points in the opposite direction. The literary structure of the account, especially that in Luke, seems to me to point in favor of the thesis that the resurrection account (or better, the passion-resurrection account as one) is a demythologization of the dying-rising savior myth. For quite in contrast to the substance of a myth, the substance of the passion-resurrection account is about an unsubstitutable series of transpirings concerning an unsubstitutable individual, whose unique identity is, for the description, not ineffably behind but directly in and inseparable from the events related in the story.

A myth's capacity to convince lies in its echoing a widespread inner experience which cannot be directly or univocally expressed. "Did this happen?" or even "Could this have happened?" are not appropriate questions to ask in the presence of a mythical account. We must rather ask concerning a myth, "What elemental aspirations or motions does it express?" or "To what transcendent dimension of truth does it unite us?" The truth of myth is religious or primordial rather than factual or historical. But the resurrection account, by virtue of its exclusive reference to Jesus and by virtue of its claim that here he was most truly manifested to be who he was in his human particularity, allows, even forces the question: "Did this actually take place?"

It *allows* the question. For this above all is one thing that novelists and historians have in common, that they deal with specific actions and specific human identities. And if a novel-like account is about a person who is rightly or wrongly assumed to have lived, *the question of factuality is bound to arise precisely at the point where his individuality is most sharply asserted and etched.* I have argued that both by virtue of the meaning of identity in general and in regard to the location of Jesus' identity in the Gospel account in particular, his individual identity is not given in an inferred inner state behind his teachings, but directly, i.e., in the report of the transpiring of an actual series of occurrences in which he was what he did and in which he was manifested. It is at this point then that the transition from literary analysis to historical affirmation or denial as well as to theological truth claim should be made. And this point is the complex unity of the passion and resurrection account, not the account of his earlier ministry.

I also said that the passion-resurrection account *forces* the question concerning its factuality. For what the authors are in effect saying (once again Luke in particular, though this time he is joined by John and by Paul in 1 Cor. 15) is that the being and identity of Jesus in the resurrection are such that his nonresurrection is inconceivable. (This does not mean that his resurrection *is* conceivable, any more than saying that God is that than which a greater cannot be conceived means that he is the greatest conceivable, or than saying that God cannot be conceived as not existing means that his existence *can* be conceived.)

In a sense (if I may put it in a manner totally uncongenial to them) the synoptic Gospel writers are saying something like this: "Our argument is that to grasp what *this* identity, Jesus of Nazareth, is, is to believe that, in fact, he has been raised from the dead. Someone may reply that in that case the most perfectly depicted character, the most nearly life-like fictional identity ought also in fact to live a factual historical life. We answer that the argument holds good only in this one and absolutely unique case where the described identity (the "WHAT" of him) is *totally* identical with his factual existence. He is the resurrection and the life; how can he be conceived as not resurrected?"

It may be dubious wisdom to make Luke or John speak like a late eleventh-century theologian. Yet something like this argument seems to me to be present in the resurrection account. All that one leaves out in putting it this way is the fact that the affirmation of Jesus' resurrection is not like that of an ordinary fact, i.e., simply denotative, but rather overwhelmingly affective ("existential"), as befits a unique fact which is unlike other facts in being at the same time an absolute personal impingement. But I see no reason for trying to validate either the meaning or the truth claim concerning Jesus' resurrection by an elaborate description of its existential appropriation. That this is the only way to grasp it, I do not doubt, and in another context the fact might well have to be underscored; but that the elaborate description of the appropriation makes it or discourse about the resurrection in any way more intelligible does not seem to be the synoptic authors' point. The passion-resurrection account tends to force the question of factuality, because the fact claim is involved as part of the very identity that is directly enacted and manifest in the story as an event sequence. One could presumably still see this as a literary feature or part of the description of the account, and therefore either leave the fact question suspended or answer it separately in the negative.[19] But one cannot deny that for the authors or, perhaps better, in the story and as part of it, the fact question was inescapable and bound to be answered the way that they did answer it. It seems difficult, further, to deny that in that case the question of fact *tends* to be raised beyond the literary analysis of the account. And how might one come to answer it in the affirmative? Presumably by a kind of movement of thought similar to and reiterative of that of the original authors. But we have gone somewhat afield in these few remarks, for we have given some reflections concerning the transition from a literary description to historical (in the wider sense) and theological argument and affirmation.

I return to the description of the account, nonmythical and clearly involved in stating that in the case of this singular individual, manifestation of his identity involves his actual living presence. Who he was and what he was, did, and underwent are all inseparable to the authors from the fact *that* he was or is. (The reverse is obviously equally true: that he is brings with it the manifestation of who he is and what he did. The affirmation of the particularity of Jesus, together with stress on its importance, accompanied by the denial that any significant cognitive content is given with this particularity seems to me a silly game.) Once again, if in his resurrection he was most of all his identity as Jesus of Nazareth, then it was here most unequivocally that they could say that he lives. The authors, particularly Luke, are saying that as raised from the dead he exists. And saying this is for them inseparable from saying

---

19.This seems to me to be the upshot of the intriguing first part of George Santayana's *The Idea of Christ in the Gospels* (New York: C. Scribner, 1946). Santayana seems to be saying that even if one must understand the gospels as poetry, they have to be seen as unique poetry in which miraculous facts are indissolubly wedded to ordinary events. The endeavor to demythologize the story or to transcend its mythology ontologically would, for Santayana, spell the ruin of the story. For it is not mythology in the first place. To raise the question of fact concerning the story is likewise to do it damage by separating out fact from the poetry that embraces fact and indeed makes untranscendably miraculous fact part of itself. On the purely and prosaically historical level, of course, one would have on these grounds to enter a judgment against the credibility of these events.

that as raised he is most clearly Jesus of Nazareth, whose being it is to be and to be unambiguously the embodiment and redeemer of Israel, he that should come, the Christ, the Lord, the Son of Man, the manifestation of God.

Such seems to be the significance of the words spoken by the "two men" to the women at the empty tomb, even before Jesus himself was manifest. "Why do you seek the living among the dead?" (Lk. 24: 5) they ask, as though it were a matter of self-evidence, a direct implication of who he is, that he is alive; as though instead it were startling not to think of him who is "one who lives" (New English Bible) as living but as dead. The fourth Gospel, as though commenting on this perspective, extends Luke's identification of Jesus' being alive with his very identity to an all-embracing generalization: "I am the resurrection and the life" (Jn. 11: 25). He defines life. He is life. How can that which or he who constitutes the specific defining difference of something be conceived to be the very opposite of what he thus defines—except through sheer contradiction in the conception? To conceive of him as dead is the equivalent of not conceiving of him at all. Hence the question, "Why do you seek the living among the dead?" constitutes a startling reversal of what we would ordinarily expect to be self-evident and what most stunning. (The difference between Luke and John is that Luke stresses that Jesus is his being, i.e., "to live," only in the transition or bond of events constituting his being, from life to death to resurrection, whereas in John, Jesus' being as the resurrection underlies or encompasses his every manifestation and its acceptance. There are no crucial events or transpirings in time sequence in John, for whom history is subject manifestation. The transitions are from veiledness to manifestation or glorification, and from unbelief to belief, "death" to "life," "darkness" to "light.")

In explanation of what they have just said, the two men add immediately: "Remember how he told you, while he was still in Galilee, that the Son of Man must be delivered into the hands of sinful men, and be crucified, and on the third day rise" (Lk. 24: 7-8). The reiteration of this prophecy, first spoken in anticipation and now in fulfillment, accompanies all the Gospels like a steady refrain (in this chapter of Luke alone it occurs three times in various forms: 24: 6 f, 25 ff., 44 ff.). It is the primary content of what little we have in the way of description of Jesus' life in the earliest preaching of Christians. In the present context the saying is obviously designed to serve as commentary explanation for the question, "Why do you seek the living among the dead?" Had he not foretold them what would come to pass? But I think one may safely say that it is designed to do more than that. It focuses his identity as one who lives, who is life and not death. He lives as the one who cannot not live, for whom to be what he is, is to be. But who or what he thus is, is unambiguously Jesus of Nazareth; and as Jesus he is the Son of Man, the one whose history, whose being as self-enactment in his unique circumstances it was to be delivered into the hands of sinful men, to be crucified, and to rise again. The prophecy (here taken as fulfilled) is the content of his identity as the one who lives. The content of the prophecy is not synthetically but analytically related to the question, "Why do you seek the living among the dead?" Who and what he is, what he did and underwent, and that he is, are all one and the same.

The relation between these verses (Lk. 24: 5 and 6, 7 and 8) is similar to that between Exodus 3:14 and 15. In response to Moses' query after his name, God tells Moses to convey to the children of Israel that "I AM" had sent him unto them. Immediately, as though in explanation which says the same thing over again, God adds, "Say this to the people of Israel, the Lord, the God of your fathers, the God of Abraham, the God of Isaac, and the God of Jacob, has sent me to you...." The reference to God's "I AM" is not synthetically but analytically related to the reference to him as the God of Israel's particular history. For him to be, and to be this specific one, are the same. Similarly, for Jesus to be and to be as Jesus the Son of Man and Israel's redeemer are one and the same thing. Once again: his identity is so unsubstitutable now that he can bring it to bear as the identifying clue for the community which becomes focused through him. Indeed, the New Testament will ask just this of men: to identify themselves with the identity, not of a universal hero or savior figure, but of the particular person, Jesus of Nazareth, the manifest presence of God in their midst, who has identified himself with them.

What kinds of affirmation would be involved in belief in Jesus' resurrection? I think it would mean much more nearly a belief in the inspiredness of the accounts than that they reflected what "actually took place." I have directed attention all along to the descriptive structure of the accounts and not the historicity of their contents. But at one point a judgment of faith concerning the inspiration of the descriptive contents and a judgment of faith affirming their central factual claim would have to coincide. The New Testament authors, especially Luke and Paul, were right in insisting that it is more nearly correct to think of Jesus as factually raised, bodily if you will, than not to think of him in this manner (even though the qualification "more nearly... than not" is important in order to guard against speculative *explanation* of resurrection). This judgment that they were right is in part at any rate a matter of a particular understanding of what identity means, what and where the identity of Jesus is to be found most directly in the Gospel accounts (i.e., in the crucifixion-resurrection sequence) and where the transition from the literary description to factual, historical, and theological judgment is to be made: precisely in that sequence. I think further that both because what is said to have happened here is, if true, beyond possible verification (in this sense unlike other "facts"), and because the accounts we have and could most likely expect to have in testimony to it are more nearly like novels than like history writing, there is no historical evidence that counts in favor of the claim that Jesus was resurrected. This is a good thing, because faith is not based on factual evidence. To what historical, natural occurrence would we be able to compare the resurrection for purposes of cognitive assimilation? On the other hand I believe that, because it is more nearly fact-like than not, reliable historical evidence *against* the resurrection would tend to falsify it decisively, and that the forthcoming of such evidence is conceivable. In other words, if true it is unique, but if false it is like any other purported fact which has been proved false—there is nothing unique about it in that case. Again this is a good thing, because if it were not so, in what genuine sense could Christian faith be said to be historical and to involve a historical risk? Until such evidence comes along, however, it seems to me proper to say (despite St. Thomas and Hume who insist that every fact, without exception, can be doubted until shown to have taken place, which in turn is a matter of evidence rather than logic) that there is a kind of logic in a Christian's faith that forces him to say that disbelief in the resurrection of Jesus is rationally impossible.

Whether one actually *believes* the resurrection is, of course, a wholly different matter. "God raised him on the third day and made him manifest, not to all the people, but to us who were chosen by God as witnesses..." (Acts 10: 40-41a).

Excursus: Hermeneutics, Identity, and "The Historical Jesus"

The recent literature on the twin problems of our knowledge of the Jesus of history and the transition, historical as well as existential, from there to the kerygma involving his name, is extensive and growing. By fairly general consent the latter-day discussion received its heaviest single impulse from Ernst Käsemann's essay, "Des Problem des historischen Jesus," *Zeitschrift fur Theologie und Kirche,* 51 (1954), 125-153, translated in E. Käsemann, *Essays on New Testament Themes,* tr. W. J. Montague, Studies in Biblical Theology, 41 (Naperville, Ill.: A. R. Allenson, 1964), pp. 15-47. The focal discussions in the American literature are: James M. Robinson, *A New Quest of the Historical Jesus,* Studies in Biblical Theology, 25 (Napperville, Ill.: A. R. Allenson, 1959), revised and expanded in a German edition, *Kerygma und historischer Jesus* (Zurich: Zwingli Verlag, 1960); and a critical review of Robinson's book by Van A. Harvey and Schubert M. Ogden, "How New Is The 'New Quest of the Historical Jesus'?" in C. E. Braaten and R. A. Harrisville, eds., *The Historical Jesus and the Kerygmatic Christ* (Nashville: Abingdon Press, 1964), pp. 197-242, originally published in a German translation as "Wie neu ist die 'neue Frage nach dem historischen Jesus'?"*Zeitschrift fur Theologie und Kirche, 59* (1962), 46-87. For surveys of the literature and problems see Hugh Anderson, *Jesus and Christian Origins* (New York: Oxford University Press, 1964) and W. G. Kümmel, "Jesusforschung seit 1950," *Theologische Rundschau,* Neue Folge 31, 1 (January 1966), 15-46.

The reader should be cautioned that Harvey's and Ogden's essay is exclusively critical and systematic in nature and in no sense a review of Robinson's monograph in the light of an independent examination of the New Testament. Harvey and Ogden neither argue any generalizations about the shape of the Gospel accounts of Jesus' life, death, and resurrection, nor do they examine any specific texts. The result of their general procedure is that, whatever the hermeneutical problem(s) of the New Testament may be, it is in one sense declared to be insoluble; in another sense, it is solved before it arises.

I do not wish to engage in any lengthy discussion of the actual status and significance of the "hermeneutical question" in New Testament and theological studies. However, I should like to raise the question if the whole problem has not perhaps been exaggerated altogether out of proportion to its actual significance. The reason for that possibility lies in the fact that off and on now for 150 years or more, theologians in the traditions of German Idealism and now Existentialism, who have carried on the discussion on hermeneutics have been accustomed to take for granted two assumptions: (1) That the written word (especially in the case of the New Testament writers) represents not the proper expression but the frozen "objectification" of the mind that lies behind it; (2) that the proper way to grasp one's own intention, indeed identity, as well as that of others, is by entry into the basic self-reflective act of the self, into that which is never "merely given."

The dominant (often wholly unqualified) scheme of understanding involved in this conception is the one I have labeled the "subject-alienation" polarity. The adoption of this descriptive scheme, as a device for the examination of the principles of Biblical interpretation, if it is not balanced or supplemented by some other analysis of human intention, identity, and their accessibility, obviously has built into it a guarantee that its very question can never be answered. How *can* the "objectified" written page actually bring us in contact with the "unobjectifiable" sub-ject-reality in back of it, if the relation between them is in principle one not only of difference but of contrast? The endeavors to ameliorate or modify the statement of this gap have been many and earnest, as for example in the recent "post-Bultmannian" discussion carried on in the shadow of the later Heidegger's ontology by such scholars as Gerhard Ebeling, Heinrich Ott, and Ernst Fuchs; but in principle the gap remains. It is this built-in guarantee which accounts for the fact that even though the *terminology* of the hermeneutical discussion has changed appreciably—becoming ever more complex, esoteric, and abstruse as the endeavors in recent decades to "overcome the subject-object split" have become linguistically more and more difficult—its *substance* has hardly changed at all since the days of its theological inception through Schleiermacher. How could it be otherwise, given the funda-mental fact of the ongoing similarity of the understanding of the self that informs the whole discussion? Given a one-sided and absolutely consistent description of the self as nonobjectifiable self-reflexiveness, or at best as a subject concretized only in a "word event," and hence given an ever doubtful conjunction of public and personal meanings on the written page, the hermeneutical discussion can obviously be guaranteed an ongoing, indeed indefinitely perduring status. Even if we discount the possibility that the seriousness of this issue has been exaggerated, it does not seem likely that it represents a "new frontier" in theology.

Now, if we do indeed suppose that there is a serious hermeneutical issue, it is presumably before us when two differing conceptual schemes are to be brought into one common context for the conveyance of meanings contained in each. In the case of theological-Biblical exegesis the common context is apparently agreed by many commentators to be that of self-description. Concerning the hermeneutical issue, two things may be said about Harvey's and Ogden's essay. (1) They do not ques-tion the inherited scheme of "existentiell" understanding of the self (hence agreeing at least in principle to the importance of the hermeneu-tical problem), though they quite properly see the insurmountable diffi-culties which the scheme offers for the "historical" picturing of anybody, including Jesus of Nazareth— difficulties which Robinson had com-pletely overlooked in his original adoption of this "new concept of the self." (2) Since they do not examine the New Testament itself, Harvey and Ogden never get into the position of having to pose even the possi-bility of independent conceptual patterns of the New Testament, which might, or on the other hand might not, then become problematical for the modern reader.

The first point enables them to suggest that the hermeneutical problem with regard to the knowledge of the intention of the "historical Jesus" is insoluble. The second point enables them to solve the hermeneutical problem before it arises. For, though they disagree with Robinson over practically everything else, they are perfectly willing to adopt his (and other existentialist theologians') oversimplified and at the same time ineffable principle of "self-understanding" as the common and proper context for self description, the understanding of man in the New Testament, and its account of Jesus' significance. The only difference between them and Robinson at this point is that he thinks that this principle makes "the Jesus of history" accessible to us, whereas they are properly dubious with regard to the direct accessibility of anyone (even to himself) on the basis of this principle, let alone the direct accessibility of Jesus. But whatever the remote "existentiell" selfhood may be for them (and however it may be grasped, inferentially or in some other way), it is clear that for them as for Robinson the true identity of a person lies in "existentiell" self-understanding, whether clear and accessible or obscure and inaccessible. It is this mysterious and (for Harvey and Ogden) remote "someone" that is addressed by the "kerygma" and lies somewhere in the depths of the self-reflexive life.

But surely there is no reason why we must declare ourselves bound, a priori as well as exclusively, to this understanding of identity, let alone assume it equally simply and without question to be applicable wholesale to the New Testament. To do so provides a clear instance of the ease with which the unmodified alienation or "nonobjectifiability" schemes turn into a "ghost in the machine" position, especially when used in connection with examination of narrative material.

Van A. Harvey's recent *The Historian and the Believer* (New York: Macmillan, 1966) may move in the direction of a modification of the position on identity assumed in his and Ogden's essay. However, since the issue is not directly addressed it is obviously difficult to assess his position. In any case, despite the author's skillful analysis of the pertinence of different kinds of historical explanations for theological argument and his departure from German thought forms, it is not clear that he works with any other notion of identity. His use of the "perspectival image of Jesus" (pp. 268 ff.), for example, functions in a way surprisingly similar to the claims of those engaged in "the new quest for the historical Jesus," who bring together Jesus, the kerygma, and ourselves by the common concept of "existentiell" selfhood. Here as there we find the same ambiguities, especially that of relating a basically undeterminable historical occasion to what appears to be a mysteriously and privately self-originating perspective of faith, i.e., a perspective for which it is extremely difficult to specify any external impulse, either from an actual historical occasion or from the transcendent source of that and all other occasions. To what extent this self with its perspective is basically characterizable as an agent self is also difficult to see. In other words, Harvey appears to leave carefully ambiguous the question if the self of faith is ever so genuinely in the public domain that narration of an historical or literary kind would be absolutely indispensable either to its own determination or to its connection with a wider spectrum of public events. The same ambiguity, by extension, characterizes the issue whether the God who reveals himself as trustworthy does so in any way remotely analogous to public and teleological activity that would have to be narrated in order to be understood.

What Harvey carefully leaves ambiguous, Ogden clarifies beyond possible doubt. All crucial action, human or divine, becomes for him reduced to "self-understanding," the really constitutive factor of our being and that "act" in the depths for which external instantiation in word or deed is a merely secondary and separable expression. Here God becomes the transcendent ghost in the historical or worldly machine and man the ghost inside the cells of his body. The characterization of either as historical agent in this context is obviously a totally Pickwickian use of the phrase. See Schubert M. Ogden, "What Sense Does It Make to Say,'God Acts in History'?" *The Journal of Religion,* XLIII (January 1963), 1-18.

THE IDENTITY
OF
JESUS CHRIST

PREFACE

This essay is a theological experiment first undertaken a few years ago. It was originally entitled *The Mystery of the Presence of Jesus Christ* and published in serial form in 1967 in *Crossroads*, an adult education magazine of the Presbyterian Church, U.S.A. It was an experiment in two senses. First, much of my thinking developed in the process of writing. Despite an overall outline that depends on a simple formal implication, I did not fill in details on a preexistent intellectual map. The work grew as it went along. From a basic conviction to which I found it difficult to give precise form, the essay took on complexity, scope, and breadth of implication as I continued writing. At every single point of its development the immediate next step looked tentative, even though the underlying conviction and the essay's final aim remained firm.

Secondly, the essay was an experiment because it tested out, as only thoughts committed to paper can, the basic conviction itself, that Christian faith involves a unique affirmation about Jesus Christ, viz., not only that he is the presence of God but also that knowing his identity is identical with having him present or being in his presence. It is of course true that we never really know what we think until we actually say it. In that sense the conviction just summarized gained force as the essay grew. But it is equally true that we change our minds, and when I say that the essay was an experiment I mean most of all that I was constantly aware of a certain tentative character to the technical pattern in which I had cast the conviction, i.e., the basic concepts I used and the appropriateness of the logical scheme in which they are linked.

Specifically, I would not now put nearly the same stress on "presence" as a category. It is, among other things, deeply implicated in the twin dangers of a mystification and of loss of morality to religion which result from making personal acquaintance or personal knowledge the model for what transpires between God and man in religion or Christian faith. I agree with the recently emerged consensus among a good many

53

theologians that "revelation" is not a wholly unambiguous or satisfying central concept for stating what Christianity is all about. Furthermore, the governing model for construing "revelation" among modern Protestant theologians, that of a "non-propositional" personal encounter, is even more problematical. When you come right down to it, most of us would hesitate to claim that we encounter God or Christ directly, the way we encounter our friends and relations or even the limits of our own potentialities and powers. And if we qualify the description by speaking of an "indirect" encounter, have we anything important or even intelligible left? An indirect encounter is really a way of conceding that while there is someone there, we haven't met him or aren't meeting him right now. It is difficult to deny at least a degree of justice to the accusation that "revelation," as construed by neo-orthodox theologians, is a way of intellectualizing the relation between God and man by riveting it to the phenomenon of consciousness or one of its several derivatives. Similarly there is justice in the cognate criticism that even then "revelation" turns out to be so non-informative as to lack all intellectual content.

It is one thing—and a good one—to use, and to speak informally of the religious use of, phrases like "the presence of God" or "the presence of Christ," especially if one can avoid associating them with the modern theological set notion of revelation. But elevating the word "presence," as I did, to the level of an indispensable systematic or technical concept governing theological analysis made me come at least within hailing distance of the tangles I have just mentioned.

I was obviously still very much preoccupied and trying to come to terms with a philosophical and theological tradition that had been dominant in Protestant theology since the early nineteenth century; and in the concept of "presence" I was trying to sum up what all its variants had in common. It was Kant's transcendental ego, transformed into Idealist subjectivity or romantic consciousness, and heightened to the point of a unique perspective on self, others, and the universe at large. The present was the crystallization of this self-positioning in time and history which, far from being merely an aspect of human experience, actually constituted the self. It could therefore be known only by the performance of the original self-positioning motion itself and never at second hand. Talk about the self and its constituting itself in or as its present moment was therefore never a mere description but a coaxing—an elicitation in which interpretation, understanding, and the persuasion to adopt, indeed to *become* the depicted point of view were one and the same thing.

This notion of "presence" seemed to me to be the distillate of the philosophical conceptuality under which such otherwise very different people as Hegel, Schleiermacher, Kierkegaard, and the dialectical theologians of the 1920s set forth their religious and theological proposals. In the light of this common conceptuality the very notion of revelation, which was supposed to represent a break with the sour theological grapes of the early nineteenth-century fathers, was no more than an instance of the dialectical children's teeth being set on edge. And the aftertaste remains, so far as I can tell, in the mouths of a good many of the grandchildren!

Even as I wrote I was well aware of the possibility that finally turned out to be the result of my inquiry into the christological use of "presence." For in the end it all came to the claim that the specifically Christian affirmation of the presence of God-in-Christ for the world involves nothing philosophically more high-flown than a doctrine of the Spirit, focused on the Church, the Word, and the Sacrament, and the conviction of a dread yet hopeful cutting edge and providential pattern to mankind's political odyssey. Originally I constructed some philosophical models for the mode of the presence of God or Christ from the aforementioned nineteenth-century tradition —and then proceeded to knock them down. If I were writing the essay over again, I would not even do this much. And if I found in the process of theological reflection about Jesus Christ that I had to refer to "presence" as a technical category, I would confine myself to saying that *if* one thinks about him under this rubric one cannot conceive of him as *not* being present. Further than that I would not go. Similarly, if the cognate category of divine self-revelation were appropriate, one should say no more than that God-in-Christ could not be conceived as not revealing himself or not being revealed, even though this means neither that he must reveal himself (as Hegel claimed) nor that this is necessarily the most appropriate way to conceive of him.

But the *substance* of the essay's argument is not sufficiently marred by its appeal to the logical implication of Christ's presence from his identity to call for drastic reworking. Furthermore, its *form is* sufficiently dependent on that implication to prevent such wholesale revision. For that double reason I decided to let it stand, a few relatively minor changes (and a concluding meditation) apart. The reader will have to judge the soundness of the decision. I request his patience if he finds this decision, drawn from apparently contrary estimates of the substance and form of the argument, initially puzzling, in the hope that the essay itself will resolve the hiatus.

Letting the essay stand in its original form also means that certain possible anachronisms are allowed to remain. For example, I made use of a scholarly interpretation of Gnosticism which took the whole Gnostic scheme, including the dying-and-rising-Savior rhythm, to be a mythological representation of human self-alienation and reconciliation. This identification was not surprising, given the prevalence in the interpretation of intellectual and cultural history of that same Idealistic-Existentialist conceptuality which then governed "revelation" theology. I gather that the pertinent historical scholars have now changed the signals, and I would therefore designate the syndrome more loosely which I describe as "Gnosticism" in Chapter 6(and by implication in Chapter 3). More than that is not at stake, since the syndrome I exhibit there is both perennial and *sui generis* and therefore easily identifiable under whatever name.

A literary-critical friend asked me why I did not take on weightier works than those I discuss in Chapters 7 and 8 under the theme of modern "Christ figures." The answer is that I am not a literary critic and do not possess the skill to deal with the likes of Dostoevsky's Prince Myshkin or the hero of Faulkner's *A Fable*. Besides, each of the works of fiction I analyzed illustrates a certain sub-type of the species I was concerned to identify. I had a theological and not a literary point to make and can only hope that I did not in the process do injustice to those works that I did examine. To those interested in the analysis of the Christ figure as a literary genre I refer to the excellent work by Theodore Ziolkowski, *Fictional Transfigurations of Jesus* (Princeton, N.J.: Princeton University Press, 1972), which covers the whole literature, with the one puzzling omission (so far as I can see) of D. H. Lawrence's "The Man Who Died."

Crucial for the argument of the essay is the twofold scheme for the formal description of human identity, under an intention-action pattern and under a subject-manifestation pattern (Chapters 4 and 9 and —as applied to Jesus—Chapters 10 to 13). While I have not changed my mind about the propriety of either, I would want to be a little more tentative about the second, since it may suffer from some of the same genetic defects as the category "presence," viz., too heavy an infestation of the vagaries and dogmas of its Idealist parentage. I do still regard it as serviceable for the purpose for which I used it, but I would now want to supplement both patterns by exploring the formal analytical devices which sociologists of knowledge and Marxist literary critics use to identify the relation between individual personhood and the contextual social structures.

II

But most important is the fact that I am of the same mind now about the essay's central affirmations as I was when I wrote it. Among these are a few to which I want to draw attention. I remain convinced that a sound basis for good dogmatic theology demands that a sharp distinction be observed between dogmatic theology and apologetics. With few exceptions, the theologians (and philosophers of religion who have wanted to make a case for Christianity) have been preoccupied ever since the beginning of the eighteenth century with showing the credibility or (in our day) "meaningfulness" of Christianity to their skeptical or confused contemporaries. Certain basic patterns reappear consistently in this apologetic procedure.

For instance, certain fact claims, especially about the veracity of crucial parts of the Gospel story, have been defended because they are thought to be indispensable to the beliefs that constitute part of the essence of Christianity. More generally, arguments from evidence as well as inherent credibility have surfaced again and again in modern apologetics. It is argued—on the basis of the shape of the physical universe, the moral life, the experience of contingency, etc.—that there is a strong rational presumption that God really exists or (in our day) that God-talk is not vacuous or else reducible to covert talk about something actually quite different. Again, it is argued that the inherent constitution of human being together with the incomplete, forward-moving shape of history makes inherently rational the assumption that history, far from being chaotic, is ordered toward a revelatory climax. Again, it is argued that the testimony that Jesus really did rise from the dead is sufficiently reliable and close to first-hand to make natural explanations of the rise of the "Easter faith" unsatisfactory.

On the other hand, there are those who claim that Christianity whatever its professed beliefs, is accessible as a viable possibility only as one learns to dispose oneself in a distinctively Christian way. In that case the apologetic move is to point out the Christian in comparison and contrast to other life stances, the Christian (or religious) use of language to other ways language functions. And then suggestions are made about how people get into position for moving in this direction. Maybe moral seriousness, maybe a distinctive experience of "depth" in human life— usually some appeal to a condition of basic incompleteness, basic need, a primordial relation to divine transcendence, or some combination of these—is made in order to persuade us that in our hearts we knew all along what we weren't willing to admit, viz., that we cannot get along without divine succor. There is always an appeal, in this kind of apologetic, to a conjunction between one's own, autonomous life quest and the divine grace. Our path toward that conjunction, in terms of which the event itself is at least partially understood, is assumed to be the indispensable condition for understanding Christianity. It is the logical or interpretive context in which theological language and theological dogma are taken to make sense.

In other words, in this view the rationale of how one comes to believe comes to control, indeed to be virtually identical with the logic of belief, i.e., the meaning and interconnection of dogmatic statements. This holds true, whether the apologetic is of the first, evidential and speculative kind or of the second, more nearly personal sort. The same tyranny over the way Christian concepts mean is exercised by the various endeavors to combine the two apologetic procedures, for instance, the argument that there are indeed concepts or fact claims which are part of the faith but that the logical condition for understanding and believing them is to see them not as "neutral data" but as personally pointed "pro me." They are meaningful only in the process of "understanding" (where understanding is equivalent to life appropriation) or in the context of the form of life that constitutes the use of Christian concepts, etc., etc.

Whatever my convictions about the uses of apologetics in Christian thought, the present essay, in contrast to the position just stated, affirms a sharp distinction between "meaning" in dogmatic theology and such apologetic interpretations of Christian faith. It is an inquiry into one sort of basis for dogmatic theology and as such ignores apologetical issues. The order of belief is logically a totally different matter from that of coming to believe or the apologetic justification of Christianity. Suppose—quite theoretically—that someone believed that the theological explanation for his own and other people's faith is God's predestinating grace. It really would matter little to the logical or dogmatic status of that belief whether the way one came to have faith was gradual nurture, a religious experience, the exercise of neighborly human affection, the upheaval of finding oneself in despair over human irreparable guilt, or even reflection on an argument.

For myself, I am quite persuaded that there is no single road to Christianity, either as a matter of universal principle or in practice. I am convinced that the passionate and systematic preoccupation with the apologetic task of showing how faith is meaningful and/or possible is largely out of place and self-defeating—except as an *ad hoc* and highly various exercise. In this arena an ounce of living is usually worth a pound of talk, and especially of writing. I am therefore persuaded that none of these ways of coming to belief or indicating the context in which believing and Christian language is meaningful is a necessary (or even a necessary though insufficient) logical condition for the meaningfulness of dogmatic language. And even if I did believe the apologetical exercise to be more useful than I do, I would still wish to insist on the distinction between the logic of dogmatic statements and that of apologetics.

On the other hand, I am persuaded that it is possible to state the logic of Christian belief, i.e., the basis and mutual coherence (though not necessarily the necessary mutual implication) of Christian concepts. Nor do I think of this as an arid, religiously fruitless intellectual exercise. It is a clarifying operation that may well bring in its train a sense of Christian life and a vision of the enormous outreach of Christian faith. On these matters, as on others, the essay will have to speak for itself. I want to emphasize that I am well aware of, but not terribly distressed by, the fact that my refusal to speak speculatively or evidentially about the resurrection of Christ, while nevertheless affirming it as an indispensable Christian claim, may involve me in some difficult logical tangles. Even so, I believe this is a better way than the contrary path (taken, for example, by Wolfhart Pannenberg) and a religiously significant way at that. Dogmatically, belief that Jesus is Lord, grounded in believing Jesus' death and resurrection, is itself the explanation for the enablement of (and so mirrored in) a life of faith, hope, and love. Whatever one's experiential sequence, the dogmatic explanation proceeds, and proceeds with confidence, in this order—Lessing and Kierkegaard notwithstanding. The logic of religious discourse (if I may use an overworked phrase from contemporary technical jargon) is odd, connecting things and categories that may be disparate in other contexts, for example, the mode of factual affirmation with that of a religious life. This is indeed not to claim the reverse, viz., that the self-involving quality of religious statements IS the indispensable logical condition or interpretive setting for the intelligibility of the doctrine that Jesus is the crucified and risen Savior. It is to affirm very simply that, unlike other cases of factual assertion, that of the resurrection of Christ shapes a new life.

III

The kind of theological proposal consonant with this essay rests on a reading of the Gospel narrative to which I have applied the term "realistic narrative." About it I want to say two things, first something about its distinctive character, and then something about the use of the term "hermeneutics" involved (for example, in the subtitle to the book). Realistic narrative reading is based on one of the characteristics of the Gospel story, especially its later part, viz., that it is history-like—in its language as well as its depiction of a common public world (no matter whether it is the one we all think we inhabit), in the close interaction of character and incident, and in the non-symbolic quality of the relation between the story and what the story is about. In other words, whether or not these stories report history (either reliably or unreliably), whether or not the Gospels are other things besides realistic stories, what they tell us is a fruit of the stories themselves. We cannot have what they are about (the "subject matter") without the stories themselves. They are history-like precisely because like history-writing and the traditional novel and unlike myths and allegories they literally mean what they say. There is no gap between the representation and what is represented by it.

Now it is important to note that since the beginning of the eighteenth century, and at an accelerating pace with the development of historical criticism, this coincidence of the story's literal or realistic depiction with its meaning has been taken to be the same thing as the claim that the depiction is an accurate report of actual historical facts. This identification of two different things is a classic instance of a category error. No matter what gave rise to this confusion, its consequences for biblical interpretation have been momentous. It aided decisively in the spread of the common critical view that the meaning of the realistic biblical stories is the occurrences which they report, whether accurately or inaccurately, or else that their meaning is the reconstruction of the historical situation which is the most likely explanation for the text's being written and taking the shape it did. Others, by contrast, felt that reference to specific historical occurrences is simply not the likely meaning of such texts, but that reconstruction of their- original contexts is also not an adequate reading. However, given the category confusion that had developed, a realistic narrative reading of the stories was no longer available as a logically independent option. As a result, the only alternative to some form of historical reading of the texts was to interpret them in some way that insisted that the coincidence between the representation or depiction and what they are *actually* about is only apparent and not real. First allegory and then myth came to be the non-historical classifications into which the realistic narratives were fitted. And many commentators simply threw the two contrary kinds of interpretation together and consistency to the winds, making the stories more or less depictive (and thus historical) one moment, while declaring in the next that their true "subject matter" lies beyond the depictive statements.

Now insisting on the integrity and distinctive character of realistic narrative is finally less important than exhibiting the case exegetically. The crucial test is to take a significant instance that appears to exhibit these features and see whether the claim is actually fruitful when put into operation. This is especially true since the suitable procedure for elucidating the category—and the stories by means of it—is probably not best dignified by being called a method. As if it were composed of a series of distinctly demonstrable steps which together form a whole, subject to independent description, and then, as a separate and subsequent procedure, applicable to the textual materials to be exegeted! In the instance of realistic narrative interpretation the exegetical practice is indispensable to the theory of exegesis, and ruled use governs the statement of the rules actually used. Therefore the amount of theory involved is minimal. There should be enough to elucidate what is actually being done in exegesis, and no more.

It should be clear, then, why the exegetical chapters of the essay (Chapters 10-13) are of greatest importance to the author, and why the fit between the exegetical material and the hermeneutical devices, viz., the category of realistic narrative and the two formal schemes for human identity description, is equally significant. In a book published this year *(The Eclipse of Biblical Narrative* [New Haven: Yale University Press, 1974]), I sought to point out the category error to which I have just referred, together with something of its background and its eventual ramifications. But fully as important is the endeavor to show how exegesis *can* be done—and hopefully done better—if the error is avoided. Hence my stress on the attempt in the present essay to provide at least an outline of a possible realistic narrative reading of the Gospels, together with some of the hermeneutical instruments appropriate to such a reading.

The aim of an exegesis which simply looks for the sense of a story (but does not identify sense with religious significance for the reader) is in the final analysis that of reading the story itself. We ask if we agree on what we find there, and we discover its patterns to one another. And therefore the theoretical devices we use to make our reading more alert, appropriate, and intelligent ought to be designed to leave the story itself as unencumbered as possible. This is additionally true because realistic stories, perhaps unlike some other texts (a matter that would have to be determined by examining each kind in its own right), are directly accessible. As I have noted, they mean what they say, and that fact enables them to render depictively to the reader their own public world, which is the world he needs to understand them, even if he decides that it is not his own real world.

I hope these remarks will help to indicate why I use the term hermeneutics in one particular way. Hermeneutics I define in the old-fashioned, rather narrow, and low-keyed manner as the rules and principles for determining the sense of written texts, or the rules and principles governing exegesis. This is in contrast to the more recent, ambitious, indeed all-encompassing view of hermeneutics as inquiry into the process that goes into understanding or interpreting linguistic phenomena. In the latter instance, hermeneutics becomes practically equivalent to general philosophical inquiry; and the language-to-be-interpreted becomes shorthand for a whole philosophical or theological anthropology, a view of man as language-bearer.

For two reasons I shy away from this perspective as an instrument for biblical and theological inquiry. In the first place, it seems to me to be one more version of religious apologetics. This is especially true in the hermeneutical school that first appeared among theologians about two decades ago. (Its American adherents called it the "new hermeneutics.") Unlike parallel but quite different endeavors to state general theories of interpretation, such as those of Freudians or Structuralists, this school of thought is heavily beholden to Idealist antecedents, especially in its reliance on the notion of the "hermeneutical circle." This term means not only that in utterances whole and parts have to be understood through each other, but that any explicit interpretation presupposes a logically prior, low-level, or implicit understanding. In effect this means that any interpretation rests on a shared structure of distinctively human being between interpreter and what is to be interpreted. Hence the pronounced tendency among theologians who have appropriated this outlook is virtually to identify understanding with decision or negative or positive life appropriation of what meets them in the phenomenon to be understood. Hence the use of hermeneutics in the service of a religious apologetic of the second, i.e., personal variety.

Secondly, general theory here dictates to, not to say overwhelms, exegesis and subject matter in the case of at least one kind of text. I have stressed repeatedly that in realistic narratives the depiction coincides with what it is about. The story renders the subject matter, not only by its ordinary and generally accessible language, but by the interaction of character and happening. Persons and publicly accessible circumstances are indispensable to each other, even as they are irreducible to each other. In their interaction they form the story and thereby cumulatively render its subject matter. They render it— and thus the sense of the text—to the reader, no matter how he disposes himself toward the story on a personal level. The negative point to be made is that the broad theory of hermeneutics we have been talking about simply cannot account for this kind of exegesis. And if a general theory of interpretation cannot explain how an exegesis that can actually be done is possible, just how general is it? The position in this hermeneutical philosophy, of which the "hermeneutical circle" is a typical aspect, is that the specifically human element, the dialectic in which man is himself and language is distinctively human, is what any exegesis must uncover. Public circumstances, social context, and structures, all become meaningful only as they are related, systematically and internally, to the specific self-world of the text as appropriated through interpretation. The true subject matter of any significant, not "merely" scientific or analytical text is thus reduced to the self-understanding or self-and-world understanding manifest in it, to the possibility for "existence" or the "linguistic event" which constitutes the subject matter, or to some similar thing. When this view, with its claim to omnicompetence in interpretation, is applied to realistic narrative, not only is the subject matter turned into something other than the story and what it depicts, but even what is supposed to be the true subject matter is nothing except in and by the relation and family resemblance between it and the interpreter.

Now this may be a very useful point of view for some ways of going at some specific linguistic phenomena and some kinds of texts. (The same thing may obviously be said of other general theories of interpretation also.) But it is useless as a theory for describing the exegesis of a realistic narrative *qua* realistic narrative or, at the most ethereal level, as an ontology for explaining a world in which the interaction between incident and character forms the web of continuity. And thus, until a more adequate general theory of hermeneutics comes along, we shall have to stand by our more modest view of hermeneutics, appealing to just enough theory to describe the rules and principles used in an actual exegesis, and no more, even if it means that we have only fragments of one or several theories rather than a single all-inclusive theory of interpretation.

As a final postscript I want to emphasize that there may well be many ways of grounding and doing dogmatic theology. I wish to claim no more than the legitimacy (and not the *sole* legitimacy) of one that proceeds by way of inquiry into the meaning of Jesus Christ in Scripture and the Christian tradition. To that limited extent I wish to identify myself with the problematic that has generally predominated in modern theology. My hope is that the exegetical and accompanying hermeneutical inquiry will show that, no matter whether one is a believing Christian or not, one can make sense of the Gospel story in its own right, and that making sense of it that way entails important consequences for a theology based on this narrative.

In the old-fashioned tradition of appeal to the "gentle reader," I must beg his indulgence if the following list acknowledging my intellectual debts is abnormally long. But then, the time-span covering first the making and then the remaking of these reflections was abnormally long, and many people helped along the way. Furthermore, there is sheer pleasure in remembering this kind of debt. Actually I should mention not fewer but many more names, especially those of a good many graduate students at Yale University over the years. Dennis Shoemaker, then an editor of *Crossroads,* coaxed this essay in its earlier form out of me with patient resourcefulness. In various ways my thought on the topics covered has been stimulated and challenged by conversations with J. Harry Cotton, Nils A. Dahl, Gordon K. Davies, Peter C. Hodgson, Robert H. King, George A. Lindbeck, Wayne A. Meeks, Paul W. Meyer, John H. Schutz, Claude Welch, John F. Woolverton. All of them also read large parts of the material at one stage or another of its development. I am grateful for their help and friendship. To Louis Pressman I am indebted for aid in preparing the new preface to the book. The typing skill of Julie Swanson and my administrative assistant, Theodora Ross, is matched only by their kindly patience.

Two friends and colleagues, each with a distinctive point of view (which is certainly not that of this book), have shared most closely the development of these thoughts over the years. In gratitude for their sustained intellectual companionship and for the friendship of which it is the expression, this book is dedicated to William A. Clebsch and David H. Kelsey.

Ezra Stiles College
Yale University
July 19, 1974

H. W. F.

Introduction

THE APPROACH
TO THE PROBLEM

Our concern in this essay is to discuss what is meant by the presence and identity of Jesus Christ. At stake is a simple question: How shall we speak of Christ's presence? I shall, of course, not try to prove that he is present, but simply ask what belief in his presence involves for Christians. Our inquiry has to do with how we can talk about the relation between Jesus Christ and Christians. Obviously, this does not mean that I shall claim to know the secret of how this relation becomes established, or even show that it is real or possible. People do not often find such arguments convincing (even if they are legitimate), especially if they believe—as Christians do—that God has his own way of moving the human heart, a way that is not simply another name for a series of human actions or reflections.

I shall not, therefore, write a rational defense of the possible or actual truth of Christian faith. I would not deny that Christian belief has a certain rational order intrinsic to its own nature, but that is another subject. This is not an essay in apologetics. Nor am I going to use faith as a convenient assumption on the basis of which to expand implications for Christians, once they begin to reason from their belief in Christ's presence to them. In other words, I am not going to write an outline of dogmatic or systematic theology that takes for its presupposition faith in the presence of Jesus Christ.

At the outset, I should like to raise two questions. First, why should we talk about the relation between Christ and believers in terms of Christ's presence and identity? Second, why should we talk about it at all, if we are offering neither dogmatic theology nor a rational argument for the truth of Christianity? As to the first question, I simply wish to argue that it is legitimate and appropriate to do so. We could have taken some other path—for example, an exploration of what Christians believe. An examination of the Creed would be an instance of that kind of inquiry. It would represent the use of dogmatic theology, of which we have just spoken, but for a different purpose, namely, as a way of expressing our actual relation to Jesus Christ. Or we could have tried to state first how we are related to ourselves, other persons, society, our natural environment, and have argued from there that an analogous relation to God or Christ is possible. Or we might have asked a question such as, "What does it mean to say that Jesus Christ died for our sins?" Again, we could have tried to discern the relation between the believer and his Lord in the pattern of Christian living or Christian worship, in the shape of the church or of the world at large. In short, there are many ways of raising the question of how Christ and believers are related. Some of these ways will enter this discussion, especially in the concluding section. To put that relation under the inclusive heading of "presence" is only one procedure. Although not necessarily preferable to some others, it is surely legitimate.

On the one hand, most of us are sharply aware of the limits of our time span here on earth, a fact that heightens our sensitivity to the persons and events contemporaneous with us. We often remark on the fact that this is a very good time in which to be alive or, contrarily, that we were born in the wrong age or out of due season. Either way we indicate a sharp awareness of ourselves and the place we occupy and of the people and things contemporaneous with us. This comes pretty close to a strong sense of presence. On the other hand, the powerful impact of Christ's presence is perfectly evident from testimony of those who wrote down what those who had been contemporaneous with him said about him. Further, the New Testament proclaims the promise that he will be present again in an as-yet-undisclosed future time (or future mode) for which his followers hope. And, interestingly enough, he is also said to be present now, between these two times: "Lo, I am with you always, to the close of the age" *(Matt. 28:20)*.

Nonetheless, these three times of his presence—past, present, and future—do not join together in the fashion in which succeeding historical eras merge one into the next. He is not present to us now as he was present to his disciples in the days of his flesh. How he will be present to us in the future, we simply cannot say. We recollect that there have been arguments and reflections from the early days of the church to the present concerning Christ's "real presence" in the Sacraments. And, at least from the Reformation on, Christians have inquired concerning the spiritual presence of Christ in the words of Scripture and of the sermon. In the nineteenth and twentieth centuries the same kind of reflection has been expressed in the question of the "contemporaneity" of Jesus to each distinct, subsequent historical era and individual life. Sometimes this "contemporaneity" has to do with personal piety; sometimes it is directed more to social situations and hopes for the future. Summing up, then, we may say that, both from our own sensitivity to things and from what we find in the New Testament and Christian history, it is appropriate to speak of the relation between Christ and believer as one of *presence to each other.*

But there is a second question to be considered. Why should we talk about the relation of Christ and believers at all, if neither the unfolding of Christian beliefs in dogma nor defense of the truth of Christianity is our intent? To consider that question, we must first of all draw some distinctions that concern not only different kinds of people, but even different aspects of our own indivisible and individual being. Concerning the presence of Christ, there are believers, nonbelievers, and people who are in transition from one place to the other, from unbelief to belief and from belief to unbelief (though some members of the Christian tradition—e.g., very stern followers of Augustine and Calvin—would deny the possibility of the latter move).

Such distinctions between belief and unbelief and the pilgrimage from one to the other are obviously not only *between* but also *within* people. A person may actually be at several stages of the process of pilgrimage at the same time. We should be fools to try to estimate precisely at what stage or just which kind of person any human being is.

The believer will talk about the relation or presence of Jesus Christ in one way, the nonbeliever in another, the pilgrim in yet a third. Essentially, what I shall write about constitutes a reflection within belief. In a sense, therefore, there is no argument to be developed. I do not make a certain assumption on which I then build an expanding series of consequences or inferences leading to the discovery of some final, wholly new conclusions. Also, I do not try to justify the grounds on which I make my primary assumption. Concerning that assumption, I shall simply appeal to the consent of believers. Nor shall I pretend to inform them about their belief of which they were hitherto ignorant, so that now they will both believe and understand for the first time. Instead, I shall simply try to explore a certain notion and what is contained in it, and suggest that there is one order rather than another for thinking about its component parts.

This exercise is, in one sense, merely technical; in another it may make a crucial difference in the interpretation of the gospel. The governing conviction in this essay is that in Jesus Christ identity and presence are so completely one that they are given to us together: We cannot know *who* he is without having him present. But I also want to suggest that if we begin with the often nagging and worrisome questions of *how* Christ is present to us and *how* we can believe in his presence, we shall get nowhere at all. It is far more important and fruitful to ask first, *Who is* Jesus Christ?

But I want to warn the reader that my procedure may appear to be the reverse of the program just set forth. In fact, I shall first examine the notions of presence and of the presence of Jesus Christ, trying to indicate in the process that reflection about Christ's presence leads us neither to that presence nor to an understanding of his identity. Only thereafter shall I actually examine the ideas of identity and the identity of Jesus Christ, in the hope of being led also to the elucidation of the idea of his presence to the believer. Talk about Christ's identity and presence should be in that order, rather than the reverse, even though identity and presence are one in him as he relates himself to us.

THE POINT OF THIS EXERCISE

What is the use of such an exercise? This is where the distinctions between believers, nonbelievers, and pilgrims become important. For the believer, first of all, there is a certain pleasure—I am afraid a rather laborious one in the present instance—in thinking about the relation between Christ and believers. That pleasure involves gratitude for the fact of the relation, as well as a clarification of the ideas or concepts implied by it and a proper ordering of their parts. But we must further consider what place there is for rational reflection within this personal relation to Christ. Sometimes we feel that reflection is extrinsic to or foreign to that relation, perhaps even harmful to it; at other times we may feel that it is an intrinsic part and expression of that relation—as if there were a presence of Jesus Christ in our thinking and not only in our prayers and our overt action. By and large, then, reflection about the presence of Christ is, for the believer, a pleasurable exercise in arranging or, as I should prefer to say, ordering his thinking about his faith and—in a certain sense—a praise of God by the use of the analytical capacities.

It will be evident that this exercise of ordering and of praise, involving neither new evidence for the truth of Christian faith nor the development of fresh claims based on prior statements, is in one perspective an empty exercise. That is to say, it is a purely formal and circular procedure, an exercise in clarification, adding no new information and providing no new conclusions. In other words, we talk about the relation to Christ as if it were already established and simply wanted a kind of descriptive expansion. In a way, our procedure is simple, perhaps even as naive as this: Inquiry about Jesus' identity establishes that he is to be defined as one who lives. To live is to have presence. Hence, when we think about *who* he is, we must think of him as present.

Thought about a relation between Christ and believer must be formal and circular. However, by contrast to thought about it, the relation itself ought to be a continual discovery about something completely new and concrete. But if the relation itself is so concrete, can thinking about it be less so? Not to the unbeliever, who cannot talk merely-formally about the identity and presence of Christ, because he believes he has never been in contact with either, to say nothing of having contact with their unity. And so we raise the question about the presence of Jesus Christ, not, this time, as believers, but as nonbelievers or pilgrims.

Before we go on to reconsider the question in this light, let us restate our assumption: *To have Christ present is to know who he is and to be persuaded that he lives.* In our knowledge of Jesus Christ, his presence and his identity are completely one. We cannot properly think of him as not present, as we can think of others without their real presence. Whether, then, we begin by asking about his presence and go on to his identity, or reverse the procedure by beginning with reflection about his identity—only to realize that it involves the affirmation of his presence—we have a circular notion. But even though it is circular, it is not one of those "vicious" circles that falsely claim to provide us with new, factual information about a subject on purely logical grounds. The reason is, of course, that, whether wholly apart from or partially within the movement of reflection to and fro concerning presence and identity in Jesus Christ, the believer affirms that Christ is present to him. Hence, the believer's delight in ordering the use of his mind concerning these two elements. Nothing more is involved for him.

We have already mentioned another claim to be made in this essay: That the right order for thinking about the unity of Christ's identity and presence is to begin with his identity. If we proceed in the reverse fashion, we are apt to impair that simple praise of God with the mind, of which I have spoken. Instead, we might begin to use our reflections about Jesus for purposes that we should actually eschew, e.g., showing nonbelievers how faith in Christ or the idea of his presence might be "possible," "meaningful," or "real." The claim that it is more important to ask *who* Jesus is than *how* he is present is not intended to downgrade the importance of the latter question. On the contrary, if its enormous significance is to be grasped, it must be relegated to second place in the order of development. For it receives an implicit answer through what we say about who Jesus is. Although our ultimate concern, therefore, is with the affirmation of Christ's presence, we shall actually think at greater length about Christ's identity.

THE UNBELIEVER AND THE PILGRIM

This preliminary reflection on the substance of this essay is designed to indicate the difference between the believer's and the nonbeliever's situation concerning the use of the exercise of talking about the identity and presence of Christ. For the believer, we have agreed, it is a purely formal procedure, useful in praising God with the mind. For the nonbeliever, however, it cannot be that and nothing more. If Jesus' presence and identity are indeed given as uniquely unitary in our relation to and knowledge of him, and if therefore one cannot talk about him without knowing him, the nonbeliever is bound to expect something more than formal talk. This is so because, although he is not himself aware of such a presence, he nevertheless notes that Christians claim they are. The reflective thought of the believer about his faith, which is actually quite admittedly nothing more than the formal ordering of his thinking, *must* be much more than that to the nonbeliever if it is to mean anything to him at all. For the unbeliever has been told that he cannot know anything significant about Jesus Christ except Christ be present to him.

Purely formal talk that is not talk in the course of becoming actually acquainted with the one talked about is, in this instance, meaningless to the nonbeliever's mind. This very circularity and formality makes such talk devoid of any significance for him. What it can mean to the unbeliever is only a clarification of the procedural order of reflection of those who think about the content of belief. But even this is apt to be discouraging to the nonbeliever, because he finds it to be such an unlikely order. In any other case with which both believers and nonbelievers are acquainted, to know who somebody is does not logically involve his presence. The claim that there is such an identity between them in the case of Jesus Christ means that there is no direct connection in talk or thought between the believer and the nonbeliever in regard to the relation of Christ to men. In fact, the situation is that there is no transition from the one state to the other that one can indicate; for precisely what is to the one most meaningful in the mode of reflection about Jesus is most meaningless to the other.

But what, then, about the pilgrim, the one who is in transition from belief to unbelief or unbelief to belief? Are we really to try to speak of the point at or the process by which the transition is made? Undoubtedly not in our context, if at all. It may well be that if it occurs at all in talk, it does so when one turns from *reflection* about Jesus Christ to *proclamation* of him. Perhaps, on the other hand, it has very little to do with any kind of talk and much more with the eloquence of a consistent pattern of life that has seemingly suffered an inexplicably wounding and healing invasion, rare though that sort of thing is. But how are we to say? We have already committed and restricted ourselves to a kind of reflection that refuses to speculate about how the possibility or reality of Christ's presence (or for that matter its impossibility or unreality) is to be explained. The pilgrimage between belief and unbelief may be made by means of something other than talk, by change in the mode of talk from reflection to confession, proclamation, or self-involvement, or in yet other ways.

Every path must be considered possible for the pilgrim—even the incongruous one that such a transition (in either direction!) occurs in the process of purely circular discourse concerning the unity of Christ's identity and presence. In the latter case we are really saying that belief is at once novel and happening now and yet already presupposed whenever it happens. And it may be necessary to say something analogous about unbelief. However, we have already ventured too far away from our own rules and into comment on a variety of equally possible paths of transition from one stance to the other. It is best not to go farther, but to practice the reserve we imposed on ourselves at the outset. Whereas it is clear, then, what reflection on the unity of presence and identity in Jesus Christ involves for the believer and the nonbeliever, its status for the man in transition must remain a puzzle.

PART I

THE PROBLEM OF PRESENCE

Chapter 1

CHRIST SHARES HIS PRESENCE

One way or another there has been a Christian belief that Jesus Christ is a contemporaneous person, here and now, just as he spans the ages. To the non-Christian and the "natural," unbelieving man in us, all this is, of course, a very difficult claim at best. How can one think that somebody once on this earth now lives eternally and that he does so in such a way as to be accessible to all subsequent generations? The difficulty becomes disconcerting when the claim is extended to say: To believe in Christ is to believe that he shares his presence in a very particular way with you personally. To be sure, this claim is not made with equal stress by all Christians. Some talk more of Christ's presence in or with the church, rather than with individuals. Others find the notion of Christ's presence distasteful to deal with directly, letting the matter rest as an implication. Still, whether it is presence to "us" or to "me," whether the claim is held explicitly or implicitly, the claim is there. In many ways Christians acknowledge Christ as personal presence, and this is deeply troubling to the nonbeliever.

In our own time the difficulty of considering the personal element in Christ's presence is compounded. Detailing actual personal experience requires moving well into one's own and one's neighbor's private sphere of life. This can be particularly embarrassing because, in modern life, the private and public sectors are quite different, something not nearly so true for Christ's early followers. The practice of public confession of private sin in the presence of the Lord and his congregation was an appropriate action in the first centuries after the church's birth and, to some extent, perhaps even as long as the nineteenth century in North America. Today, such an invasion of private life seems a much more dubious thing. The dissociation of private and public spheres, whether good or bad, has been long in the making. It is not over yet, despite the present fashion of a reverse movement, allowing the media to bring the private person before a vast impersonal public. There is still something awkward if not specious about the direct public display of private experience—sexual, psychological, or religious. Members of Christian churches who have undergone the shock of group-therapeutic endeavors to weld them together into a common body on the basis of a radical challenge to their private reserve, their hostilities, etc., know of the tense question about the genuineness of such procedures

Mixed in with the awkward relation between public and private experience is the troublesome issue of the inner certitude of faith. It is a question that afflicts Protestants in particular whenever the issue of *how* Christ can be present is raised. Christians often become earnest, insistent, and zealous advocates of the credibility of a faith in Christ's presence. Perhaps this is due to the vividness of their sense of that presence perhaps to the opposite sense. It may be that a believer is not really sure and cannot really believe unless he can convince others. Both lack of certitude and dissociation of private and public experience make talk about "presence" a dubious kind of testimony in our modern cultural setting. Thus, it is wiser to approach the question of what it means to speak of Christ's presence indirectly rather than head on. We shall, then, in the interest of indirection, be first governed by the question, Who is he? We must try to comment on the claim in the introductory section that the very affirmation of his identity also involves the claim to his presence. But we shall have to emphasize the fact of his presence as an abiding mystery. It is a mystery because there is no precise parallel to it in ordinary human knowledge. Even though there is a firsthand quality about a person's identity when he is present, so that the two are in fact given together, still they are in principle separable items of understanding. Ordinarily, we can think of a person as a special, unsubstitutable human being without his actual presence. But the Christian claim is that this cannot be done with Christ. The nonpresent reminiscence of him is that of an ordinary or extraordinary, vaguely or sharply portrayed mortal and not that of the Christ.

Except for outright spiritualists, most of us believe that the identity of a person is intimately linked with and not merely remotely attached to his bodily presence. Indeed, it is silly to ask who a person is if he has not been present somewhere, and presence means that he had or has a body. To have an identity means among other things to have, nay, to *be* a body, a human fact. There is a unity between who any man is and his factual presence in embodiment. Still, there is a great difference between this and the claim we have made concerning the unity of Christ's presence and identity. To ask about any other man, *"Who is* he?" does not bring him into the questioner's spatial presence. We can think of anyone without having him actually before us, and certainly our thinking of him does not constitute his presence.

In the case of Jesus Christ, however, Christians claim we cannot even think of him without his being present. But it is not the power of our thinking that makes him present; it is he who presents himself to us. Furthermore, we do not have the capacity within ourselves to hold the unity of his identity with his presence in our minds. If he is effectively rendered to us in this unity when we think of him, it is due to his powerful goodness. Its bestowal, in effect, means that we may not think his presence and identity apart from each other. If we do, we no longer think of Jesus Christ, but of some ephemeral ghost of him, whether we call that ghost the "historical Jesus," supposedly portrayed by the Gospel, or the "Christ of faith" who is an ineffable and indefinable spiritual force in human experience.

But even though there is no precise parallel between the unity of identity and presence in Jesus Christ and their coincidence in ordinary human existence, there is an area of resemblance between them. The *difference is* that we can *think* the two elements of personal being apart in any other man, but not in Jesus Christ. The *similarity is* that in both cases they are, in point of fact, given together in any and every individual. To pursue the similarity: Even if our knowledge of a given person's identity does not depend on or require his specific and physical presence, every time we think of him there is a sense in which that person is "present." When a person whom we have met is identified, his identity—or that which makes him uniquely the person he is in distinction from all others—is recognized through the aid of memory and imagination. If we are to know his identity, we require, if not his physical presence, then the closest thing to it—his presence to us on the inward plane, passed along by memory and its less earthbound twin, imagination, from the physical to the inward remembering and thinking level.

Most likely, even a person of the historical past whom we have not met, such as Napoleon, Washington, or Lincoln, must be present to us in some manner in the imagination if we are to know in any significant way his identity—that set of describable characteristics that makes him who he is and none other. The imagination is the cement by which, in ordinary experience of absent human beings, the separable elements of identity and presence become joined effectively for our own imagined representation of these persons. But in all such cases, unlike that of Jesus Christ, the imagination, or the person doing the imagining, is *not forced* into uniting the content of imagination with the grasp of *actual* presence. Here, then, the similarity between ordinary apprehension and the apprehension of Jesus Christ comes to an end. For in his case we are forced to consent to the factuality of what we represent to ourselves imaginatively. We must affirm that to think of him is to have him actually present.

IDENTITY REQUIRES PRESENCE

Jesus Christ is known to the Christian believer in a manner that incorporates ordinary personal knowledge, but also surpasses it mysteriously. To the non-Christian, this mystery becomes an insurmountable difficulty, for there is no precedent for it in personal acquaintance.

Now this special mystery of Christ's presence, as we have sketched it so far, is irrevocably connected with certain attendant claims. There is, as we have already stressed, no presence of a person, whether in fact or imagination, that can be conceived without a physical or historical, a spatial or a temporal locale. In the case of factual rather than imagined presence, this locale is obviously no mere matter of our own necessary representation of a presence to our imagining selves. Instead, the physical and temporal locale must pertain to the person present himself. So the claim that Christ is present, although signifying much more than certain attendant physical and historical claims, must have such assertions for its basis. One must, in short, say that he was raised from the dead, ascended on high, and from thence imparts his Spirit. In fact, Christians do claim that he is wholly unique as one who lived and died in Nazareth and Jerusalem and is now present as that very same person because he was raised from the dead. His having been raised from the dead is not his presence now, but it is the necessary local basis for his presence now. The manner and means of his new life after death as well as the mode of his presence now constitute a different question, and for some, perhaps, a very difficult one. But we shall have to insist that whatever these are, they are the fit instruments of showing forth who and what he uniquely is. The means of grace are the presentation of Jesus Christ and of no one else.

The factual basis necessary for the claim of presence makes it imperative that we pay close heed to what the facts are, as every fact human or otherwise bears identifying marks. For that task we must turn to the New Testament and attend the story that narrates the identity of Jesus— in the manner in which any human fact is identified by his particular story. Before we do so, however, we must point up the importance of the corresponding idea of presence, the meaning of that word, and why we choose nonetheless to begin with identity instead. Why is the notion of presence more problematic than that of identity in this particular context?

Chapter 2

THE ENIGMA OF CHRIST'S PRESENCE

We must specify the idea of "presence" more closely before we turn to the Gospels to see how they delineate the "identity" of Jesus. I have already indicated in what way the notion of presence undergoes change when applied to Jesus Christ rather than to other persons. In the instance of Jesus Christ we are forced to consent to the actual presence of the one imaginatively represented, even though he is not apprehended by the outer senses. This is not the case with other persons.

But not only does imagination have to perform special feats in regard to the appropriation of Jesus' presence; there is the additional fact that, although talk of Jesus Christ's presence is proper in some ways, in other ways it is not. We must now try to delineate the difference and in the process indicate why we should talk positively first of the identity of Jesus.

The word "presence" is one of a number of personal terms that defy definition. But sometimes description can help where definition is difficult. The first and most obvious sense in which presence is used is that of physical proximity. Though we have suggested that the claim to Christ's presence must have a spatial and temporal basis, it is obvious that the phrase "the presence of Christ" does not mean his physical proximity to us. The necessary substitution of imagination for the work of the senses is enough to remind us of that fact. Most of us feel intuitively that belief in a physical or even quasiphysical, extrasensory presence of Jesus Christ involves the conjuring up of some highly abnormal visions. Most Christians do not talk of Christ's presence now in terms of physical space and time.

CHRIST'S PRESENCE AS SACRAMENT AND WORD

The idea of physical proximity may, however, also remind us of a different way of communion with Christ, one that does not smack of hallucination or abnormal visions. We call this manner of his presence "sacramental," and this, in the tradition of the church, has been the meaning nearest to the actual physical presence of Christ. But, however near in meaning physical and sacramental presence can be said to be to each other, they are not identical. In the Sacrament of the Lord's Supper the Lord is said to be present in such a way that he actually communicates himself. That is to say, he is the real celebrant and the agent of Communion. Nevertheless, though sacramental presence is claimed to be a real presence, it is not a physical presence. Though it is the nearest thing we have to the physical presence of Christ, it is not identical with the latter.

In addition to physical proximity and relation and the corresponding sense of the sacramental presence of Jesus Christ, the term "presence" also denotes symbolic, especially verbal, communication between human beings. As we have said, the Sacrament of the Lord's Supper puts us in mind of the physical presence. Does human communication likewise merely remind us of "the Word of God," or do we actually mean the same thing by words human and divine? Orthodox Protestants, though insisting that the Word of God and the words men speak are quite different, do believe that the term "word" may be applied literally to God's speech just as it is applied to man's. By and large, this means that they find God's presence more nearly in his Word, i.e., the text of the Bible and the expository sermon, than in the Sacrament. Traditionally, the situation has been the reverse for Catholics. The doctrine of transubstantiation has meant for them that Christ's presence in the Sacrament is to be conceived in a manner similar to the proximity of other substances.

In both instances, Word and Sacrament, we have a hint that their use is not literal, but analogical, when applied to the presence of Jesus Christ. We shall assume that this is indeed the case. Even then, there may be an order of priority between them that makes one the prime analogy, the other the secondary analogy to the presence of Christ. I shall not try to settle that question here. For present purposes, the important thing is that they are both analogies. In the process of analogical conception each must undergo drastic change. The transposition of physical to sacramental presence involves a picture for the senses, but on the inner plane of imagination rather than on the outer plane of actual vision. Similarly, the transposition of verbal communication to the Word of God involves an extended use of human language, such as metaphor or simile, rather than verbal communication by means of direct divine-human discourse. Granted that verbal forms and visual pictures are not disconnected, since, after all, we are unitary beings and our imagination shares in that unitariness, extended verbal forms, such as parables, are nonetheless rather different from inner-visual pictures. Something of the difference, as well as the unusual shape which verbal form assumes in Christian usage, is indicated by the way in which Protestants connect "the Word of God" with human experiences: That Word, they are apt to say, is an event and a moral action rather than a literary discourse evoking admiration for its use of imagery, such as a poem.

If it is at all appropriate to speak of a typical Protestant art form, it would presumably lie at the juncture between a strong verbal imagination and a strong moral sense. I can think of no more classic illustration of that juncture than that great challenge to the Christian life that is, at the same time, cast into one enormous figure of speech (allegory), Bunyan's *The Pilgrim's Progress*. When these two things pull apart and the imagination responds to the Word of God as a work of art rather than a challenge for decision and conformity of life, the presence of Christ becomes distorted into an aesthetic thing. A kindred distortion can no doubt enter the visual or sensible imagination, quite apart from the other danger to which it is subject, that of physical hallucination.

It is doubtless true that Christianity cannot exist as a strong force without providing food for the imaginative life—sensible, verbal, or some other form—as the cement of the real world with the religious affirmation. The present decline of Protestant Christianity in particular is due in part to a failure in imagination, which may or may not have been historically unavoidable. But it is also well to remember that a purely imaginative or aesthetic response has never been regarded as the right or central response to the presence of Christ. Christians are called upon to *practice* the presence of God or of Jesus Christ, not simply to contemplate or imagine it.

The notion of Christ's presence may involve the danger of reduction to hallucination or that of weakening the moral fiber by a reduction of religion to the level of the free play of the imagination. It may also come to be used as a theoretical term in such a way that one believes he knows nothing of Jesus Christ unless he has figured out some sort of *theory* of his presence. Needless to say, when the term "presence" has become just a question of theory, it no longer has any use in describing the relation between Christ and believers. But the fact that a term can be distorted does not make it inappropriate.

THE "PERSONAL" RELATION OF CHRIST TO BELIEVERS

In the introduction to this book we commented on the fitness of the term "presence," summarizing the case that both our own sensitivity to things and what we find in the New Testament and Christian history make "presence" an appropriate term for the description of the relation between Christ and believers. So far in this chapter we have indicated certain uses of the term that point at once to its legitimacy and to its questionableness when applied to this relation. But we have not yet discussed the strongest claim for its use. That is quite simply the fact that "presence" is a highly personal term and implies personal ties that are linked only by such phrases as "physical proximity" and "verbal communication." We may surely take it for granted that the New Testament and Christian tradition lead us to believe that the relation between. Christ and believer is in some sense personal. Hence, the fitness of "presence" for the description of that relation.

Let us then turn to the personal meaning of "presence." It is, of course, sometimes used of nonpersonal beings or objects, but then in an odd manner. A particularly striking building, for example, may be said to have "presence," but in such a case a kind of transfer has been made. The "presence" of the building is due in large part to its being the manifestation of architectural force, the fit embodiment of design. We should say in any case that "presence" as a term is related, not to mere physical proximity as such, but to the physical proximity of human beings.

"Presence" also has less literal and more metaphorical uses. When we say that a person has "presence" or even *is a* "presence," mean that a certain power inheres in him. It is a quality resident in that person himself rather than one lent to him by something external, such as an office or a position of authority. In the New Testament, and also in modern parlance, the term "charisma" is used to describe at least one form of that personal power.

In a fashion less metaphorical than the use of "presence" to describe inherent power, and yet not so literalistic as physical proximity, there is a pair of terms whose qualities depict an aspect of "presence." The terms are "sharing" and "turning."

In the present context, the word "sharing" means that a person can take public facts and data and talk significantly about them with others and, in the right situation, even make them vehicles of self-communication. In the mutual presence of two or more people, public and personal meanings, descriptive and expressive functions of language, may become fitly joined by significant conversation. Further, and perhaps most natural to many, "sharing" suggests our breaking a candy bar, a sandwich, or a sum of money in half for another's sake. But it may also mean the sharing of one's presence, and this is similar to what we call "communion." It is the word, the look, the gesture that passes between friends and lovers, indicating that to regard the self as encased within walls and communicating with others as though by code-tapping on the wall is not always correct. Our communications are not always inferences or hints or mental X-rays conveying shadowy pictures. There is such a thing as communion, no matter how distorted it becomes; and most of us would be willing to say that breaks in communication, or experiences of alienation, are just that, i.e., *breaks,* rather than the normative or usual state of affairs. If the latter were the case, if human life were distinguished by isolation with only occasional breakthroughs into communication, there would really be no problem of communication between people, because we should not expect that communication could or should normally take place. Sharing indicates the fact that a person can give himself in public and personal communication without losing himself and that he can be received. Sharing means, furthermore, that this action takes place over a period of time. It can, up to a point, become a continuing state of affairs, with a rhythm or continuity of its own.

"Turning" is not a wholly different thing from "sharing." It simply draws attention to the fact that states or acts of shared presence have a beginning and also an end, that they are initiated and received. There is such a thing as making oneself present to another, which can be called turning to the one with whom we wish to share. There is also turning away, often in the final agony in which a curtain is drawn over an episode. Turning may be a response to someone else's act or address; it may be prior to the latter or the two may be simultaneous. But in all three instances, it is still both a spontaneous action and one initiated by persons. At the level of personal experience, spontaneity governs both turning and being turned. In other words, acting and being acted upon tend to go together in such a way that it is not always possible to determine who is acting and who is being acted upon. And because we can turn and be turned, we can also share.

PRESENCE TO OTHERS MEANS PRESENCE TO ONESELF

Because acts of sharing and turning are self-initiated, one cannot be present to others without being present to oneself. The reverse is also true: One cannot be present to oneself without being present to others. The significance of this mutuality becomes graphic when one discerns its opposite, which, whether in fiction or reality, has the appearance of a madness that has its own peculiar poignancy and terror for onlookers. This madness possesses a particularly haunting quality and is characterized first by a maniacal concentration of personal presence, or a power exercising itself with exhilarating and yet paralyzing and destructive effectiveness upon others as well as itself. This is followed by the collapse of the person, leaving an empty shell of quiescence and passivity, which is in frightful and complete contrast to the previous maniacal and fierce concentration of presence and is underscored all the more by an occasional dumb and menacing look.

Thomas Mann describes the transition of the composer Adrian Leverkuehn, the Doctor Faustus in the book of that title, from such acutely self-present and destructive power into final madness. The description is of almost unbearable force, a classic instance in which the person collapses under the weight of his own power, a spent tornado. There is another instance of this collapse in Franz Overbeck's account of Friedrich Nietzsche's descent into madness, an account that is in many ways similar to Mann's in describing the hyperpresent person, increasingly present, it seems, only to himself, who then becomes an empty shell.

When we find a shell where there had been acute presence to self and charismatic presence to others, we sense how much in the case of human beings their presence is the equivalent of their whole being. We sense also the inescapable mutuality of presence to oneself with presence to others. In the collapse of presence we grasp as its contrary, not absence, but the loss of everything—the loss of sheer being, of the cohesion of presence with identity that makes up personal being.

Earlier we suggested that Christ's sacramental presence can only be analogous to and not literally the same as physical proximity. Similarly, we said the Word of God is analogous to, but not the same as, human, verbal communication. If now we think of Jesus Christ's presence in the personal terms of sharing and turning and self-presence and presence to others, do we have to qualify its meaning as we did when we thought of presence as physical or verbal? Not precisely. By contrast with the physical or verbal, the personal sense of "presence" does say just what believers want to say of Jesus Christ. It is not used merely analogically. Nonetheless, there are difficulties inherent in it. They arise from the fact that the fully personal use of "presence," when applied to Jesus Christ, is not qualified like the other two, but rather *completed* in a way that is beyond our imagining and conceiving.

Our difficulty here is precisely the contrary of the difficulty in the previous uses of "presence." First, we do not know a situation in which turning and sharing coincide completely, and yet this is what we would want to say about Christ's (or God's) presence. His faithfulness is constant. "Lo, I am with you always, to the close of the age." In any time span—that of our life, of our era, of history—he is always and already there, ongoingly and without interruption. We cannot step out of the relation in which he has joined with us, if he continues; and when we initiate ourselves into the relation, he was already there before us. Yet we also want to say that he is not riveted to that relation; he is free to turn toward and away from men. To have him as our contemporary does not deny that in a different way he was contemporary once and in a yet different one will be present again, as though he had not been present ongoingly. Furthermore, our turning to him may *coincide with,* but is not *identical to,* his turn to us. Our turn is not his turn. His freedom to initiate and terminate remains unimpaired; yet it is one with his constancy and faithfulness. This complete coincidence or identity of sharing and turning we can neither imagine nor conceive.

Secondly, the same thing would have to be said about the complete coincidence or identity of self-presence and presence to others. Like turning and sharing, these two things must converge toward each other in personal experience, but they do not coincide. One may well say, as we have suggested, that my presence to myself and to others may each be the condition for the other. Without their mutuality, I may suffer that complete collapse of being about which we spoke as the opposite of presence. Yet we cannot imagine the complete unity of presence to oneself and presence to another person. We have no experience of this, though Christians have always spoken of love as its foretaste. That unity in which one person experiences another as completely from the inside as he experiences himself, without absorbing the other, can be found only in the Triune God. But for us such a relationship is completely beyond imagining—an empty hunch that somewhere there must be unity of inside and outside experience between persons. The problem is parallel to that of envisaging the unity of Christ's presence and identity; indeed, the two issues involve each other. If that complete unity is actually given to us, the formal talk about it makes good sense; otherwise, it remains idle chatter.

What, in fact, has happened in our reflection on the personal use of "presence" in regard to Jesus Christ is that we have come to the situation envisaged in the introductory essay, in which we said that all our reflection about the presence and identity of Jesus Christ has to be purely formal, assuming that coming into his presence has already happened. The term "presence" in this formal use is perfectly applicable to him. Indeed, in this application our understanding of the term is mysteriously completed—if in fact the presence about which we are trying to speak, Jesus Christ himself, is given in, with, and through that purely formal set of descriptions of presence. If, in other words, his identity is given in unity with his presence, we may rest perfectly content with this formal description. Without that unity, the application of personal presence as a formal notion to him becomes at best empty, and at worst vicious, because it is idolatrous. We are bound to raise the question of Jesus' identity in the course of speaking of his presence and as a way of speaking of his presence, since otherwise talk of his presence dissolves into illusion or covert talk about the human self.

Chapter 3

DOES JESUS HAVE HIS OWN PRESENCE?

We began by saying that comment on the presence and identity of Christ can be no more than formal or circular talk. They are not established by argument. Our task is one of reflection within belief. Concerning the unity of Christ's presence and identity, we said that in this case imagination and judgment are forced to acknowledge him as present. Further, the unity of presence and identity must have a physical and temporal basis in his resurrection. In the last chapter we asked just what is involved in the notion of presence, to see in what manner the term applies to the description of the relation between Christ and believer. We concluded that it does indeed apply, but in a qualified way and in any case in a thoroughly formal manner. Even at that, "presence" implies all along the need for a reference to the specific identity of Jesus, of which we have not yet spoken, in order for us to say anything significant concerning him.

The believer will find this sort of exercise just what he expected it to be—a merely formal one. As we said earlier, it is in its own way part of the celebration of the divine glory and mystery. To the nonbeliever, however, the exercise is not really significant at all, except if he can make the transition from purely formal consideration to a concrete apprehension of Jesus' presence. Many a time the believer will be tempted to support this endeavor, in the hope of helping the nonbeliever over what appears to be an insurmountable barrier. But suspiciously often the effort seems to result in failure. Let us see how this happens by examining a hypothetical attempt to come to terms with Christ's presence without giving prior attention to Christ's identity.

DOES JESUS' PRESENCE DEPEND ON THE RESURRECTION?

The problem that immediately appears is in connection with Jesus' resurrection. The question that has to be faced is this: Does Jesus' presence depend upon his being raised from the dead? Further, in what sense may we consider the resurrection to have meaning? That is to say, does Jesus' presence depend upon a literal and physical resurrection, or is it possible to think of the resurrection symbolically? It is obvious that if Jesus' actual presence is something more than the memory of a departed person or the presence of a ghostly being, the resurrection must be understood in some sense as having happened. A dead Jesus who has not been raised, whether literally or symbolically, can hardly be said to be present with us now. Traditionally, there have always been some who have argued strenuously that the possibility of Christ's presence depends on his resurrection. They have argued first for the credibility of this miracle (and of miracle in general before that). This procedure in turn resulted in fruitless arguments concerning "evidences" for the resurrection of Jesus. I do not want to go into them. If they were ever aids to faith, nowadays they are not.

However, one may still have to try to picture that for which he cannot argue: Must we not be able to imagine the resurrection of Christ if he is present? At the level of the imagination, this means that we should have to try to think of a reversal of the ordinary physiological processes when we represent the resurrection to ourselves. Surely that is at best a difficult task for the imagination. The imagination is used to combining things not united in the everyday world and even of surpassing such things gloriously. From such combinations come poetry, music, and sacrificial deeds, but the actual *reversal* of things is another matter, raising questions that admit of no easy solutions. There is, as we have said, a spatial and temporal basis for Christ's presence, and it must be grasped through the imagination (at some points with the secondary aid of historical science). Thus, we picture in our minds the incarnation, Calvary, and the discovery of the empty tomb. But we must add that the closer the imagination comes to the precise, focal point of that spatial and temporal basis, i.e., to the miraculous act of Jesus' being raised, the closer it comes to its own breakdown point. Moreover, seeking to picture these things is to come dangerously close to being diverted from the fact of Christ's presence to the believer. This thoroughly ambiguous result is probably as far as we can take this problem. That ambiguity undoubtedly does not prevent belief in Christ's presence, but it indicates that any argument for Christ's presence that is based on the imagination will not get us much farther than the argument from evidence.

There are many people who recognize the futility of taking such roads toward faith. They cut the Gordian knot and try to grasp the concrete meaning of presence, distinguishing it sharply from its union with Jesus' identity as crucified and risen Savior. Even if the physical resurrection of Jesus is granted, they say, its miraculous quality serves to *separate* him from our ordinary experience in the actual world or in the imagination, instead of bringing him to it. His resurrection is as though a man had escaped into a wholly different dimension of existence, about which we can know nothing. The manner in which he would then confront us has about it the eeriness that accompanies the story of the raising of Lazarus. It is as though we were being stared at with blank eyes capable of evoking in us only that inner terror that bespeaks our reaction to the presence of an absence—an absence that is similar to nonbeing. Even if resurrected (or especially if resurrected), Jesus is as inaccessible to us, whose lives are confined to this one lifetime and one lifespace, as if he were on another planet with which there is not even the minimum communication of undecipherable radio signals. At best, therefore, the person trying to get from formal talk to a concrete grasp on Jesus' presence, and trying to do so by way of belief in the resurrection, will have a difficult time. It is likely that he will finally come to think that Jesus' presence as resurrected might be something unto Jesus himself, but not anything to us. We cannot imagine it as *shared* presence, as *turning* to us.

JESUS' PRESENCE AS THE WANDERING STRANGER

Indeed, one might well go on to say that he would be more nearly present if he had not been literally raised from the dead. This saying is not nearly so strange to modern ears as it might at first sound. Theologians, from Schleiermacher in the nineteenth century on, have tried to speak of the presence of Jesus Christ in a fashion that would avoid raising the question of Jesus' bodily resurrection. They have done so by connecting the presence of Christ directly with the interior life of the Christian. His presence has been understood, as it were, as the presence of Spirit to spirit mediated through historical events.

Many theologians and ordinary Christians have given up arguing for a miraculous presence from the miracle of resurrection, in order that they might be able to imagine Christ's presence more nearly "religiously," personally, or in a this-worldly manner. We have witnessed what is, all considered, a rather surprising phenomenon with regard to the acquaintance with Jesus, especially in this century, both among folk who are and those who are not overtly Christian or theologically inclined. After having faded from the imagination of sensitive men during the eighteenth and nineteenth centuries, Jesus has reappeared to the inner eye of imagination in the twentieth. His reappearance to contemporary imagination, however, is neither in the orthodox garb of the miraculous Savior raised from the dead nor in the form of the great moral example of heroic action. Instead, as he is frequently depicted in the imagination of present-day writers of fiction, Jesus is the archetypal man, or the pattern for authentic humanity. He is the *stranger*—as we all are—in this harsh and hostile universe. Our spirit's longing is infinite, our capacity for good and evil— though seldom fully exploited—is likewise unbounded. We have no destiny on these alien shores other than death. Where our essential home is, since it is not in this world, we do not know. All we know is that it is neither here nor in a superworld of immortality and eternal personal life—a world in which miracle originates and which is miraculously similar to this world.

In just this wandering estrangement, Jesus is our embodiment or representative. It used to be said of him by people who had broken with the heritage of Christian orthodoxy that he was not a supernatural Savior, but the greatest of the race of moral or historical heroes, the moral example *par excellence*. But Jesus as the incarnation of the wandering human stranger is something different. A great deal of the New Testament story lends credence to this strangely moving interpretation: In Jesus, the typical human situation finds its most concentrated symbolical expression. He has no known human ancestry, no earthly progenitor to establish his identity on earth. As early as the moment of his conception and birth, it is symbolically the case that he has no place to lay his head. The story repeats itself in his wandering ministry, when, unlike foxes and birds, he has no resting place. How symbolic of the real essence of our humanity from which we so often run away into the false hiding places of earthly security!

His end is altogether of a piece with the rest of the story. It is not to be understood as a singular and unrepeatable happening, qualitatively distinct from all others (as, for example, in traditional Western Catholic and Protestant "satisfaction" theories of Jesus' obedience and death). On the contrary, his death is unique precisely and paradoxically because he, unlike others, surrendered all claim to uniqueness by his act of dying and so became one with all of us. He surrendered all false security of reputation by which men try to escape from their true humanity and its ultimately anonymous quality. He died, in other words, on behalf of all men, including those, indeed especially those, who are ignorant of the intimate relation of their own essential humanity with that portrayed by his death. That is why his death speaks to men in such an elemental way, and why they can identify with him in sympathy and even in antipathy. Men realize their own destiny in his destiny, but from this they try to escape, each to a little place of his own, separate from his fellowmen—wealth, position, reputation, ideological causes—anything to establish victory in the quest for one's own particular identity. Jesus, by contrast, is truly "the man for others," the one to whom all things happen and who takes all upon himself in such a way that he becomes the true pattern for all humanity; and yet it is he from whom we try to run away in the quest for our identity—believing the quest to find ourselves to be something significant in its own right But since Jesus is here so identified with ourselves, the running is as much from ourselves as from him. There is the man with whom all men can be identified.

By contrast, moral substitution, an innocent Savior dying a unique and unshared death on behalf of the guilty to satisfy the wrath of a literally offended deity, looks like poor fare. It envisions, we may think, a mechanical as well as an immoral transaction, and our relation to such a terrible and ruthless God as well as to that sort of Savior remains purely external and mechanical—if indeed we are not repelled by such propitiatory sacrifice.

And yet, in another way, even the idea of substitutionary death is capable of metaphoric or symbolic transformation because it speaks to a primordial element in all of us, an element that we cannot possibly articulate. We are united by something even more profound than imagination to the One who bears our universal homelessness. He becomes identified with us as our common archetype, and as such is more nearly a substitute representative for us than he is our moral example. This is true especially of his passion and death. He has no other life than that of all humanity in its homelessness, and his death is its death. The upshot of this reflection is that if we do not use the idea of penal substitution literally, but symbolically, it may be combined very nicely with the thought of Jesus as the universal stranger.

The conclusion to the Gospel story fits the same theme. He has no place to lay his head even in death. He has not even that final vestige of a specific historic identity, the final resting place that supplies a person with the remnant of identity that has been his peculiar claim on this earth—the headstone on his grave. No, *his* tomb is unmarked and empty; it can have no headstone.

And now, it would appear, Jesus rises from the unidentified tomb, symbolically empty, to diffuse his mysterious presence into the imagination and consciousness of human beings, which is the true location of his identity and his life. That, indeed, perhaps we want to say, is his presence, his proper life— not the grave nor any limited and circumscribed earthly temple, not a heavenly and literally conceived counterpart to it, but the depth of men's communal and individual life. It is as though this figure reminded us at once of a past and a future that have nothing to do with literal and historical time, but with intimations of immortality, with our own childhood and that of the race at large, with a similarly timeless future not embodied in any special place or state, but involved with the agony and triumph of human suffering at all times. His conception, birth, life, death, resurrection, and ascension become, in this view, poetic expressions of a dimension of our own existence that belongs to no literal time and place, but to the common ground and horizon of man's true spirit—veiled from sight, but no less real for that.

The condition of his presence to such modern imagination, then, is that he is not literally raised from the dead, but is rather raised symbolically. His resurrection is the symbol of our ascending (or descending) to another level of our being, so that his presence is diffused into and made to represent all mankind seeking to grasp its own basic longing and true hidden spirit. In this view, he cannot, after the fashion of orthodox belief that emphasizes his literal resurrection and ascension, *own his own presence,* or possess a life of his own, for to do so would mean that he is at a different level from our own true being, as if he were on another planet, gazing vacantly at nothing. Owning his own presence there would preclude sharing it with us. No, in order to be present to our imagination, to share our presence, he must be raised symbolically rather than literally.

NO DIRECT ACCESS TO JESUS' PRESENCE

Something like this is the view which tries to speak directly and concretely of Christ's presence. It must reject the merely formal talk of presence, which connects Christ's presence with reference to his unsubstitutable identity by which his presence is self-focused, a presence to himself as well as to us.

When the Christian speaks of Christ's presence, he means that Jesus *owns his own presence and yet turns and shares it with us.* Thus the Christian is forced to part company with the imaginative view discussed above, precisely because what is to him essential about Jesus is left out— his *real* presence. In contrast, Jesus, raised from the dead, is present to himself and therefore can and does share his *real* presence with us.

The result of these reflections seems to be that, regarding the presence of Christ, there can be no real communication between at least one sort of believer and one sort of nonbeliever; for the nonbeliever cannot agree to this claim, except as he tries to make it concrete for himself by losing Jesus' self-presence and identity in his presence to us. In the nonbeliever's view, if Jesus is resurrected from the dead and owns his own presence as a person in his own right, he has no presence to share with us. Only if he is not literally raised from the dead and, hence, does not own his own presence, but diffuses it into our imagination and consciousness, can he share his presence with us. This either/or suggests something of the significant gulf between the believer and the nonbeliever that appears when the believer's purely formal reflection on

Christ's presence and identity is turned into the nonbeliever's endeavor to grasp that presence concretely in his own personal reflection. The endeavor to explain how the process of change from unbelief to faith takes place, the change from presence to absence, or from one interpretation of Christ's presence to the other, is doomed to failure.

Does this mean that there is no communication at all between the Christian and the non-Christian concerning Jesus Christ, and no transition from the one state to the other? Indeed, such communication would seem to force the Christian to distort all that he wants to say about Jesus, for he would have to talk about Jesus as if his presence were a problem, or as if his presence could be detached from his identity and confined to his imagined presence in us, or as if his identity were no more than the presence of humanity at large.

When faced with such problems, the Christian may want to turn away from the very notion of "presence" as a useless trap and, more especially, from reflection about Christ's special way of being present. He may indeed want to concede that, in a rather formal or abstract sense, "presence" may be a useful term for describing the relation between Jesus and believers. That is to say, it is better to talk of his presence than of his absence or nonbeing. But the endeavor, which we have described, to represent the presence of Christ in and to our presence may well mean to the Christian the total diffusion of Jesus into our presence so that he no longer has any presence of his own. The cost of being contemporaneous with him would then be, it seems, that he no longer *owns* his own presence or, if he does, that we cannot apprehend or comprehend that fact. He cannot *turn* to us; he can only *share* with us what he no longer owns for turning. For his turning to us is accomplished only in *our* imagination or perhaps *our* moral decision. There is then a way of talking about the presence of Christ that is, for the Christian, not appropriate to the description of Christ's relation to the believer. It is that of talking about Christ's presence before talking about his identity, of trying directly and concretely in our talk to grasp the presence of Christ. What is grasped is empty space—the shadow of our own craving for full and perpetual presence.

PART II

THE PROBLEM OF IDENTITY

Chapter 4

IDENTITY—
A PERSON'S UNIQUENESS

How are Christians to describe what they believe to be the *presence* of Jesus Christ? At the beginning of this book we said this question could not be answered directly. But even though my claim is that the description of Jesus' identity must precede talk about his presence, I have tried to suggest first the problems that arise if we reverse the order. In Chapters 2 and 3 we began to explore the difficulties that inhere in the word "presence." We noted, first, that there is no precise parallel between the presence of Jesus Christ and the way we think of the presence of other persons and, secondly, that the use of imagination in regard to Jesus cannot adequately represent his presence to us as the resurrected Lord.

Is there, then, another means by which we may know the presence of Christ? At the beginning of this book, we stressed the claim that the identity and presence of Jesus are uniquely related, so that to know *who* he is is also to know his "real" presence. We have assumed that this is true for Jesus in a way that it is not true for others, but we have found that to begin with reflection about his presence leads us to a painful dilemma: If we insist on the purely miraculous nature of Christ's resurrection, our imagination will find him to live unto himself, but in a sphere in which he is not really present to us. Or if we still insist on imagining that he shares his presence with us, his resurrection then becomes a symbol—though an indispensable one—and his identity merges into that of humanity in general. The dilemma, in short, stems from the fact that we cannot reach the singular identity of Jesus Christ by starting simply with his presence. If we still insist on the total unity of presence and identity, as indeed we must, we must begin at the other end—with his identity.

Something like this order or sequence—identity first, then presence—is suggested by biblical exegetes when they stress that the Spirit, who is one with Jesus Christ, could not come before Jesus had withdrawn from the world as a physical being. For large sections of the New Testament, especially Luke and John, a temporal distinction must be made between Jesus' identity as a historical person and his presence to us in his Spirit. We must speak about the identity of Jesus before we can talk about the presence of his Spirit.

IDENTITY—THE SPECIFIC UNIQUENESS OF A PERSON

Now let us come directly to the question of "identity." First, what do we mean by the word? We have been speaking of identity as if this word did not have the kind of problems associated with it that the word "presence" does. But actually the word "identity" is, if anything, more difficult.

All sorts of people—historians, philosophers, and psychologists, as well as poets and writers of fiction—have talked about the meaning or use of the term "identity." Loosely speaking, the word indicates the very "core" of a person toward which everything else is ordered, like spokes to the center of a wheel. It is that something which, if one knows it, provides the "clue" to a person.

Identity is the specific uniqueness of a person, what really counts about him, quite apart from both comparison and contrast to others. Even a contrast between two things means that there must be a common basis for judgment between them. The uniqueness of a person, however, goes beyond the possibility of contrast or comparison with others. One person may, in fact, be the possessor of qualities, even physical properties, that are almost identical to those of another, yet each of them has his own identity. A person's identity is the total of all his physical and personality characteristics referred neither to other persons for comparison or contrast nor to a common ideal type called human, but *to himself.*

The point is significant. Comparative and contrasting reference of characteristics and qualities to other human beings and to a common abstract model of what it is to be human must indeed be present if we are to know anything about a particular person. But such a reference does not constitute his identity. A person's identity is the self-referral, or ascription to him, of his physical and personal states, properties, characteristics, and actions.

To this point we shall return later, but we must now go on to say that identity does not refer simply or exclusively—as we may have seemed to suggest thus far—to the integration of all physical properties and personal characteristics. Identity has, in addition, a temporal refer-

ence, indicated by a term much in vogue in contemporary thought—
"identity crisis." This term often indicates that a person may lack a sense
of identification with something else—a meaningful community or some
other significant point of reference for his life. But, more significantly,
the term may also refer to the lack of identification a person senses
within himself concerning his own past, present, and future. A "crisis"
of identity in this sense is said to exist when a person senses an alienation
from his own past to the extent that it is possible to say that the present
self is not related to the past self. A person may arbitrarily and artificially
reconstruct his past or suppress it altogether. Identity, without this type
of crisis, means that a person is one and the same over a period of time,
that there is a connection or unbroken relationship between the past
and present experience of the same self.

IDENTITY AS SELF-AWARENESS

When we ask how the continuity or connection exists that affords a
person self-relatedness of his past and present, we discover the real complexity of our question about the nature of identity. Only the self can
constitute the bond of connection by which the self of the past passes
over into the present, then to edge into the future. It is I who integrate
myself, including my past and present.

Søren Kierkegaard, in his enigmatic fashion, attempted to describe
how the self constitutes the bond of connection that at once takes the
past, the present, and the future into a single relationship. He wrote:
"Man is spirit. But what is spirit? Spirit is the self. But what is the self?
The self is a relation which relates itself to its own self."[1] Kierkegaard seems
to be saying that the self is the source of its own self-relatedness, that
nothing external to the self can constitute (though it may aid) the continuity between the past, the present, and the future that real identity
requires. Identity, or the temporal continuity of the self, occurs when
the sides or sequential aspects of the self are related to the same self that
is doing the relating between them.

To push our question farther, and ask just what constitutes the
relating factor inherent in the self, raises a hornet's nest of problems
concerning which contemporary philosophers do not agree. For example, consider the problems involved in the term "introspection" or a
description of the means by which self-relatedness (and hence "identity") occurs. Does introspection produce genuine knowledge of the
"core" of the self? This is to ask if we know ourselves in some way different in principles from our knowledge of others (as the term "introspec-

---

1. *The Sickness Unto Death* (Princeton: Princeton University Press, 1944), p. 17.

tion" would seem to imply). But then how, precisely, do we know others? Perhaps we need to ask, Is knowledge of either ourselves or others intuitive (immediate) or is it inferred (based on observations of physical and psychical states and behavior patterns)? Implicit in this last question is the troublesome distinction between the means by which we know *about* a person and knowing the real identity of the person himself who stands "in back" of his behavioral characteristics.

The analysis of these questions, however, important and valid as they are, goes beyond the scope of our general inquiry. Hence, we shall touch upon them only peripherally, insofar as they are pertinent for our thinking. Nevertheless, since the term "identity" seems to require the concept of self-relatedness in some fashion, we cannot altogether avoid probing into what constitutes the factor that relates the past, present, and future of the self to itself. It may well have something to do with self-awareness, or the knowledge of oneself as reflected, for example, in memory. Hence Augustine, "There [i.e., in memory]...do I meet with myself, and recall myself—what, when, or where I did a thing, and how I was affected when I did it."[2]

IDENTITY AS MORAL RESPONSIBILITY

But, then again, it may be that the factor to be stressed regarding the analysis of identity is not so much self-awareness as it is moral responsibility. When one takes responsibility *now* for the private as well as public consequences of a past deed or decision of his own, he establishes or at least affirms the fact of identity in the shape of self-continuity from past to present. Further, if we make the assumption that moral responsibility is a prime relating factor between a person's past, present, and future, we have come close to another area in which identity may be analyzed—the area of *conscience*. But the main reference in the description of the self as conscience is not the relation between past and present in the self. Rather, conscience chiefly refers to an interior dialogue within the self concerning actions past, present, and future. In this dialogue a disinterested observer or critical evaluator talks with me from within. Just whom he represents within me is a question answered differently by different theorists. Some have said God, others the free self, others the society in which the self lives.

So far we have suggested that identity occurs at the point of total integration of the self by itself. It is the specific form of one's interior self-disposal. When such integration occurs, a person is seen as unique,

---

2. *Basic Writings of Saint Augustine,* Whitney J. Oates, ed. (New York: Random House, 1948), vol. I, p. 154.

without comparison or contrast to any external point of reference. The point of reference is purely *internal* to the individual person who constitutes a self-relatedness that is continuous over a period of time. Similarly, we have suggested that internal or self-reference constitutes the physical and personal attributes of a person into a single and unified pattern rather than two parallel series of self-relatedness. But when we seek to discover the relating factor— sensing that it may be something like self-awareness, memory, moral responsibility, or conscience—the temptation is to turn it into a point of reference constituting a superadded attribute of the person. An attribute such as conscience is viewed in that case like a characteristic such as good humor, firmness, blue eyes, etc., except that it is supposedly capable of acting as a pole around which all other factors are integrated. Such a conclusion is questionable if for no other reason than that the search for distinguishing signs or manifestations of this superfactor draws a blank. For example, if we ask what, in addition to all a person's observable and describable qualities, characteristics, and states (both physical and personal), makes a person the unsubstitutable person he is, we find nothing discernible. A person is what and who he is just by the way he holds all these things together and orders them; and to tell how he does that, all we can do is to refer to the same qualities and the way they are ordered.

IDENTITY—NOT A "GHOST IN THE MACHINE"

What we have attempted thus far is to take cognizance of a difficult puzzle that the sages of Western culture since the time of Plato and Aristotle have not been able to solve: *Is the identity (or the "soul") a distinguishable factor over and above all describable characteristics and the one that integrates them all? Or is it simply another name for the integrative pattern they form?* It is important for us to understand that there is such an argument, but also that we need not and must not enter into it. It was carried on by ancient philosophers, medieval theologians, post-Reformation philosophers, and also by nineteenth-century thinkers who wanted to believe in evolution without giving up belief in the reality of self-developing vital spirit in man. If we now enter into this argument, we have in effect gone beyond our own task of purely descriptive talk and into metaphysics. That is to say, we should have to claim that before talk about the identity and presence of Jesus is possible, we should have to settle the issue of whether human identity depends on the affirmation of the reality of the human soul. That is precisely what I am not going to do. Our talk is from within belief and, in regard to this as well as other philosophical questions, purely formal and descriptive. We take the presence and identity of Jesus for granted, just as we do human presence and identity. And we are simply trying to discover how the description of one helps in the description of the other. Moreover, we are saying that, for this limited purpose, the theory of the "superadded factor" is not helpful. Both physically and personally, a person's identity is his self-referral beyond comparison and contrast. That self-referral is not a mysterious X in back of the physical and personal characteristics. For descriptive purposes, a person's uniqueness is not attributable to a super-added factor, an invisible agent residing inside and from there directing the body, or what Gilbert Ryle has called "a ghost in the machine." (This does not adjudicate the metaphysical question of the nature and reality status of the substantial soul.)

The most we can do with identity description (as distinguished from metaphysical explanation) is to indicate that the self relates itself to itself. Apparently, we cannot come up with any single factor within the self that has unifying power. But even if we avoid settlement of the metaphysical dilemma about the soul by sticking solely with descriptions rather than explanations for what it is that is describable, there is nevertheless a problem that we must face. We know that the self is not disconnected from the fundamental modifications it undergoes, but it is also true that we may discern the continuity of a person within these changing states, properties, and actions. All of us know that there are actions so typical of a person that when we see them we say, "That's him, all right!" But that very same person may reappear at another time in an action that is totally different in character from his previous behavior. Still, this new action may be so important that we now say, "What he did just now represents all that he now is." Just for that reason we should then go on to say with astonishment, recalling the previous actions, "My, how he's changed!"

We undergo this experience frequently, and it offers no difficulty. Still, it is mysterious, certainly for explanation if not for description of identity. Identity description is the ingathering into a connected story of both stages. On the one hand, we have to say that that to which changing actions, states, and properties are ascribed or referred is nothing more than they themselves under a certain focus, the focus of self-referral. And when the actions, states, and properties change, their change is the self's change. On the other hand, no set of changing states, properties, and, in particular, set of actions, exhausts the self in such a way that it cannot also provide the *bond of continuity* between these distinct acts, states, and properties which it is.

We shall have to undertake a further refinement of our understanding of identity later on, in connection with the interpretation of the identity of Jesus in the Gospel story. I want to indicate now a distinction to be explored more fully at that time.

First, there is a kind of description indicating more nearly the way a particular person is himself at a given time than the unbroken continuity of his identity. We try to follow at that point the path by which someone's particular intention develops into action. There is a real or hypothetical "inside" description of that transition, of which all of us are aware but of which it is not easy to give an account. The intention is not an independent mental "thing" having a spiritual life of its own in back of the act embodying it. Intention and action are one process. Yet it is obvious that there must be a distinction between them, for not all intentions are carried into action. Now the whole person may be described under the pattern of "intention-action" description. For a person is not merely illustrated, he is *constituted* by his particular intentional act at any given point in his life. This kind of identity description we shall be calling "intention-action." The judgments formed in respect to a person's intention and action are in answer to the question, "What is he like?"

Secondly, when we try to describe the unbroken continuity of identity through its changes, we do so by raising the simple yet puzzling question, *Who is* the person under consideration? In other words, we ask concerning the *subject* or the particular identity manifest in a set of actions, in a particular bodily pattern, in the words he speaks, and in the name given to him. I shall call this attempt to describe human identity through continuing placement or location "self-manifestation" description. Both of these types of identity description will be employed in connection with our inquiry into Jesus' identity as set forth in the Gospel story.

Chapter 5

THE SAVIOR AS SPECIFIC MAN

We have just spoken briefly of identity in two ways. First, we described it as an intentional act, suggesting that a person is as he acts. What he does in a connected sequence of events over a limited period of time tells us what he is like. Here the focus of attention is on the person's intentions and actions as they can be reported in a narrative account of his life. In this type of identity description, we are concerned about a person's specific deeds as the focus of identity.

Secondly, we have spoken of identity in terms of a person's manifestation as a total being. Here the emphasis is not on the specific acts of a person, but on the continuity of the person as he persists through all the changes that take place in his life.

Can either of these two types of identity description be used to describe the identity of Jesus Christ? The answer to this question will be prescribed for us by the New Testament itself. Not theoretical argument for the possibility but its exegetical application will dictate the success or failure of the enterprise.

We have been dealing, thus far, with formal categories of identity. We may note that such intellectual instruments have a habit of taking charge of the materials to be described. With this warning before us, our task, nevertheless, is to see if these two kinds of identity description can help us ascertain what the New Testament says about the identity of Jesus Christ. We shall try to determine this by actual commentary on the New Testament, especially on the Synoptic Gospels. In doing so, we shall not ask how we can make what the New Testament says about Jesus significant in our present life, but simply, "What does the New Testament say about Jesus?" Expanding that question, we want to know if the narrative account of the New Testament concerning Jesus falls into any significant states or transitions of development and, if so, whether they cast any light on the identification of Jesus as the narrative's chief character.

In this undertaking, identity description is designed simply to furnish us with ways of thinking about the person of Jesus as he appears in the narrative of events in the Gospels. The usefulness of this kind of analysis, however, will depend on the extent to which it may vividly portray aspects of the Gospel narrative, without damaging the integrity and flow of that narrative by the imposition of artificial intellectual categories or structures. In other words, if these categories and concepts are suitable formal instruments, they should enable us to see who Jesus is without determining better than the text itself the meaning and importance of what the Gospels have to say about him. These categories should serve as organizing patterns to help us understand the actual structure of the text and bring it into relief together with the story's content.

PRELIMINARY ASSUMPTIONS

There is a twofold assumption involved in the hope that identity description is useful for this purpose. First, it is assumed that both the New Testament writers and we ourselves hold in common some of the same sorts of description of human identity and, furthermore, that the identity of Jesus which the New Testament discloses—along with the clue it gives to the identities of other human beings—is of vital importance within the New Testament itself.

Secondly, we assume that the category of "identity" heightens rather than interferes with the description of the uniqueness, specific character, quality, and actions of human beings—and in this case, of course, Jesus of Nazareth, as he is presented in the actual text of the Gospel story. Indeed, identity description is intended to help us concentrate attention on what happens to Jesus, without pushing us into the more remote regions of the underlying assumptions and convictions of the Gospel writers that may govern the text, or into the question of the relation of our own attitude to the structure and content of the text.

It is, of course, true that every author—including the writers of the Synoptic Gospels—writes from some governing convictions and with some theme or intention in mind, even if it be no more than the telling of a good tale. Obviously, the Gospel writers wanted to do much more than that. But we cannot with any certainty tell their convictions and intentions apart from the narrative text. In other words, we shall not cull them out of the Gospel as separable themes. To do so without regard for the narrative pattern would make these convictions as thin and uncommunicative as it is to paraphrase the meaning of a poem or a novel by distilling it out and separating it from its language and imagery or its story and then presenting it in a didactic form. We lose the meaning together with the work that way.

Now the cases are obviously not completely parallel: The Gospel is neither a poem nor a novel. Still, it is in large part and at crucial points a story. Hence we must say that culling the author's intentions out as separable objects of special importance, though possible, is so one-sided that it demands immediate correction by a view that looks for the Gospel's significance in the narrative structure itself. The intentions of the authors must be seen in that context. Further, we do not arrive at the convictions and intentions of the authors by supplying them out of our own frame of reference and then attaching them to the Gospel writers. As obvious as this point seems to be, it is of more than peripheral importance.

There are, of course, differences between our own world view and those of ancient writers. But this fact should actually make one extremely cautious about claiming for the Gospels convictions and outlooks appropriate to our own understanding of the problems of the self and of the universe. Without such caution we tend to consign the things that do not fit our world views to ancient mythical beliefs or, at best, to mythologized expressions of what the Gospels and we hold in common. Precisely because we must insist that the story has an integrity in its own right and yet want to affirm some important affinities between patterns of meaning in it and those we ourselves understand, we have to be extremely wary about supplying the Gospels too freely with our own profoundest convictions or our analyses of the structures of distinctive human being.

If we must exercise such care in limiting the scope of the intellectual tools with which we read the Gospel narrative to determine the *author's* intentions, or the understanding of life and world pervading the text, we must be even more careful with regard to Jesus himself. In other words, if the convictions and intentions of a Gospel writer and the understanding of existence manifested in the writing cannot be ascertained except by sticking to the story as it is told, how much more difficult it is to grasp the conviction and intention of Jesus about whom the story is told! Now it would not do for us to say simply and straightforwardly that we have *no* knowledge of Jesus' intentions or disposition as they are embodied in the Gospel writer's convictions concerning him and in the narrative text. To take the matter even farther, we shall not dogmatically assume that just because a high degree of speculation is involved, we know nothing concerning Jesus' own understanding of his identity and mission through these writings about him by other men. Nor shall we dogmatically assert the opposite, viz., that we have reliable knowledge of his disposition and self-identification.

About Jesus' intentions and his own convictions concerning his identity, one simply has to listen to and weigh specific proposals made by historians, always realizing that they are and will remain speculative and therefore only more or less likely or credible. Furthermore, it is always possible that the degree of a claim's credibility is proportional to its modesty.

The important thing, however, is that we realize the limited value and reliability of such ventures. For each is more limited in value and more speculative as it takes us farther beyond the narrative text and forces us to rely more and more heavily on the independent power of our own interpretative devices to unlock the significance of the story.

WHERE JESUS IS MOST FULLY HIMSELF

When we turn to the figure of Jesus in the Gospels, our perspective in earlier chapters forecasts what will be for many a problematical outcome. If we regard the Gospel narrative simply as such—i.e., as a story (whether fictional or real)—the individual, specific, and unsubstitutable identity of Jesus in the story is most fully set forth in his resurrection appearance. Indeed, in the Gospel story the human person of Jesus of Nazareth becomes most fully himself in the resurrection. Moreover, the focusing of his full identity in the resurrection is what enables him to turn and share his presence with his disciples.

Luke, in climaxing the resurrection with the ascension story, highlights the fact to which the mysterious veiledness of the resurrection appearances had already pointed. Jesus has a location of his own, and only as he is able to withdraw from a common location with men to one distinctly his own, does he turn to share his presence with them in the Spirit. In a way, the narrative's emphasis on Jesus' having his own location or self-presence is made clearest in the story of Paul's conversion. When Paul asked the bearer of the lordly voice in his vision on the road to Damascus to identify himself, the reply was, "I am Jesus" *(Acts 9: 1-5; 26: 1-15).* And even more pointedly, as if to specify the identity as closely and unsubstitutably as possible, "I am Jesus of Nazareth" *(22:8).* What we have here is the claim that the presence of Jesus after his death is fully identical with who he was and what he did in the flesh before his death. He is none other than Jesus of Nazareth. His presence is self-focused and not diffused.

From all we have said earlier in this essay, it is evident that many of our contemporaries who wish to identify with Jesus as the mysterious archetypal presence do not agree to what we have just said. From their perspective the outcome of our questions concerning Jesus' identity in the Gospel narrative may well be quite unfortunate. By claiming the unsubstitutable singular identity of Jesus in the resurrection, and the self-focus of his presence there, we are in their eyes denying the very possibility of the presence of Christ now.

In connection with the search for the direct presence of Christ, we mentioned the tantalizing symbolic quality of so many of the signal events in the Gospels. There was his virginal conception and his home-less birth and, later on, the lack of a place to lay his head. In addition, there was the representative nature of his death and, finally, his ultimate nonentity. And then, as a fitting paradox, there is his universal presence, symbolized by the emptiness of his tomb. To these events we may add certain mythological elements with which they fit nicely. (I prefer to call these elements "stylized" to indicate their connection with conventional late Jewish and Oriental-Hellenistic thought.) The titles of Jesus come especially to mind, particularly his association with the Messianic, qua-sipersonal, and supernatural figure of the Son of Man. Such a title adds grist to the mill for those who try to understand Jesus' identity as sym-bolizing all mankind in its mystery and strangeness.

It is always tempting to put much, if not all, of what is told about Jesus in the Gospels into an explanatory context of this sort: Here was a perfectly extraordinary figure of charismatic presence; what could be more natural than that the stories of his life and death, his teachings, and his mysterious representative identity should be grasped by fitting them into the religious molds of the Jewish and Oriental-Hellenistic world that were readily available? The story of the resurrection would be the fitting capstone to the mythologizing process. It would be the most appropriate symbolic way of grasping the mysterious sense of what it is to be human, to gain our identity and presence in the midst of our homelessness in this world.

In other words, to say that the Gospel story and its climax in Jesus' resurrection focused sharply on his singular identity and self-presence meets with stern objections. Not only does this view eliminate for many the possibility of Christ's presence, but in their view it is not even faith-ful to the identity of Jesus' portrayal in the Gospel story. Their argument is twofold. First, they claim that in order to grasp the real story of Jesus it is necessary to go behind the story told in the Gospels in some such manner as we illustrated earlier. The example of Jesus as the wandering human stranger is only one among many. Secondly, they argue that the Gospel story most likely supports their view of human identity because it is the commonly held view. Moreover, it supports the element of myth in the religious matrix out of which early Christianity arose. The New Testament, so it seems, shares the common heritage of mythological religion.

It is in pursuit of the latter issue that we are driven to the suspicion of mythology at the very heart of the Gospel story, the sequence from his passion to his resurrection—the group of events that provides the climax toward which the whole story of Jesus is ordered. It is indeed true that mythological, saving gods died and rose again in liberal numbers in the ancient Mediterranean world, especially at the time of the birth of the Christian community. Also, segments of the Jewish community were expecting the resurrection of the dead at the coming of the Messiah. In other words, the common cultural backdrop and similarity in themes which the Gospel narrative shares with other redemption stories is bound to raise the question concerning whether the Christian story is at all unique. This being the case, I shall not attempt to evaluate the *historical* reliability of the Gospel story of Jesus or argue the unique truth of the story on grounds of a true, factual "kernel" in it. Instead, I shall be focusing on its character as a story. As for history, I shall take for granted only what most commentators agree upon: that a man, Jesus of Nazareth, who proclaimed the Kingdom of God's nearness, did exist and was finally executed.

We began this chapter by affirming our intention to apply the fruits of our identity analysis to the figure of Jesus in the Gospels. We affirmed in a preliminary way that this is appropriate because the Gospel story presents Jesus' identity as that of a singular, unsubstitutable person, especially in the sequence from his passion to his resurrection. This view of the Savior's identity we now find challenged. We must therefore make a detour before proceeding with our attempt to understand Jesus' identity from the reading of the Gospel. In the next chapter we shall try to distinguish the Gospel story of the Savior from a common savior myth of the period. It is a myth that has many affinities with the view that Christ is genuinely present only if he is symbolically, rather than literally, raised from the dead. In the two subsequent chapters we shall pursue the issue of the identity of the saving figure—whether that of Jesus or of someone modeled after him—in the modern literary world. Only then shall we be able to return to our prime task, that of tracing Jesus' identity in the Gospel story.

PART III

DISTORTIONS OF CHRIST'S IDENTITY

Chapter 6

REDEEMED REDEEMER IN MYTH AND GOSPEL

Since we have turned from the question of the presence of Christ to that of his identity, we must ask if Jesus' real identity in the Gospel story is like that which is indicated in the savior myths that were current in the time when he lived. It seems safe to say that there were at least two kinds of myths pertaining to the dying and rising savior god, both of them influenced by and influencing early Christianity. One kind of myth is an aspect of "mystery religion." It was an ecstatic, sometimes orgiastic kind of religion, in which secret rites, especially of initiation, opened the door for a sense of elemental participation in the constantly reiterated rhythm of death and rebirth, a cycle that binds man and all organic nature together. In ritual reiteration we sense our kinship with the fertility of nature, with the mysterious loss and renewal of her strength, and with the pulsating life flowing in both nature and ourselves. The ritual killing of an innocent animal victim and being sprinkled with his blood, the sexual orgy, the dance, are some of the ways by which the primordial unity of all nature is represented and enacted. At the level of mythological representation, this primordial renewal is mirrored in the story of the dying and rising savior god.

But there was at least one other, much more individualistic and sophisticated form of the dying and rising savior myth. Its endlessly proliferated varieties are gathered together under the collective heading of Gnosticism. The mythical accounts of the Gnostic savior's death and rising are usually precise, detailed, and allegorical, involving the personification of abstract entities like "truth," "depth," and "creator." Here myth functions in a far more deliberate way than in the mystery religions. In other words, its function is that of a reflective, intellectual pointer to something else, mysterious and hidden in the depths of the self.

The myth in Gnosticism is not, as it is in mystery religions, the celebration in story form of the immediate unity of life in nature and man. Instead, it is more nearly designed to evoke a kind of interior insight. Yet this insight is not simple and capable of straightforward intellectual representation. Far more than an explanatory scheme, the insight is the process of the discovery of a certain awareness—the awareness of the harmony, disrupted and regained—of a man's identity beyond his life in nature and society. Indeed, life in nature and society is a profound distraction or "scattering" of man's essential being. Life is understood as "fallen," and the burden of being alienated from oneself or "fallen" is really the same as being born into this life.

It must be emphasized, however, that the mythical expression "fall," as used in Gnostic thought, is not pressed to the point that death would become the equivalent of the true return home to oneself. On the contrary, death is at best an equivocal friend. The return to oneself from the "fall" into this life comes much more nearly with the shock of recognition of the alienated nature of life and with the new insight of the depth of this recognition—a recognition so profound that its reflective expression can only be symbolical. For the Gnostic, this means that truth always points to an ineffable, inexpressible inner unity best articulated by the word "silence." Since that unity or silence cannot be directly expressed, it finds one of its indirect (or mythological) statements in the account of the dying and rising savior. This savior is at the same time divine savior and—what really amounts to the same thing—archetypal man, standing for the qualities of falling and returning in all those who gain insight into the true state of things.

We are actually in a curious position in undertaking such an account of Gnosticism. First, there is the endless diversity of Gnostic types, not easily brought under a common heading. Secondly, the experts are by no means agreed as to whether or not the motif of the redeemer, both in need of redemption and redeemed as well as redeeming, is central for Gnosticism. Finally, just because the Gnostics seem to have seen myth as the indispensable expression and not as the imperfect shape of true thought—understood as interior personal meaning—they do not provide us with an interpretative "clue" by which the myth may be grasped. Obviously, they would think that the only way for us to understand what they were about is to learn the same insights they had, no matter how we may express them with our own symbols and myths.

But let us, until better instructed in wisdom, assume that something of Gnostic thinking *can* be described and that the dying and rising savior or redeemed-redeemer motif is indeed part of that structure. Is it, then, similar to the death and resurrection story in the Gospels? Certainly the possibility cannot be denied, just as the pattern of mystery religion also shows significant parallels to early Christianity. But there are also some clearly discernible differences. One is that the New Testament story deals simply and exclusively with the story of Jesus of Nazareth, whether it is fictional or real, and not with anybody else or with every man under the cover of Jesus' name. Another is the manner of the savior's activity, concerning which there are at least four interrelated distinctions between the Christian and Gnostic stories. These we shall now examine.

GNOSTIC AND CHRISTIAN
UNDERSTANDINGS CONTRASTED

In the first place, the Gnostic redeemer and the redeemer of the mysteries have to be redeemed from a syndrome of things, among which are the savior's own alienation and death which he, as archetypal man, standing for all mankind, has undergone. This seems quite clear for Gnosticism, since projection into historic, natural reality in itself constitutes man's self-alienation. This is, of course, not so for early Christianity.

To exist in human history may well mean the incurrence of guilt, the Christian equivalent of alienation, but existence and guilt are not identical. The redeemer in the Christian story is one man who, in the course of his career, incurs no guilt of his own from which he would have to be redeemed, although indeed he must be saved from the power of death and evil, both the evil that guilty men inflict on him and the evil of demonic powers.

Secondly, despite the fact that the Christian, unlike the Gnostic, redeemer is not self-alienated, his need for redemption appears to be far greater. His powerlessness and helplessness in the face of death, his fellowmen's sins, and the evil of other God-opposing powers seem far more drastic and complete than in the case of the Gnostic redeeming, archetypal man, who is both the fallen and the redeeming figure.

In the third place, far more drastically than in other schemes, in the Christian story it is precisely the savior's complete need for redemption and the fact of his death that have saving efficacy. They do not constitute simply a transient stage in an organic rhythm of dying and rising, the totality of which would be the saving process. I do not mean to say that the story of the resurrection is not a fitting, indeed necessary, climax to the narration of the redeeming events. But each event in the story—passion, death, resurrection—has the sort of uniqueness, integrity, and finality one finds in lifelike reports, fictional or real, in contrast to mythical stories. The connection of each event with the preceding and succeeding ones is not such that there is a bond suggesting some inevitable dialectic of the human psyche or external fate. Instead, the bond between the events is such that each succeeding occurrence is perfectly appropriate to what went before, and yet each has a certain accidental or contingent, rather than inevitable, quality about it. So the bond between events in the Gospel story simply has no meaning and does not exist apart from the occurrence of the events themselves in their sequence within the story. In this way, then, Jesus' death in the New Testament story is a unique event having its own integrity or finality within the sequence, in a way that the organically linked dying-rising motion of the other schemes does not. Of course, his redeeming efficacy comes to a climax only in his being himself redeemed; and yet the singularity of each event in the sequence means that the irreducible fact of his completely helpless need of redemption is the only path by which he redeems others. "With his stripes we are healed."

Finally, in the Christian story Jesus redeems others, not only by his helplessness, but also by the congruence or harmony of his helplessness with his perfect obedience, his moral purity. He becomes *vicariously* identified with the guilty in their need by undergoing the same need in innocence and purity. By contrast, the Gnostic redeemer saves the alienated by being himself alienated and by indicating the organic unity of alienation with purity.

This contrast has forced Christian thinkers, from the earliest days on, in two directions at the same time. They have had to insist, almost to the point of heresy, that Jesus' identification with the helplessness of the sinners for whom he died was so complete that there was a mysterious coincidence between his purity and their sin. But with equal propriety they refused to pursue that theme to its final conclusion. This they did because that very coincidence or identification is and must remain one with Jesus' deliberate and *vicarious* adoption of the other's guilt, rather than a mysterious *organic* identity of guilt and innocence in his own person. The proper ambivalence on this issue concerning Jesus' uniting unique purity with radical identification with sinners has been suggested by the apostle Paul: "For our sake he made him to be sin who knew no sin, so that in him we might become the righteousness of God" *(II Cor. 5:21)*.

THE REAL DIFFERENCE BETWEEN
THE GOSPEL STORY AND OTHERS

But the chief obstacle to a simple and straightforward parallel between the story of Jesus and other redeemed-redeemer accounts lies neither in the difference between the saving qualities and action nor in the difference between redemptive needs. It is simply the unsubstitutable person about whom the story is told—his unsubstitutable deeds, words, and sufferings—that makes the real difference. Such exclusive reference to the person of Jesus as is found in the Gospel story is characteristic of neither Gnostic nor mystery religions. The Gospel story's indissoluble connection with an unsubstitutable identity in effect divests the savior story of its mythical quality. The Gospel story is a demythologization of the savior myth because the savior figure in the Gospel story is fully identified with Jesus of Nazareth. The early Christians would substitute no other name.

This exclusive identification of the savior figure with Jesus was quite uncanny. In the first place, the writers allowed no human substitute for Jesus. This was vitally important to them, and on this crucial point they all agreed. In the second place, they tended (though with some exceptions) to have the human person, Jesus, bestow identity on the savior figure rather than the reverse. In Mark's Gospel, for example, the Messianic Son of Man figure is still strongly to the fore, almost detached from a historical mooring in Jesus, but then—and one can almost sense the surprise of the author—it becomes necessary fully to identify the Son of Man with Jesus of Nazareth. This is also true of the Christ figure in Paul's letters and of the Son in the Fourth Gospel. In all these cases, it appears that the identification was both unavoidable and radically complete.

This complete identification of the savior figure in the Christian story with Jesus of Nazareth accounts for the radical nature of the redeemer's need for redemption in the Gospel story. He, the savior, became just as helpless as the human brethren with whom he was completely one—a statement that needs qualification only in the case of the Fourth Gospel. The savior's helplessness and purity are in the Gospels' telling perfectly identical with the story of Jesus' unique identity, past sign, and death as told by the Gospel narrative. This fact alone is sufficient to account for all the differences between the early Christian narratives and other redemption stories.

We said that there are two chief differences between Christian and Gnostic redemption stories. First, in the Gospel story, unlike the Gnostic stories, the savior is completely identical with a specific human being, Jesus of Nazareth. Secondly, they differ in their accounts of the manner of salvation and of the savior's activity. These two differences are, in fact, one, for the second is really founded on the first. The story of salvation and the savior in the New Testament narrative is completely one and the same with the story of Jesus' singular obedience in passion and death.

In the New Testament narrative, the savior's action is not independent of the savior himself, as it is in the Gnostic myth, for which there is no identity between the savior story and a specific, individual human being. The glory of Gnosticism is the opposite of that of the Christian story. The Gnostic savior story remains an undivested and undivestable myth; in the New Testament the myth is demythologized because the story is a self-enactment in word and deed of a specific person.

If this analysis is correct, certain consequences immediately follow. In the first place, the Gnostic myth represents a surprising exception to the claim that in Jesus Christ alone presence and identity are completely one. In a certain sense, the Gnostic savior's presence is indeed totally at one with his identity; and through him those privileged to gain deep insight into the mystery of things reach the same state. They reach, that is to say, a kind of full self-possession at the deepest level, a grasp of the mystery of their human identity within the compass of an infinite universe. To reach this point seems to be the goal of the savior myth. The savior is the primeval man, in whom the innocence, alienation, and redemption of all those who have true insight is mirrored. Indeed, when they behold him they behold themselves. His being is nothing other than their presence to themselves or, to put it another way, their grasp upon their own presence. This merging of the primordial man, the fallen and rising redeemer, with the realization of human self-presence is possible only because it takes place out of time; in other words, because it is a myth. This unity of men and redeemer in the Gnostic myth is paralleled by the organic unity—also taking place out of time—between fall and redemption. The two things, alienation and redemption, finally come to be one and the same thing. In effect, this unity of opposites means that one's identity and the acceptance of his nonidentity are one; presence and nonbeing or lack of presence are one.

What we are saying cannot, for the true Gnostic, be expressed non-mythically. To go beyond myth is to go beyond all articulation. The only state of final truth left after that, the ultimate font of all true identity and presence, is silence—from which all speech issues, the infinite, unplumbed abyss of being whence all truth comes and to which it returns. In that abyss all true identity and presence are one, because neither is self-focused. The result of this lack of focus is that true identity is equivalent to having none. So, too, one's presence is totally diffused. The abyss of being and nothingness are one and the same. In other words, the unity of presence and identity in the Gnostic myth lies in the acceptance of the common loss of both. This insight into ourselves—into the common nonentity of our presence and identity—is what the "rising" of the savior comes to mean in the Gnostic savior accounts.

Secondly, our analysis implies a clear contrast between this strenuous and finally direct grasp of the unity of one's presence and identity within the Gnostic savior myth and the unity of presence and identity in the Christian savior. For one thing, the unity of the latter lies solely in the savior's own singular, unsubstitutable, and self-focused being. It is neither the presence nor the identity of humanity at large. For another, the unity is grasped in a conceptual sequence, identity first and presence second, a clear indication of the importance of the self-focused nature of the savior's being. Finally, Jesus Christ's presence and identity are not known directly through our own insight. To know Jesus one must indeed know who he is; and before he can be known, he must be able to withdraw from our grasp and turn to us from his own presence. He does indeed withdraw and then turn to us before we can share his presence or—to put it another way—his "Spirit."

In short, our detour has emphasized the claim that the savior of the Christian story cannot be confused with mythological savior figures. As we have noted and shall explicate later, the Christian savior story is that of Jesus himself. He determines the story as the crucial person in the story. Hence, his identity is not grasped by a knowledge of savior stories, including those which appropriated his figure to represent them.

Chapter 7

JESUS CHRIST AND
MODERN CHRIST FIGURES

A full justification of the Christian description must await the detailed examination of the Gospel narrative in Chapters 10-13. In this chapter I shall try to sketch a figure who is in some ways reminiscent of the Gnostic savior, and in others of Jesus in the Gospel story. This figure, appearing frequently in modern fiction, goes by the term "Christ figure" because of his apparent resemblance to the Christ of the Gospels.

What is a "Christ figure"? At the risk of forcing a lot of diversity into one ill-fitting straitjacket, we must try a definition. To begin with, we must say again that our task is the purely formal one of setting forth the identity of Jesus Christ as being one with his presence and that the proper order for thinking about our task is to begin with questions about his identity. In other words, acquaintance with Jesus Christ is already presupposed in our analysis. His identity as Savior is therefore already assumed. Hence we, unlike literary critics, can try to define what a "Christ figure" is without examining the whole range of literary specimens that could be cited. We take the New Testament picture of Jesus as our norm, and there we find three interlocking features. Let us examine these in order then to get at the distinctions between Jesus and the "Christ figures" of literature.

First, there is the cosmic scope of his redeeming activity. This scope comes into view in the story about him through the use of certain stylized elements, chiefly the Messianic titles that are applied to him. But it is also evident in the miracles, Jesus' preaching, his death, and his resurrection. All these point to the unusual character of this man. In conjunction with his identification as the Son, they heighten the impression of unusual power, amounting to cosmic scope, that is present in him.

Second, there is the personal and unsubstitutable center that is

Jesus, his personal uniqueness. This is the element in the story which stands in such marked contrast to the Gnostic savior myth. The savior figure of the Gospels is fully identified with this individual person as he enacts his identity in the history of his events and in his unique "style," that of perfect obedience first in power and then in powerlessness.

In the third place, there is a certain pattern in that unique personal existence which provides the bond between the individuality of the Savior and the cosmic scope of his activity. The "perfect obedience" referred to in connection with his irreducible individuality is already part of it, but there is more to the pattern. It consists chiefly in the quality that made him an individual who nonetheless incorporated humanity at large into himself. The pattern is that of an exchange, the substitution of his innocent back for the guilty by carrying the load of all who suffer with them and even for them. Invariably the pattern recalls to the New Testament writers, and later to Christians, the figure of the obedient and suffering servant in Isaiah, Chapter 53.

Taken by itself, there is no clear indication that the suffering servant of Isaiah is Messianic in status or cosmic in outreach. The figure only assumes such lofty proportions when the pattern exhibits the unique, unsubstitutable individual who is at the same time the universal Savior, Jesus. In him the suffering servant becomes both a unique individual and the universal Savior. Furthermore, there is provided in the pattern of the suffering servant a continuity between Jesus and the history of Israel, and hence a way of identifying the followers of Jesus with one another.

It is worthy of note that this pattern of exchange between guilt and innocence is at least in some respects reminiscent of the Gnostic pattern of alienation and reconciliation, fall and redemption, in the redeemer figure. However, we must recall the differences between them, which we outlined earlier. The mystery of the vicarious assumption of guilt by the obedient man, Jesus of Nazareth, is different from the organic unity of innocence, alienation, and redemption seen in a mythical savior figure who falls, dies, and then rises. Nonetheless, the pattern of exchange between the redeemer and those in need of redemption is a way of bringing the suffering servant pattern into significant contact with the world of savior myths into which Christianity was born.

THE CHRIST OF SCRIPTURE, THE REAL CHRIST FIGURE

A Christ figure must have all three elements—universal redeeming scope, the unsubstitutable personal identity in which the scope is enacted, and the pattern enacted by that person's history. It is therefore important to say that obviously—by definition—the Christ figure's identity is already preempted by him who actually is the Christ of Scripture. In short, there can be no Christ figure because Jesus is the Christ, unless an author depicts the figure in terms of a particular identity and pattern wholly different from that of Jesus' story. But in that case it would not make any sense to talk of a Christ figure at all. To speak of Christ involves an enormous claim—a claim so large that it is made *exclusively* of whomever it is made. The claim is that *in one unique case* identity and presence are so completely one that to know who he is to confront his presence. In him and in him alone, so the claim goes on, are also to be found these three elements by which the "Christ figure" is identified. It is either one unique figure of whom this holds true, or no one at all. And in that case, a reiteration of his particularity in somebody else becomes impossible.

In this and the next chapter I shall try to illustrate the unwarranted confusion of certain mysterious persons in literature with Christ figures, and also the doubtful success (from a Christian perspective) of stories endeavoring to depict either Jesus or a figure identical with him. The closer such stories press toward their goal, the less convincing they are. The Christ figure, it has been suggested, has three aspects—universal scope, individual identity, and the pattern of saving action uniting them. We shall look at three stories, each in its turn embodying at least one of these qualities. Herman Melville's *Billy Budd* presents us with a figure of cosmic outreach. Nikos Kazantzakis' *The Last Temptation of Christ* tells the story of Jesus of Nazareth in novel form. Graham Greene's *The Power and the Glory* (to be looked at in the next chapter) sets forth a version of the pattern of saving action in the form of an exchange.

MELVILLE'S BILLY BUDD

In a negative but quite graphic way, we may illustrate the confusion we are trying to avoid from Herman Melville's mysterious and moving story *Billy Budd*. Billy is a sailor impressed into the British navy and serving as foretopman on H.M.S. *Indomitable* during the critical revolutionary period at the end of the eighteenth century, when the memory of recent naval revolt still hangs heavily in the air. In the presence of Captain Vere, commanding officer of the *Indomitable*, the evil John Claggart, the ship's master-at-arms, falsely accuses Billy of plotting mutiny. Dumbfounded by the lie, Billy strikes out blindly at his accuser, accidentally killing him. Captain Vere, though convinced of Billy's innocence, believes that the letter of the law must be followed. A court martial condemns Billy to death by hanging. To call the hero of this tale a Christ figure is totally misleading, and to judge it by its success in portraying that figure would be to consign the work to undeserved failure.

To the bluejackets of H.M.S. *Indomitable* and their fellows elsewhere, a chip of the spar from which Billy was suspended was indeed "as a piece of the cross." So, too, Billy's hanging seemed to be his ascent, very much as Jesus' crucifixion in John's Gospel was his glorification. In connection with it, indeed, there is a Johannine reference to the vapory cloud in the east as "shot through with a soft glory as of the fleece of the Lamb of God seen in mystical vision." But far more significant than these and similar hints of parallels to the story of Jesus are the striking differences. Here was no "Second Adam." Billy Budd was purely the first Adam, an innocent barbarian—as innocent of the civilized fear of death as he was of "the thought of salvation and a Savior." The ship's chaplain, beholding him, "felt that innocence was even a better thing than religion wherewith to go to judgment."[3]

The innocence was indeed such as to remain unspoiled and untouched by the act that forced Billy to enter into this harsh legal world and, by entering, come in conflict with it. Billy's blow, felling the evil Claggart, was involuntary. He had not become sufficiently personal to do voluntary evil. Billy or Baby Budd was the embodiment of strength and beauty, a peacemaker to boot, though a fighting one. Masculine, and yet with a grace suggestive of femininity, he was completely unself-conscious and equally fully innocent of his background—a foundling. He was illiterate, and he stuttered.

His speech impediment was like some foreign disturbance, inflicted by the impurity of civilization, demanding speech from him. Like the wicked Claggart, the stutter was a sign that evil—that full development of human beings and of society—will foist itself on innocence wherever it finds it. But even though evil can bring innocence to defeat, it cannot corrupt it, at least not in the case of the primordial Adam. So Adam falls, but in such a way that the fall itself can be redemptive. It is an abidingly innocent fall, consummated in the transfiguration of the very sacrifice the evil world extracts from the innocent man. Though evil annihilates innocence, it cannot corrupt it; but in the consummation of that act of annihilation, evil itself is also destroyed and innocence transfigured. The light of that transfiguration casts its healing rays on the world, forever ensnared in the harshness of those legal and moral structures that come in the wake of evil. Though nothing in the world is changed materially by this illumination, the world has been touched unforgettably by a moment of truth, the touch of innocence. There is healing in the contact with the falling and transfigured innocent man. The innocent culprit himself is the redeemer. His healing power touches those who

---

3. "Billy Budd, Foretopman," *The Shorter Novels of Herman Melville* (Greenwich: Fawcett Premier World Classics, 1967), pp. 271, 264, 262.

condemn him (Captain Vere) and those who stand by.[4]

Billy Budd is no particular person. He learns nothing and can himself neither develop nor shape the events in which he is the chief ingredient. He is helpless and remains innocent. Though redemptive, he never combines his innocence with the guilt of others in such a way as to be close to the danger point of divesting himself of his innocence. It is true that he is reckoned among the transgressors, but the discerning reader will never mistake him for one, a mistake that always remains present as a real possibility in the Gospel story. The rhythm of Billy's being—innocence, fall, transfiguration—is perfectly organic and harmonious, just like that of the mythical man who is at once the primordial, alienated (but not guilty) man, and the redeemer.

In short, we have a redeeming man, but no Christ figure here. Billy is the first Adam as fallen but abidingly innocent redeemer, achieving cosmic scope through elevation to mythical status at the expense of specific, personal being. To turn this remarkable story into an echo of Christian redemption is to judge it by a false category.

But there are other stories involving Christ figures in which we find something of a reversal of the pattern of *Billy Budd,* because their hero becomes a particular man. At times this means the sacrifice of universal scope, at times a drastic alteration in the individual pattern of saving action—if indeed we wish to judge it by the story of Jesus in the first place.

KAZANTZAKIS' THE LAST TEMPTATION OF CHRIST

Nikos Kazantzakis, in his passionate novel *The Last Temptation of Christ,* presents us with a completely individual person, very much a man of flesh and blood. But his passion is greater than his tempestuous desires. Indeed, his desires become his servants even as they beset him, and he conquers them in the continuous spiritual struggle in which his mission is forged. The man's name is Jesus, and there is no mistaking him.

The novel tells the story of Jesus, the cross-maker of Nazareth, who fashions the crosses on which the Romans kill the Zealots who seek to bring nearer Israel's day of deliverance. He does it in order to escape the obsessive force that is upon him and that possesses him from within. But the force that separates him from ordinary men drives him on, nevertheless. Beyond the temptation of sensuality, beyond the temptation of ascetic withdrawal, the struggle rages on toward the fulfillment of his

---

4.See the illuminating remarks on *Billy Budd* by Richard W. Lewis, *The American Adam* (Chicago: University of Chicago Press, 1955), pp. 147-152.

mission, which is to bring the world to an end and bring in the Kingdom of Heaven. And there is, he discovers, no other way to do this except by his own death. In the original Gospel story, Isaiah, Chapter 53, provides the saving pattern for interpreting the Savior's passion and death; in Kazantzakis' novel, the same chapter provides the reason why the Messiah must die:

> "But he took upon himself all our pains;
> He was wounded for our transgressions,
>   he was bruised for our iniquities;
> And with his stripes we are healed.
> He was scourged, and he was afflicted,
>   yet he opened not his mouth:
> Like a lamb that is led to the slaughter,
>   he opened not his mouth...."

This, Kazantzakis' Jesus tells his disciples, was spoken about him: "They have been leading me to the slaughter ever since the day of my birth."[5]

The author, in his prologue to the novel, explains something about its sequence: "Every moment of Christ's life is a conflict and a victory. He conquered the invincible enchantment of simple human pleasures; he conquered temptations, continually transubstantiated flesh into spirit, and ascended. Reaching the summit of Golgotha, he mounted the Cross."[6] But it is of the essence of the novel that this is not yet the end. Now follows the last temptation, which lends the book its title.

There is a theory about salvation in Christ held by Protestant scholastic theologians of the seventeenth century, who followed the Gospel story closely—a theory that reaches back at least to St. Anselm's *Cur Deus Homo?* It says that Christ gained infinite merit for our salvation in two ways: first, by his active obedience in fulfilling the law; second, by his passive obedience in undergoing the propitiatory sacrifice imposed on him by God. In one way we may say—in the spirit of this theory—that his death (and also his resurrection) was the reward God gave him for his prior active obedience. Active obedience, it seems, ceases with the passion; passive obedience is embodied in the crucifixion. Or else we may perhaps say that the two coincide completely on the cross.

But for Kazantzakis, there is no passive obedience of Christ. So the last, and indeed greatest, temptation to be overcome actively—as every temptation must be—comes to him on the cross itself. Against the

---

5. Nikos Kazantzakis, *The Last Temptation of Christ* (New York: Simon and Schuster, 1960), p.426.
6. Ibid.,p.3.

tempting dream of a contented domestic life, he consents to the crucifixion and makes it inwardly his own, just as he had already done outwardly when, at his insistent behest, Judas Iscariot had betrayed him to the authorities, so that his mission might be fulfilled. This inward consent is the conquest over death.

> "He uttered a triumphant cry: *It is accomplished!*
> "And it was as though he had said Everything has begun."[7]

This is the Kingdom of Heaven. No doubt there is here a man who is a particular individual in a passionate, paradigmatic, and poignant way. There is likewise no doubt of his quest for cosmic outreach. He sees the salvation of the world as the goal of his struggle. The author tells us in his prologue: "This book was written because I wanted to offer a supreme model to the man who struggles; I wanted to show him that he must not fear pain, temptation, or death—because all three can be conquered, all three have already been conquered...."This book is not a biography; it is the confession of every man who struggles."[8]

There is a certain pattern in the Gospel story—quite in harmony with the doctrine of active and passive obedience—that presents a transition from power to powerlessness in the actions of Jesus (though suggesting that the two, power and its opposite, also continue to exist together) as we get closer to the crucifixion. With it goes another pattern, that of an increasing dominance of God's initiative over that of Jesus in the last stages of the Gospel story. The pattern of salvation is that of the ironic saying of the chief priests, scribes, and elders, "He saved others; he cannot save himself" *(Matt. 27:42)*.

The Last Temptation of Christ manifests something like a contrary pattern. Increasingly, as the story goes past Jesus' cross-making days, the initiative passes into, rather than out of, his hands. His death, with his inner consent to it, is the apex of his struggle, the victory of his initiative over death itself. For, as Jesus had said earlier to his disciples: "You must always be tightly girded and ready...for the great journey.... Death is the door to immortality."[9] He is, as he rightly calls himself, "Saint Blasphemer." In contrast to Billy Budd, he is the fully human individual whose spiritual struggle elevates him to divinity.

The point I want to make about this book is really very simple. This is not a Christ figure, or at least not a successful one. The individuality of Kazantzakis'' Jesus is bought at the price of sacrificing the Jesus of the

---

7. Ibid., p.496.
8. Ibid. p. 4.
9. Ibid. p. 400.

Gospel story and substituting another man for him. The outward events are, loosely speaking, the same. The person shaping and undergoing them is someone else. At some points—such as in his teaching on love— he fills out the picture of the Jesus so fragmentarily represented in the Gospels. At other points, as I have suggested, his identity, as he enacts, it is so different as to amount to a sheer contrast to the obedient Jesus of the Gospel story.

But not only do we have a different individual from Jesus in this story and, in that sense, no Christ figure. With the different identity goes a different saving pattern. Despite the appeal to Isaiah, it is simply impossible to see in the novel the element of passivity set forth in that chapter and in the Gospel story as indispensable to the pattern of salvation. A sheep led to the slaughter? No, rather a superman going to his triumph. And it is of the essence of the superman that he does not share his struggle. By contrast, while passivity may not be identical with sharing in either Isaiah, Chapter 53, or the Gospel story, they do seem to require each other. ("He saved others; he cannot save himself.") But in Kazantzakis' novel, the man for whom Christ dies is the strongly struggling rather than the weak, passive, helpless man. Each such fighting man walks his own unshared road of agony and triumph, whereas the weak and vacillating fall behind. There is no evident way in which the novel's pathetic and sinful disciples— other than Judas, who is strong in his own right—have any vital and significant share in Jesus' deed. Did he take upon himself the pain of these weaklings? Was he wounded for their transgressions, bruised for their iniquities? Are they healed with his stripes? Hardly! His deed is done for and in behalf of the strong who know that they can and must accomplish all for themselves. Not Isaiah but the author's prologue provides the clue to the saving pattern: "This book was written because I wanted to offer a supreme model to the man who struggles....it is the confession of every man who struggles." Himself he saved; others he could not save, is the theme here rather than its reverse in the Gospels.

The saving individual and the saving pattern of this story are different from the Gospel story. Indeed, the pattern is so different that the universal outreach is put in grave doubt. Billy Budd's universality was bought at the cost of individuality. That sacrifice is reversed in *The Last Temptation of Christ*. It is in any case doubtful that a novelist can portray both together. But in this instance the pattern of the saving action insures that he cannot. If the novel is to be judged by its success in portraying a Christ figure, it is surely a failure. This is not necessarily to say that the novel is a failure, only that we must find other criteria for assessing its merits.

Chapter 8

THE PATTERN OF EXCHANGE

In our discussion of Christ and modern Christ figures, we have spoken of the unique coherence in Jesus of two elements: unsubstitutable individuality and universal saving scope. The result of this claim is that the place of the Christ figure is preempted once and for all by Jesus of Nazareth. There cannot be any reproduction of Christ in a fictional figure who is supposed to mirror the original. Either the endeavor is unsuccessful or the interpretation of a work of literature as claiming to present a "Christ figure" is inappropriate.

Thus far we have tried to test this assertion by examining two models. First, we looked at the distortion of a truly universal figure who lacks individuality when the Christ-figure model is imposed on him *(Billy Budd)*. Then, we examined what happens in a novel to an individual named Jesus when he is measured against the original *(The Last Temptation of Christ)*. We must now turn to the third element pertaining to the Christ figure, the pattern uniting the individuality of the Savior and the cosmic scope of his identity. There is a whole genre of literature of this sort, looking for the individuality of the saving figure in the pattern of salvation common to Isaiah, Chapter 53, and the Gospel, particularly the pattern of *the mysterious exchange of guilt with self-sacrificing purity.*

In the pattern found in Isaiah and also in the Gospel narrative, the focus of obedience is, of course, God. But because an appeal to the supernatural is not open to the novelist, the place of obedience to God—so closely tied to the Savior's identification with the guilty—may be taken by the characteristic of love, which is treated as the Savior's one and only disposition and deportment. But this, we shall claim, is an obvious distortion of the original because there is no single clue—not even love—to unlock the character and deportment of Jesus in the Gospels. As the governing motif of Jesus' life, love is far more nearly an indirect than a direct focus of his behavior. His love is a function of his mission, but his mission is to enact the salvation of men in obedience to God. Love is subsidiary to that mission, though it is one way of expressing the manner in which the mission is carried out in his action toward all men.

Though the love motif is frequently the manner in which the pattern of exchange is worked out in literary works, there is another way of representing it. The pattern of exchange, or the vicarious identity of the Savior with the sinful, is sharpened to the point that the extreme opposites in the saving figure's own character are made to flow together with a kind of mysterious harmony or agreement in his action toward other people.

There is a kind of fiction in which this pattern makes use of the New Testament in such a way that there is a paradoxical or even miraculous reconciliation of violently sharpened opposites portrayed in either a hero or antihero figure: action with passivity, moral guilt with purity, death with life, belief with unbelief, love with hate, and so forth. Likewise, there can be an extreme opposition between certain characters, which flows into a strange connection or even unity between them—even though the fate of the one contradicts that of the other and the characters remain, on the surface, in unreconciled conflict.

GREENE'S THE POWER AND THE GLORY

For an example of such congruence between extreme opposites, we turn to one of the works of Graham Greene. In his novel *The Power and the Glory*,[10] a priest of the most unworthy and soiled character—a coward, an alcoholic, and a fornicator—turns before our eyes into a saint, despite himself and while remaining substantially his old self. The author's extraordinary narrative skill in creating a self-contained and coherent world makes the episode credible. Everything in the book is pruned to the essentials and made subservient to the action and interplay of the characters, even the hideous, suffocating climate and landscape. The squalid little priest is the only representative of his church left in a remote Mexican state from which ecclesiastical activities and persons have been banned on pain of death. The novel deals with his traveling and wandering about, in the process of bringing God (the Sacraments)—more or less unwillingly—to as many of the people as he can reach, while fleeing from the arm of the law. He eludes his pursuers successfully, even when they unknowingly have him in their grip. But at two crucial points, near the beginning and end of the story, he denies escape to himself and returns to the situation he knows will trap him and bring

---

10. New York: Viking Press, 1940.

death upon him. Again, the author's skill renders these two returns credible and fitting in the macabre setting. They do not deny the character of the priest, and they do nothing to elevate him to heroism. He is, as he shows repeatedly, no hero. But, as he says of himself, "even a coward has a sense of duty," and his duty is also his fate—he cannot deny the Sacraments he alone can dispense to those who demand them. Quite consciously the little antihero fails to achieve sainthood, and in his failure he comes very close to it, as he moves to his death. Having been ordained, he knows he is a man marked by God.

Quite in contrast to Billy Budd, this man marked by God is a guilty man. Indeed, one comes to think that for consistency's sake Greene would have loaded yet other major sins on his back, if only he could have found the pertinent ones. In other words, despite the author's skill, the quest is not, to put it mildly, that of an altogether unmanipulated character; nor is the action wholly uncontrived. Greene's priest hardly even rises to the level of what we earlier described as passive obedience. No superman, he is dragged with shaking knees before the firing squad. Actively, he had sought to escape, and he consents to his fate just enough to accept it as the demand of his priestly lot. But it is of real significance that the vice of hypocrisy is not in his roster of shame. There is no pretense or spiritual pride about him to keep the virtue of humility away from him. "I am a bad priest," he admits simply and unpretentiously in situations where the confession can bring no credit to him.

Humility is a disposition towards oneself which, though not itself love, is at least open to the possibility of love for the neighbor. In a crucial scene, imprisoned for illegal possession of liquor, he learns in a completely dark, stinking, and crowded cell what it is to be "moved by an enormous and irrational affection for the inhabitants of this prison." It is significant that this is the only community that ministers sacramentally to him. Before his execution there is no priest to whom he may confess, but during his earlier imprisonment it was this group of abject human beings towards whom he bore affection, to whom he also confesses his grave sins—to them and, paradoxically yet fittingly, to the police lieutenant who is his sworn enemy. This enemy of great integrity and his own companions at the dregs of society make up the only religious community that matters to him. In the prison scene there is only one person— characteristically, she is a respectable, righteous, and pious prig—who puts herself outside the pale of this crowded human fellowship: not the murderer, nor the man and woman engaged in intercourse in the dark cell's crowded corner, only the respectably pious woman who judges her cell mates by those conventional standards which bar the one who does the judging from true human life and community. The priest, on the other hand, has learned humility. He has grasped the possibility open to it among the virtues and so expands humility into human love. The result is a marvelous—and for Greene rather rare—reciprocity. In this scene human beings receive from each other and, in receiving, seem capable of actually *accepting* the gift. The priest in particular is enhanced by this lowly little crowd of humanity.

The prison scene is in startling contrast to a previous one in which Maria, the mother of the priest's child, protects him from the police with cunning but also with a cold pity that bars just the sort of reciprocity of which we have spoken. The barrier in this latter scene falls also between the priest and his child, whom the father loves with an agonizing, vain affection that the ruined child cannot receive. In the prison there is no such barrier.

The priest is enhanced by the humanity of a few others, but he is certainly not the stuff of which saints and martyrs are made—and that, of course, is why he is one, or nearly so. Were he more like a saint, were there a fit and harmonious relation between his character and its perfection in martyrdom, he would have run the risk of just that conventional, self-righteous priggishness that would have made him, at the point of death, not a saint but a hypocrite, a self-righteous fanatic. That is just the point: The pattern of congruence in his qualities is and must be that of the congruence of extreme opposites, abject spiritual squalor with the possibility of sainthood.

It is not only the priest's character and destiny that disclose this pattern; so also does his interaction with his chief pursuer, the police lieutenant who tracks him down. The fiercely godless, socialist idealism of the officer bespeaks a complete, indeed fanatically theological, integrity and a well-nigh priestly (though iconoclastic) devotion to the good of the people. It turns out, to the priest's surprise, that his pursuer is a good man. The lieutenant, even more surprised, learns the same thing about the priest under the even less conducive circumstances of the latter's pathetic character. R. W. B. Lewis' illuminating words summarize their relation: "The exhausted and sometimes drunken soldier of God, the chaste and fiercely dedicated priest of the godless society: each one enslaved to his mission, doomed to his role and its outcome: these are the beings, the systole and the diastole, between whom the force of the novel is generated."[11] They are brothers in mortal conflict, each the alter ego of the other, each bearing the burden he inflicts on the other, each showing forth the affinity of opposition or unity in conflict with the other. Each is the other's substituted brother.

---

11. R. W. B. Lewis, *The Picaresque Saint: Representative Figures in Contemporary Fiction* (New York: Lippincott, 1958), p. 252.

IS THE PRIEST A CHRIST FIGURE OR A DISCIPLE?

Lewis rightly points to the broad hint of Jesus Christ in this story. The novel has a Judas figure, a half-caste who betrays the priest for money. There is the priest's hunted, peripatetic ministry to the poor alone, ending up in complete powerlessness in which he is placed side by side with a common criminal. Is there anything to save the novel's protagonist—and with him the whole story—from the lifeless stylization of a Christ figure whose every action, look, and characteristic become as predictable as they are artificial? We recall the priests drunkenness, cowardliness, his giggly absurdity, and squalid weakness. And we are struck—in Lewis' words—by "the grotesque disproportion between the model and its reenactment." Surely the contrast to Christ breathes life into the figure of the priest. But then we remember that, instead of mere contrast, what we may have here is the pattern of saving action—that of exchange—expressed through the sharpening of opposite extremes to a point of absurdity or paradox where they flow together in agreement. The Christ figure must exemplify such congruence in his character, fate, and intercourse with others. He stands in complete solidarity with the sinner, not with the saint. He exemplifies his saintliness only in union with squalor, his loftiness only in union with the squalid absurdity that is the common human lot. Surely, from the perspective of this novel, God's love of the world (here looking like hatred), his becoming a man, and his righteousness united only to the unrighteous, all show forth the same pattern of saving action the novel itself embodies: the unity of opposite extremes. It is precisely this element of individual saving action in the Gospel story that has now become stylized in the novel. In short, emphasizing the strange little saint's contrast to Christ into one of sheer and absurd contradiction to the Savior makes the priest actually look all the more like Christ. Absolute contrast in this case becomes paradoxical identity. The grotesque disproportion between figure and model, rather than breathing life into the figure, gives it a stereotypical identity with the model.

The implication of all this is that the little priest is saved from being a predictable and lifeless Christ figure only if he is *neither* the same as the Christ in his lofty purity *nor* identified only with men's total sinfulness. In other words, the priest is a believable human being only to the extent that he is *different* from, but not in absolute contrast to, Christ. He is credible if he follows Christ at a distance by being *patterned* after him, but by being neither the same as the original model nor its absolute opposite. Nor can he be the unity of both. It is the *disciple* who is believable, precisely because he follows Christ without trying to become Christ, at a distance rather than from too nearby, or with that intimacy of total contrast which is paradoxically one with total identity.

Is the little priest a Christ or a disciple figure? The question is not easily answered, but the answer spells the success or failure of the novel. Unlike *Billy Budd* and *The Last Temptation of Christ*, *The Power and the Glory* allows no other criterion for assessing it than the question of whether this novel presents a Christ figure or a disciple. One common and profoundly valid way of discerning the difference between Christ and some other person who is a disciple is embodied in the scene in *The Power and the Glory* to which reference has already been made: the enrichment of the priest's humanity by his presence to his fellow prisoners, an enrichment paradoxically climaxed by a money gift made to him by his mortal enemy and pursuer, the police lieutenant, who is unaware of the priest's identity. With this gesture the lieutenant joins the fellowship of humanity that blesses the priest's humanity. In that scene the priest becomes more than the focal point for the interplay of superhuman good and evil. He becomes a human being instead of a Christ figure, because he can receive and accept good. For this is surely one distinct difference between Jesus Christ and the rest of us: Nowhere in the Gospel story is Jesus' own humanity enriched by his relation with others, and so no person who is blessed in this way can be confused with him. And yet, although Jesus does not receive enrichment at men's hands, we are commanded by him to bless our neighbors and are allowed to receive good at their hands.

There are novels in which the main protagonist is more clearly a disciple than a Christ figure than the priest in *The Power and the Glory* seems to be. Pietro Spina, in Ignazio Silone's great novel *Bread and Wine, is* such a man. A Communist agitator returned to his native fascist Italy and now disguised as a priest, he constantly receives his humanity from those he encounters, for whom he is present and who are present for him. In a climactic way he receives it when he breaks bread with a man he does not yet know is a deaf-mute and learns companionship in an act of sharing greater than shared words. The black priest, Stephen Kumalo, in Alan Paton's *Cry, the Beloved Country,* is another instance of such a man who, in the process of his terrible search after his criminal son, has his humanity enriched by others, especially by his fellow priest and friend, Msimangu. In each of these instances, something of the pattern of exchange is present in muted or evident form about the man and about the intercourse between him and others. But it is kept from becoming stylized into an artificial figure or action, because there is an enrichment of the specific individual's humanity. In that context the stylized, paradoxical element takes on life, and we begin to see the figure of a disciple rather than a Christ figure.

In Chapter 6 we asked if the identity of Jesus Christ—completely one with his presence—is perhaps simply a myth, like the identity of the savior in other dying and rising savior stories. Our answer was that the Gospel story claims the Savior Jesus' identity to be solely and unsubstitutably his own and not a universal myth. The genre of the two kinds of stories is wholly different. In the last two chapters, by contrast, we examined other endeavors to represent Christ, not as a universal, mythical figure, but as a specific individual. We concluded—not surprisingly—that the endeavor is a failure. In large part this is because the place of the Christ figure is already and exclusively preempted by Jesus Christ himself, and there can be no concrete duplication of him. The "Christ figures" of modern fiction thus are unsuccessful endeavors to identify a "savior as specific man," one who would stand, in contrast to the universal figure of Gnostic myth. But a class of this-specific-man-and-no-other is a contradiction. No specific man is another specific man, and if the unsubstitutable story that establishes a man's identity finds a substitute story, even under his name, we have another person instead. The Gospel story's specific identity of the Savior is bound to be wholly different from that of any other equally specific savior, and they cannot be grouped into one class. The endeavor to make the one replicate the other and still be a unique, specific individual in his own right is bound to be a failure.

Both types, Gnostic myth and modern Christ figure, are alternatives to the Gospel story in presenting an account of salvation. The Gospel story is different from both because its "type" is wholly derived from the specific and unsubstitutable identity of Jesus Christ. The very distinctiveness of the Gospel story as a story of salvation rests wholly on the claim that the Savior is completely identical with the specific man Jesus of Nazareth.

But having said this, we must add that, even if the modern endeavors to present "Christ figures" are bound to be theological—if not literary—failures, they may be *significant* failures for the Christian in several respects. (1) They may point to the novel-like structure of parts of the Gospel story, i.e., those parts in which Jesus enacts his specific identity in a connected series of events and not simply in preaching or teaching, namely, from the meal in the upper room on. The novel is the special vehicle for setting forth unsubstitutable identity in the interplay of character and action. The latter part of the Gospel story does just that. The Christ figure, unsuccessful or not, points us to an individual savior rather than to a universal savior myth. (2) In the introductory essay I stressed that there is no telling what kind of talk—formal, proclamatory, self-involving, any kind or none at all—may have significant bearing on the transition of the pilgrim from unbelief to belief (or vice versa). In a narrower compass, the same situation obtains between the depiction of a savior figure and that of Jesus in the Gospels. In its very failure to tell us what an individual savior figure is like or to re-embody the story of Jesus, the Christ-figure story may help us grasp something of the concrete, unique meaning of the identity of Jesus Christ. On the other hand, it may not: there is no telling beforehand. (3) However, given the assumption that the Christian is already acquainted with the Savior's identity (his identity and presence being one) and that reflection about it is therefore a purely formal matter, the Christ figure is indeed a help in reflecting on the unique identity of the specific Savior Jesus —even if, or perhaps just because, the Christ figure fails in its explicit purpose of replicating the Savior as specific man. (4) Again, assuming the identity and presence of Jesus Christ as already known to the believer, the help such fictitious persons provide for formal reflection on the identity of Jesus Christ is enhanced by the degree to which they fluctuate between being Christ figures and disciples. Precisely such fluctuation throws into stark relief the uniqueness of Jesus Christ. (5) Once more assuming acquaintance with Jesus Christ, the unsuccessful straining after a Christ figure and the frequently successful depiction of a disciple aid the Christian in clarifying his description of Jesus Christ's pattern of saving action. Such discernments of the pattern of exchange, though not *sufficient* descriptions, do *help* in the description of what Christians mean when they say that Jesus Christ died vicariously on behalf of men and for their salvation.

The outcome of these reflections on savior myth and Christ figure (Chapters 6-8) is that we have been helped, certainly negatively and perhaps to some extent positively, in focusing on the unique identity description of Jesus provided by the Gospels as they tell his story. To the task of understanding that description, we must now turn.

After some preliminary reflection, we shall begin to examine the Gospels themselves to discern the identity of Jesus in terms of the two forms of identity analysis we have outlined: "intention-action" and "self-manifestation." In so doing, we shall be searching for certain patterns or schemes in the Gospels that will tell us what Jesus is like and who he is.

PART IV

THE NEW TESTAMENT DEPICTION OF JESUS CHRIST

Chapter 9

IDENTITY DESCRIPTION
AND JESUS CHRIST

On the assumption of prior acquaintance with Jesus Christ, our claim is that the proper order for describing the unity of presence and identity in him is to begin with his identity. Our actual starting procedure, however, was the reverse. In speaking first of Christ's presence, it was concluded that any answer to the question, *How* is Christ present? that is not based on the prior question, *Who* is he? would be hopelessly entangled and useless. At best, it would involve endless and inconclusive arguments about the relation of the description of the "Jesus of history" to that of the "Christ of faith," in the vain hope that adding these two abstractions together would somehow provide us with the description of one concrete person. At worst, we could expect to end up with the discovery that the endeavor to understand Christ's presence to ourselves is a projection of our own presence.

If one begins with presence rather than with identity, the question, How is Christ present? is finally answered by the mysterious movement of Christ toward us, coinciding with our movement toward him. The result of this complete coincidence or simultaneity is, in the last analysis, the ultimate dissolution of both our own presence and his. His presence is not his own; indeed, he is diffused into humanity by becoming one with it. And we, in turn, find in him the mysterious symbol expressing our own ultimate lack of abiding presence and identity. In this fashion, humanity in general or a representative portion of it, such as the church, is the community in which Christ and we become one. Humanity (or the church) then is Christ present, and to say this is also to claim that it is the only abiding presence we ourselves have. Such a presence, e.g., that of the archetypal and nameless human stranger, and our own become mysteriously diffused into each other, so that they are one and the same. This, of course, is not what Christians believe (even if the fusion of these modes of presence is taken to be the church), but it is a typical consequence of seeking to discern the unity of Christ's presence and identity by beginning with the understanding of the former.

We must, therefore, turn to the description of his identity, the delineation of which is a delicate thing, as we have already seen. We cannot, for instance, inquire into the "actual" life and character of Jesus inferred from the records. Most scholars agree that the Gospels do not furnish us with the requisite information for such a reconstruction. Nor can we probe the intentions and themes or even the cultural contexts of the Gospel writers that underlie the story. Our task is, rather, to observe the story itself—its structure, the shape of its movement, and its crucial transitions.

Reading a story, whether the Gospel story or any other, has been rightly compared to understanding a work of visual art, such as a piece of sculpture: We do not try to imagine the inside of it, but let our eyes wander over its surface and its mass, so that we may grasp its form, its proportions, and its balances. What it says is expressed in any and all these things, and only by grasping them do we grasp its "meaning." So also we grasp the identity of Jesus within his story. There are, of course, parts of the New Testament that do not tell a story, but in the Gospels, which tell us most of what we know about Jesus, his identity is grasped only by means of the story told about him.

Several demands are put on us when we inquire into the identity of Jesus Christ in the story about him. First, as we have already attempted to show, the story of Jesus is not really the story of all mankind or, at least, of men of a certain type. In other words, we had to meet the claim that Jesus' identity might turn out to be an identity shared with other storied savior figures. One such is the mythical savior figure of Gnosticism, who is not really an individual person and therefore can be represented by any number of salvation stories. Another is the fictional "Christ figure," who can be embodied in many novel-like stories. Christians claim that to identify the Jesus of the Gospel story with either of these types causes serious confusion. The identity of the Christian savior is revealed completely by the story of Jesus in the Gospels and by none other.

Secondly, knowing the identity of any person involves describing the continuity of the person who acts and is acted upon through a stretch of time. But it also involves describing the genuine changes, sometimes to the very core of a person's being, that occur both in that person's character and in the circumstances of a story. A good storyteller manages to do both things without experiencing any difficulties in the process, as Henry James suggested in a brief remark: "What is character but the determination of incident? What is incident but the illustration of character?" A metaphysician, on the other hand, who has to explain how both change and sameness, unity and diversity, can be real at the same time and in the same conceptual universe may have a more complicated time of it. But we are inquiring into the shape of a story and what it tells about a man, in contrast to metaphysical explanations that would tell us what sorts of things are or are not real and on what principles they cohere.

Thirdly, proper attention to the identity of Jesus also forces us to pay close heed to the appropriate technical and formal categories with which to describe identity. The task here is first to determine what the categories are and then to keep them from taking over the show. In other words, the tools for description easily may and often do turn out to govern with such a heavy hand the material to be described that they distort the descriptions intended. Toward the end of Chapter 4, we said that in order to determine any individual's identity it is necessary to ask two formal questions: "Who is he?" and "What is he like?" It will now be necessary to ask, What is the force of these formal questions or categories for identity description?

WHAT IS MEANT BY A FORMAL QUESTION?

But before we proceed we need to ask again what is meant by a "formal question" and why it matters so much for our enterprise. A formal question, such as "Who is he?" or "What is he like?" is one to which an answer is necessary if we are to know anything at all about a person. But more importantly, it is a question that will not force an answer that would risk overwhelming either the person or the story. By contrast, we may mention two alternate kinds of identity analysis that do take this risk and thus demonstrate the real importance of a purely formal approach to identity.

One approach involves asking how a person in a story illuminates, or perhaps merely illustrates, this or that problem of our common existence. It may also involve asking what a person is like in comparison to other persons. In other words, the description of an identity involves comparative reference to the characteristics, conditions, or destinies of some other persons or of all mankind as they may be viewed from the standpoint of a given cultural or social framework. In our day, the comparative reference is usually to the common qualities of estrangement, self-alienation, or some other basically divisive conflict that may appear within the self, between the self and its society, or between social forces. I do not wish to argue that such references are wrong in relation to the story of Jesus; I only wish to say that in this instance the category in terms of which the identity question is framed materially influences the answer, and the description is not a formal one. The *question* rather than the story becomes the governing context with which the person is identified. (In modern theology the thought of Paul Tillich and Rudolf Bultmann are typical instances of this procedure; for Bultmann in particular the question addressed to a text becomes an important principle for its interpretation.)

A second approach that tends to force an answer that distorts either the person or the story by going beyond mere formal identity inquiry is in some measure contrasted with the first. This approach does involve trying to determine a person's identity by referring simply to himself rather than to others or to humanity as an existential concern. But the attempt in this instance is made by adding a kind of depth dimension to the story's surface, which is actually a speculative *inference* from what is given in the story, rather than a part of it. This procedure enables us to write something like the story behind the story so that we can, for example, explain the consistency of Jesus' actions by reference to the consistency of his inner disposition. The story thus becomes merely the outward illustration of his unswerving inward disposition and tells only what is true about the person in any case. Here, to revert to the dictum of Henry James, incident is indeed the illustration of character, but character and disposition are not shaped by incident.

This approach involves a fundamental prior decision, one that limits the category of identity to the description of the person as distinct from the sequence of events in his own unique story. Identity is given a status independent of, prior to, and only tenuously connected with the story. Thus, in this view, an independently derived notion of Jesus' identity really shapes the story to conform to that notion. The story of Jesus, by virtue of its sketchiness, makes such an enterprise possible. Moreover, the results are often illuminating. But it is obvious that in such a process the category of identity serves more than a formal function, for it gives independent content to Jesus' person or character, which then shapes the reading of the story. (There are innumerable instances of this procedure in modern theology. One that raised considerable interest in scholarly circles some years ago is James M. Robinson's *A New Quest of the Historical Jesus.*)[12]

The two approaches we have briefly mentioned here (which sometimes are in effect one and the same) illustrate the peril of tearing asunder the person and his story in identity description and freighting the inquiry after identity with more than formal categories, even before the examination of the story begins. With this in mind, we will seek to confine ourselves as best we can to the purely formal categories expressed in

---

12. Naperville, Illinois: Allenson, 1959.

the questions, "Who is he?" and "What is he like?"

"Like" in "What is this person like?" does not indicate comparative reference to others or to humanity at large, but simply a typical state or action of a person that would properly and genuinely constitute or characterize him. Because we seek with this question to come upon a person in his characteristic stance, the question endeavors to pinpoint him in specific actions or in responses to specific occurrences that involve him. In other words, this category or question accentuates a person's *story,* the *changes* (even those to the very core of him) that he undergoes, and his *acts at a given point* or over a limited stretch of time. The question, "What is he like?" is answered by an intention-action description.

The second category for identity description is embodied in the question, "Who is he?" A much more elusive question than the first, it focuses not so much on a person's story directly, or on crucial changes in a person, as on the person himself in his ongoing self-continuity, as he acts and is acted upon in the sequence of the story's events. In other words, the second question concentrates on the steady line of *persistence* that is involved in the very idea of a person. His changes are real indeed; yet he remains the same identical person. The question "Who is he?" is answered by describing the subject as he is in and through his self-manifestations.

THE UNITY BETWEEN INTENTION AND ACTION

We shall spend more time on the second question, because its implications are harder to grasp. But to return momentarily to the first, it is essential to understand certain of its overtones. The appropriate answer to the question, "What is he like?" is: "Look at what he did on this or that occasion. Here he was characteristically himself." If there is an instance (or instances) for a given person when we can say that he was most of all himself, we should say that his action in that instance does not merely *illustrate* or *represent* his identity. Rather, it *constitutes* what he is. A person is what he *does* centrally and most significantly. He is the unity of a significant project or intention passing over into its own enactment.

Above all, in asking what a person is like, it is essential to grasp the intimate unity of intention and action. An intention, unless impeded or frustrated, is no intention and has no mental status at all except as a plan to be executed. The expression "I intend" is rightly and logically followed by a verb, i.e., an action word. On the other hand, an event that happens accidentally or without intention is an occurrence rather than an action.

Intention and action logically involve each other in verbal usage.

"To perform intelligently," says Gilbert Ryle quite correctly, "is to do one thing and not two things."[13] Hence, each has to be described by reference to the other. An intention is nothing other than an implicit action; but to say this is not to make intention and action one and the same. The necessary use of the qualifying adjectives "explicit" and "implicit" in defining each by the other makes that point clear. Wherein, then, does their unity lie?

Their unity, we can only repeat, is the irreversible passage or movement from one to the other, from intention into action. The enactment of intention always differs from the intention to enact; and each person has inside knowledge of how he passes from one state of affairs to the other directly and without a break. Our identity is constituted by the enactment of central and, in that sense, characterizing intentions, but it is not constituted by the intention alone. For in that case the intention or decision to act would account for everything, the actual enactment for nothing. On the other hand, enactment— the positive external occurrence without an ingredient of intention in it—also does not constitute a human identity, just because it does not pertain to a centered self, but only to a piece of overt behavior.

We need to say one more word about identifying a person in his intentional acts. Earlier we said that this kind of identification—answering to the question "What is he like?"—points more to changes within a person and to the person's story than to the persistence of the person in the person-story interaction. There are, therefore, limits to this manner of identifying a person. The persistence of the same person through all the changing events, and even through his own changes, is a factor still to be dealt with. It leads to the second category or question of identity description, "Who is he?" which we shall consider in a moment. But first there is the further limitation on the identification of a person in his story, that a person's story is not only the enactment of *his own* intentions or his own identity, but the enactment of others' intentions and even of unintended events as well as those not specifically intended. Things happen *to* a person that enter into the very identification of him; they are enacted or occur upon or through him. Do such external acts or occurrences become embodied in him? Do they become part of his identity, since they are woven into his story? Undoubtedly, yes, and in part by his own response to or incorporation of these happenings.

What is to be stressed here is that our categories for identity description break down at this very point. They cannot describe how external events become ingredient in a person's identity directly, i.e., other than by his own response to them. All that one can do to describe a person in

---

13. *The Concept of Mind* (New York: Barnes and Noble, 1949), p. 40.

that situation of direct impact by circumstances upon him (and not as refracted through his own response) and how he becomes himself in and through these circumstances is simply to tell the story of the events.

It is useful to point to this limitation in the applicability of the formal question, "What is he like?" For without the impingement of external occurrences on the person, there is no story and no person, just as there is none without the external enactment of one's inner intention. But whereas the latter contingency is describable in terms answering to our formal question, the former is not. These reflections are of some significance in the understanding of the Gospel story. The identity of Jesus in that story is not given simply in his inner intention, in a kind of story behind the story. It is given, rather, in the enactment of his intentions. But even to say that much is not enough. Rather, his identity is given in the mysterious coincidence of his intentional action with circumstances partly initiated by him, partly devolving upon him. The latter kind of occurrence also, in part, shapes his identity within the story.

THE PERSISTENCE, ELUSIVENESS, AND ULTIMACY OF A PERSON'S LIFE

The focus of the second category for identity description, embodied in the question, "Who is he?" is somewhat harder to specify. The task is difficult because it is unclear what the pronoun "who" asks about, beyond some apparently superficial clue, such as a person's name, or else simply the same thing we discussed under the preceding question (a person's characteristic intentional action). Beyond these two alternatives, the question apparently could refer only to that hypothetical, separable, and hidden being inside the organism, steadily unchanged, who purportedly pulls the strings by which the body puts act into effect.

But granted our dissatisfaction with all these solutions, not many of us will dismiss as meaningless the question, "Who is he?" or even the admittedly prejudicial and often overdramatized question, "Who am I?" At the very least, such questions are useful in pointing us to the necessity of taking into account the *persistence, elusiveness,* and *ultimacy* of personal life in the description of a person.

a. *Persistence.* Of persistence we have already spoken, referring to self-continuity or self-ascription over a period of time. The question, "Who is he?" obviously points us to the identity or self-persistence of a person from action to action, rather than (as does our preceding question) to the uniqueness of each action and the possibility of change at the core of the self from one act to the next.

b. *Elusiveness.* The elusiveness of the "who" lies in the fact that one's own acts *now* cannot become objects of knowledge to oneself until they have receded into the past. If we try to describe (even indirectly) what constitutes the bond of selfhood between a self's own actions, we would have to refer to the self as this elusive, present subject. Persistence and elusiveness go together.

c. *Ultimacy*. Finally, ultimacy simply means that asking the question, "Who is he?" indicates that we can describe no personal-physical states, characteristics, and actions except as we ascribe them *to* someone. At least this is true in ordinary conversation. And the "someone" to whom they are ascribed is ultimate because in ordinary conversation no person is a quality, state, or action predicable of another.

But there is still something unsatisfactory about all that we have said concerning the question, "Who is he?" We may indeed agree that the personal pronoun "who" indicates the subject in his persistence, elusiveness, and ultimacy; but these qualities are simply higher order generalizations that hold true for all identity descriptions. But the very point of asking "Who...?" was largely to escape a common characterization that applies generally to a number of persons and, instead, to pinpoint specific identity. So we are still tempted to ask, "Yes, but *who* specifically is he?"

To such a question we are forced to give indirect and not fully satisfying answers. Anything more ambitious will deny the elusiveness of the subject-self and, in effect, return to "the ghost in the machine" position discussed earlier. The specific and unsubstitutable subject-self does come provided with indispensable marks of identification, but they are also so intimately identified with him that they are, in a certain manner, himself. There is no descriptive device that can enable us to be more precisely definite than saying "in a certain manner."

The chief, though not necessarily only, means by which the "who" question is answered are a person's name and his body. In particular, the identifying status of the name is ambiguous, and the only hope for the name's serving the purpose is that the person himself will supply what others cannot —the intrinsic or organic identification between the core of himself and that name which others attached to him arbitrarily and superficially. The hope is that he will act so as to identify himself with his name as given. Only so is it really *his* name, and only thus is his name the final clue to his identity. With regard to the body, it would seem a bit more difficult to refuse to identify oneself with it.

From the particular identifying action of naming and taking a name, it is but a short step toward another—identification with a tangible or intangible community, either the one by which one has been named or some other. Such a community may be as broad as "humanity" or as narrow as one other human being. However, even though such identification is indispensable for any human being, it always comes close to identification by comparative reference and hence eludes identification of specific and unsubstitutable identity. But the device of naming suggests not only reference to a person's community setting for the purpose of identifying him, but also the use of *words* as the closest and most intimate exercise in the process of identification. The ascription of a name to a person and his self-identification with it are perhaps the most mysterious uses of a word, a mystery in back of which there is no need to go.

A PERSON IS HIS WORD AND HIS BODY

Because the subject-self is elusive and cannot be a direct commentary on that performance which is itself, the unity between the self's identity and the *manifestation* of that identity in the person's use of his name or of other words is bound to remain mysterious and indirect for any description. How is it that any word, a mere sound that ordinarily designates public and observable items like chairs and vegetables, can become the vehicle for the communication of *personal* meaning? We cannot penetrate the mystery of it, but we know it can be done without misleading others about what the words refer to. At times a man's speech is literally his embodiment. He is revealed in his words; indeed, he is his word. Sometimes this is the case when a person makes promises, sometimes when his speech sets forth the common purpose of his community, and sometimes when he verbalizes the profoundest states of his affective life. In short, a person's self-identification with his words, in particular those that we have come to call "performative utterances," is perhaps the most acute form of the unity between the subject and his self-manifestation. It is one of the bases for the coherence between public and private meaning in the use of words.

There are, we said, two identifying means by which the subject is manifest. The first is the verbal medium. The second is that of the body with its peculiar and unexchangeable location that is called *mine*. That body is properly referred to as *mine*, as the *manifestation* of myself and as I. The body is indeed possessively distinct from me. It is my body to dispose of and direct in action. There is nothing wrong with saying "I try to keep my body fit" and, by so saying, to indicate the possessive I relation to it. But it is equally appropriate to say "I keep myself fit" and thereby to point to the fact that the body is not merely a possession, but the intimate *manifestation* of myself. Neither the possessive relation to nor that of manifestation of the subject suggests that the body is a mere external accretion to the "real" self. Not only is the body the self in manifestation; it *is* the self. The body is I, or rather I am the body occupying this particular, unsubstitutable space. So we say "I" (and not "my body") walk from here to the corner. There is no way to state more simply the identity of the self as manifest in and yet identical with its embodiment.

Self-manifestation in both word and body suggests that the elusive and persistent subject can only be described indirectly, i.e., in and through its manifestation. But indirectness does not mean failure by any means. In neither case do we point to a vanishing or unintelligible fact. Instead, each form of description of the subject involves a public medium that both fitly *represents* and is the subject. The parallel between the "who" category and our earlier category ("What is he like?") is evident. In each instance there is a strong relation between the inward and the outward: intention is directly linked with enactment, the subject-self with its manifestation. Neither case has a "ghost in the machine" character, and each illustrates a healthy regard for the intrinsic significance of the outward life. It remains only to be stressed that neither description gets at a more "basic" view of the person than the other. The person is as fully described by his intention-action pattern as by the pattern of his self-manifestation.

THE SELF SEEN IN ALIENATION
FROM ITS MANIFESTATION

Both descriptions suggest the compatibility of inwardness and outwardness in personal identity. It is important to stress this point, for there is another kind of formal inquiry into personal identity that is quite contrary to this analysis. This kind of inquiry may also come under the "who" question, but its outcome is quite different. Yet because it is a common analysis of human identity or existence underlying much technical theological interpretation of the New Testament, it is of importance for us. Recall that we have stressed that intention is implicit action and that the name and the body are identifying marks of the self. But they are not, we said, merely *manifestations* of the self; they *are* also the self manifest. The self does not stand in mysterious and ineffable fashion in back of them. Rather, there is a complex of indirect identity between the self and its manifestation. Obviously, what is assumed here is that there is a real *fitness* or congruence between the self and its manifestation or representation. Now it is just this assumption which is rejected in the other form of posing and answering the "who" question.

In the analysis of a good many modern philosophers and theologians, from Hegel to Heidegger's early philosophy, from Kierkegaard to Bultmann and Tillich (including some aspects of Marxist thought), there is, at best, a real distance between *true selfhood* and its *manifestation* and, at worst, a genuine incongruence or contradiction between them. Whether the situation *must* be so may be a moot question for some of them; but at least it seems to them to be so *in fact,* when they look at the actual, external, or cultural situation of the self related to history.

The path that analysts of this sort are treading is thorny, delicate, and narrow. On the one side, lies the assumption of a real fitness, even identity, between the subject-self and its manifestation—an analysis that seems wrong to them. But the obvious alternative, that since the self is in principle incapable of realization in its manifestation, the real self must inevitably stand in back of its manifestation—a ghost in the machine once more—is also rejected with equal firmness.

As a matter of fact, however, a good case can be made out that the latter position is precisely the danger to which such analysts are subject, although they wish, without doubt, to avoid it. What they attempt is to come down between these two undesirable alternatives and suggest a description of the self that is neither back of nor yet fitly embodied in its manifestations. What they suggest is that all manifestations—not only the words and names and psychological structures of individuals, but also the whole complex of social institutions and cultures in which selves interact and are collectively manifested—are distorted manifestations of the true subject-self. As one consequence of this analysis, history becomes the ever-dissatisfied or "self-alienated" quest of the self or of humanity for its true being through the cultural forms of its own distortedness. In this fashion, the self is at once identical and yet—paradoxically—not identical with its own individual and collective forms of existence.

Certain other consequences follow from such an analysis. In the first place, there are striking affinities between it and some aspects of the Gnostic outlook. We discussed in Chapters 3 and 6 the sense of alienation in the world, of wandering through it in search of one's identity, the haunting possibility that the closest one can come to an authentic sense of identity is the fully cognizant acceptance of the state of alienation, realizing paradoxically that one has no identity of one's own. These are possibilities common to the two traditions. Parallel to this sense of alienation is the conviction that, if the self is neither a substantial, self-contained identity accessible back of outer reality nor an identity fitly embodied in its manifestation, then there is no direct way of expressing what one truly is nor even what one thinks and feels about human identity. Myths, indirect communication, and forms of language other than the ordinary and public usage of words are the only ways of pointing toward what cannot be expressed directly.

Secondly, the focus of identification in this description is on the mysterious subject who is not—in the technical language of this tradition's philosophers and theologians—"objectifiable." The subject, that is to say, is distorted as soon as it is caught, frozen, and represented in outward manifestation. What is true to its own nature in a work of art, in an action, even in a stretch of history and the understanding of it, is the intending, the deciding, the moment of doing, and not the external deposit that results from it. If one tries to understand an intention-enactment sequence, one must concentrate on the intention or the moment of decision and not on the enactment. If one tries to grasp a subject in its manifestation, one must look at the manifestation only to the extent that it mirrors the subject. In hearing a person's words, one must seek to grasp the being or the personal event within these words. But particularly in trying to grasp the meaning of a sequence of historical events, one must go back of the web of external occurrences and grasp instead the original moment of intending and doing, just as it was on the point of *passing* over, but before it had *passed* over, into external embodiment or into a specific act.

Thirdly, we must ask what happens when this analysis of self-manifestation in distortion rather than in fitness (and the accompanying conviction that a subject's being and doing cannot be "objectified") is applied to the study of the New Testament. We have already mentioned the consequences in the introduction to this discussion. The formal category of identity description under this version of the "who" question, we said, runs the risk of supplying the material content to the Gospel story rather than deriving that content from the story itself. In this type of identity description, the person and the story tend to be pulled apart, and the emphasis is laid on the "unobjectifiable" subject in back of the story rather than on the story's sequence of external occurrences.

Furthermore, this analysis of human identity tends to confront the person and story of Jesus with a prior judgment that what is important here must be judged by the criterion we have just mentioned—how Jesus and his story bear on the dilemma of the self at once embodied and yet not embodied in the historical, cultural world. That world, we recall, is in this analysis the place of human self-alienation or self-distortion. Authentic existence in the world, the genuine preservation of one's identity, lies precisely in realizing this dilemma and therefore never losing oneself or one's identity by simple identification with the world. This, then, in this alternate form of interpretation, becomes the frame of reference within which the story of Jesus is significant. Jesus himself, in his preaching and action, is seen to manifest a crucial choice against such simple identification with the world; and he, therefore, is the crucial occasion for our own decision as to who we are.

But, once again, have not the "formal" categories for identification really taken over the person and the story in this analysis? Have not Jesus and his story been forced into a preconceived pattern—whether the right or wrong one? We conclude that, instead of this, the proper procedure is first to look at the story, under as few categories and as formal a scheme of categories for identity description as possible, to see what it tells us about Jesus' identity, and we must use the same procedure in examining those who gain their own identity, by implication, in relation to him.

Chapter 10

THE ENACTED
INTENTION OF JESUS

What is Jesus like in the story told about him? We stressed earlier that in the Gospels, in contrast to Gnostic accounts, the saving activity has no role independent of the story of the individual, Jesus. The story of salvation is the story he enacts —the story of his obedience in redeeming guilty men by vicarious identification with their guilt and literal identification with their helplessness. In Chapter 3, one possible pattern was suggested for understanding Jesus' story. It could well be taken symbolically, as the story pattern of man—the wandering stranger without identity. Jesus' virginal conception, lowly birth, wandering ministry, mysteriously ambiguous identity, and even his empty tomb all lend credence to this interpretation. What we must now try to show is that the story as story—not necessarily as history—should be taken in its own right and not symbolically and that, if it is read for its own sake, it suggests that Jesus' identity is self-focused and unsubstitutably his own. He is not the wandering stranger, but the one individual so completely himself that his inalienable identity not only points us to his own inescapable presence, but also is the focus toward which all of us orient our own identity—each one in his own person and place. For he is the assurance that particular identity is not a false front for its own opposite, the loss of identity and presence.

In the New Testament story, Jesus is seen to enact the good of men on their behalf—or their salvation—in perfect obedience to God. It is not, as we have said, that love to men was his only or even his predominant behavioral quality. Rather, he was perfectly obedient, and his obedience to God was one with his intention to do what had to be done on men's behalf. In this way, his mission was identical with love for men.

But do we actually know that much about Jesus? Certainly not, if we are asking about the "actual" man apart from the story. But that is not our concern. Whether indeed the "historical" Jesus *intended* the crucifixion and in what sense whether he went freely to his death and with what motives, we cannot infer directly from the available evidence. The *believer* will, of course, find confirmation of the coming together of Jesus' intention and acts with those of God in God's raising him from the dead. He will claim that whatever Jesus' motives, the resurrection is the seal of God's confirmation upon them. Indeed, the resurrection demonstrates Jesus' acceptability to God as being obedient to God's will. But the resurrection is not, of course, an event subject to critical historical judgment; and even if taken at face value, it, by itself, tells us little about the internal history of Jesus.

We are, in fact, thrown back on the story simply as a story, regardless of whether or not it is well documented. But, then, do we actually have testimony to Jesus' obedience in his story? Here the answer is a decisive "yes." The testimony we have is not of a detailed sort. It does *not* light up the motives, the decision-making process, the internal ambiguities, or the personality of the story's chief protagonist. Nor is there, precisely at those points in the story where claim is laid to a knowledge of Jesus' intentions, any evidence whatever that there were others present or that he had shared his thoughts with them. In other words, at those few points at which the story gives an inside glimpse of Jesus' intentions, they are *not* provided in the same way a biographer or historian provides inferential or indirect clues from the witness testimony or other external data. The insight we are allowed is far more sparse and restrained than that, and yet also more intimate. It is like that of the novelist who tells us from the inside, as it were, of his subject's intentions and the bond by which they lead into action. This is what the Gospel story does at one or two crucial points; but it does so in exceedingly spare terms that do not search out the personality, inner motivation, or even the ethical quality of Jesus. The glimpse we are provided within the story of Jesus' intentions is just sufficient to indicate the passage of intention into enactment. And what is given to us is neither intention alone nor action alone, neither inner purpose alone nor external circumstance alone. Rather, he becomes who he is in the coincidence of his enacted intention with the train of circumstances in which the story comes to a head.

So the pattern of Jesus' identification in the story is at once simple and subtle, unitary and complex. When we seek to determine what Jesus was like by identifying the enactment of his central intention, we note that those who told the story about him or commented on it speak of his obedience to God's will (*Rom. 5:19; Phil. 2:8; Heb. 5:8*). Secondly, when we ask about the manner in which his obedience was enacted, we are brought face-to-face with the *coexistence* of power and powerlessness

146

in his situation. But we also note that there is a *transition* from one to the other. Indeed, the narrative points simultaneously to the pattern of coexistence and transition between power and powerlessness. Jesus enacted the good of men on their behalf in both ways. It is his vicarious identification with the guilty and, at the climax of the story, his identification with the helplessness of the guilty that provide the Gospel's story of salvation. Yet this helplessness is his power for the salvation of others. Something of his power abides and is accentuated as he becomes helpless. The pattern of exchange becomes the means of salvation. In the description of Jesus, one has to keep coming back to the ironic truth of the words of the priests and the scribes, "He saved others; he cannot save himself" *(Mark 15:31)*. These words detail the pattern of the saving action and suggest that, if Jesus had not forsaken the power to save himself, he could not have saved others. Thus, the transition from power to helplessness is at the same time the realization of his saving power. There is, then, not only transition but also coexistence between his power and powerlessness.

Finally, in discussing the complex pattern of Jesus' obedience, it must be noted that the enacted intention of Jesus—to obey God and to enact men's good on their behalf—meshes with external circumstances devolving upon him. That is to say that the exact circumstances climaxing his story were not completely initiated and executed at his behest. On the other hand, he did not passively await and accept them. In fact, his identity is revealed in the mysterious unity of his own decision and determination with the circumstances and events of his passion and death. He is identified as well by his initiation of circumstances, his response to them, and their sheer impingement upon him.

Without this narrative sequence of events that climaxes the Gospel story, we should not be able to identify Jesus by an intention and action pattern. But we must add that the circumstances making up the sequence of the story should not be regarded as fated. They are, rather, due to the interaction between Jesus and the initiative of the power he calls "Father" to the very end. In addition to the coexistence and transition between power and powerlessness, the identity of Jesus that is manifest in his obedience must be seen in the mysterious manner in which his intention-action pattern meshes or interacts with that of God in the Gospel story.

HE WAS OBEDIENT

Jesus was obedient to the will of God. This is the light in which the apostle Paul—writing before the composition of the Synoptic Gospels as we now have them—saw what Jesus did. Apparently Paul himself saw the action of Jesus that way in at least partial dependence on a yet earlier tradition *(Rom. 5:19; Phil. 2:5-11)*. It is striking that, in all four Gospels and in the other writings of the New Testament, it is the motif or quality of obedience that is stressed in regard to the person of Jesus. By contrast, there is, for example, very little mention of his faith. The characterization does not occur at all outside the Gospels (except for one uncertain reference in Hebrews 12:2, but even this seems to speak of him as the one "on whom faith depends from start to "finish,"[14] rather than the "pioneer" of faith [Revised Standard Version]). Within the Gospels, the references to Jesus' power rising out of his faith are few and ambiguous *(Mark 9:23; Matt. 27.43)*. Undoubtedly Jesus is the ground or source of the believer's faith; but if we trace the movement that goes from his teaching to his personal being, to his power for salvation, and thence to the believer's new relation to him, we cannot say that "faith" is the common underlying factor in all stages. We simply have no warrant from the sources for this conclusion. To draw it would be to claim an inside knowledge of him that we do not have. This is true not only by virtue of the sparse amount of information the Gospel story provides us about Jesus, but also because of the kind of information we are actually given. As a storied figure, it is not his faith, but his mission and his obedience to it to which constant reference is made. He is one who is "sent." All the Gospels have such self-references on Jesus' part, and the Fourth Gospel abounds in them. The counterpart of this is his consent to "him who sent me" *(Matt. 10:40; John 13:20)* and to the events enacting the purpose for which he was sent *(Matt. 26:53-54; Luke 24:26; John 12:27;18:11)*.

The implication of what we have said about the primacy of Jesus' obedience as a clue to his identity is interesting. If we were able instead to begin our understanding of him by grasping certain of his inherent personal characteristics, such as his faith—and we might add love, freedom, authoritativeness—we should be able to construct his personality from them. Moreover, the characteristic most profoundly typical of him would then be the clue to his personality and to his saving power. Now, such characteristics may be inferred from the story about Jesus, but what must be kept in mind is that they do not reside at the very center of the story. In fact, we do not possess any such profound or intimate knowledge of him. The main point is, however, that if we did have such knowledge of him, we should be able to find the center of Jesus' person within himself rather than in his story, i.e., in relation to the events of his life and the persons with whom he came in contact.

---

14. *The New English Bible, New Testament* (Oxford University Press and Cambridge University Press, 1961).

We may illustrate the point by returning to the question of Jesus and the quality of faith. We commonly think of faith as faith in something and therefore to be seen only in relation to that object. But when faith is regarded as the central characteristic of a person, then what counts is not that to which faith refers, but the quality of the person's faith itself. What is presupposed in such an understanding is that faith is a spiritual characteristic of him, a disposition that shapes his outlook and behavior patterns. It is significant that we have no such direct knowledge available from the Gospel story by which to characterize Jesus. The story and the early commentary about him show only that he was fundamentally obedient, rather than faithful, loving, free, or authoritative.

And the point about his obedience is that it is not, like these other hypothetical qualities, regarded as a quality in its own right in the story. His obedience exists solely as a counterpart to his being sent and has God for its indispensable point of reference. Jesus' very identity involves the will and purpose of the Father who sent him. He becomes who he is in the story by consenting to God's intention and by enacting that intention in the midst of the circumstances that devolve around him as the fulfillment of God's purpose. The characterizing intention of Jesus that becomes enacted—his obedience—is not seen "deep down" in him, furnishing a kind of central clue to the quality of his personality. Rather, it is shown in the story with just enough strength to indicate that it characterized him by making the purpose of God who sent him the very aim of his being.

We may suggest three consequences that result from this attempt to identify what Jesus was like from the story's depiction of his intentional action. (1) As we have emphasized from the beginning of this essay, the focus of this story, unlike that of Gnostic myth, clearly turns on Jesus as the unsubstitutable, specific individual he is and becomes through the equally specific actions and circumstances of his last days. (2) In very broad terms, Jesus' identity is centered on his moral action in moving towards a certain goal, rather than on his basic, constantly unchanging yet constantly renewed self-understanding. This fact, no doubt, provides a clue to the New Testament's understanding of how others are to see their own identity in relation to that of Jesus. The clue to that relation lies more in moral obedience than in profound self-grasp. (3) Unlike what one finds in so many Christ figures, Jesus has, in his story, a clearly personal center, a self-focused identity. It is he who makes the pattern of coexistence as well as the pattern of transition between power and helplessness flow together in their complex harmony. They are not a set of paradoxically or otherwise related states or qualities for which he is the empty personal receptacle. These states or qualities do not exist apart from his person. Instead, he makes them instruments of his saving efficacy, making them all internal to his obedience to God. There is no power for salvation in such pre-established, paradoxical qualities as helplessness and power, guilt and purity, either in themselves or apart from him. They become efficacious for salvation because they are his and because he holds them together in the enactment of his obedience to God.

THE CHARACTERIZATION OF JESUS IN HIS OBEDIENCE

The characterization of Jesus as obedient man is not simply inferred but is directly set forth at two points at which the story, in very restrained fashion, tells us something "from the inside" of the intention of Jesus' moving toward enactment. In a certain sense, this direct portrayal is at the heart of the temptation episode right after Jesus' baptism and the descent of the Spirit upon him, when he—still "full of the Holy Spirit,...and...led by the Spirit"—is depicted as rejecting the satanic temptation to tempt God *(Matt. 4:1-11; Luke 4:1-13)*.

Returning from the wilderness "in the power of the Spirit," he is shown immediately thereafter *(Luke 4:14-44)* beginning his ministry. The stress, now that he has rejected the temptation to disobedience, is on his obedient enactment of his mission. He does that for which he was sent (vv. *18, 43*). He cites Isaiah 61:1-2 to his hometown hearers:

> "The Spirit of the Lord is upon me,
> because he has anointed me to preach good news
>   to the poor.
> He has sent me to proclaim release to the captives
> and recovering of sight to the blind,
> to set at liberty those who are oppressed,
> to proclaim the acceptable year of the Lord."

> (Luke 4:18-19)

Being obedient, he can say to them, "Today this scripture has been fulfilled in your hearing" (v. *21*). At the end of this same chapter he tells his listeners that he must preach the Kingdom of God, "for I was sent for this purpose" (v. *43*).

But if obedience is to be understood as specific enactment of an intention, one needs a sequence of cumulative, unbroken events within a story. We do not have such a sequence at this early point in the Gospel story. Jesus' obedience is set forth more clearly in the events of the final stage of his career. In the early portions of the narrative, the accounts present us with self-contained blocks of material, each covering one topic. In the final portion, we begin to get a sustained and unbroken narrative, leading from event to event, starting with the preparation for the Last Supper *(Mark 14; Matt. 26; Luke 22)*. Set into the midst of this sequence is our second glimpse into Jesus' inner life (within the story) when, tempted to plead for a way out of what looms ahead, he confirms his obedience: "Yet not what I will, but what thou wilt" *(Mark 14:36)*. It marks the crucial *inner* transition point from power and scope to powerlessness. We shall speak of it again in that context. What we must emphasize now is that here, as nowhere else, the story points "from the inside" to his obedient intention. This is its focus. We should be gravely mistaken were we to put the stress of this incident on the sadness and agony of his terror and decision. They are there, and it would be equally erroneous to ignore them. Without them, as without Peter's bitter tears after his denial of Jesus, we should not penetrate below the surface and into the real center of the story's figure. The stress, however, is not on the agony so much as on the fact that in the midst of it Jesus determined to be obedient. The writer of Hebrews, apparently speaking about this particular scene, comments that beginning here Jesus actually *learned* obedience *(Heb. 5:7-10)*. Here, then, is the inner point at which Jesus' intention begins to mark his identity.

But intention, as we have said repeatedly, is nothing in itself without enactment. Enactment does not merely illustrate, but constitutes, intention. Corresponding to the transition from power to helplessness on the *inner* plane is its constituting enactment on the *outer* plane. In a measure, this is nothing short of the whole passion-crucifixion-resurrection sequence. Nothing accomplishes that point of transition from inwardness to outwardness at the point of change from power to powerlessness more clearly than Jesus' words in Matthew's report of the arrest, just after the scene in the Garden of Gethsemane. Staying the hand that would defend him against arrest, Jesus asks: "Do you think I cannot appeal to my Father, and he will at once send me more than twelve legions of angels? But how then should the scriptures be fulfilled, that it must be *so?*" *(Matt. 26:53-54)* Jesus affirms the will of God obediently by both initiating and consenting to the shape of the events that now develop in their mysterious logic.

But we said earlier that Jesus' obedience to God is also his love toward man. It is so by virtue of the coincidence of the intention of Jesus with that of God. His love—enacting the good of men on their behalf—is not to be discerned simply and directly as predominant personal deportment, but as the specific vocation entailed by his mission of obedience to God. We need only remind ourselves of the will of God embodied in the mission on which he sent Jesus, the righteous one: it was an errand of grace extended to the world. In the words of the Fourth Gospel: "For God so loved the world that he gave his only Son, that whosoever believes in him should not perish but have eternal life. For God sent the Son into the world, not to condemn the world, but that the world might be saved through him" *(John 3:16-17)*. Again, Jesus' use of the words of Isaiah 61:1 *(Luke 4:18,* cited above) puts his obedience in announcing his gospel in the terms of an errand of mercy. Here, again, the *referent* of Jesus' obedience is the will of God and his purpose, which become embodied in the climactic events of Jesus' self-enactment. The *content* or meaning of that obedience is the pattern of merciful, saving activity drawn largely from the picture of the obedient, righteous servant in Deutero-Isaiah. It is the pattern of exchange (Chapters 7 and 8). "For I tell you that this scripture must be fulfilled in me, 'And he was reckoned with transgressors'; for what is written about me has its fulfilment" *(Luke 22:37; cf. Isa. 53:12)*. In a word, "the Son of Man came not to be served but to serve, and to give his life as a ransom for many" *(Matt. 20:28)*.

But, once again, it is in the connected narrative sequence of the last events of the Gospel story that we look for the coincidence of Jesus' obedience to God and his love toward men, which is the content of that obedience. The most striking instance of that unity of obedience and love comes precisely in the process of his identification in the enactment of his intention. The sequence, we have said, begins with the preparation for the Last Supper. The crucial transition point for the enactment of his obedience through the events is in the Garden and the subsequent arrest. Shortly before, in the upper room, he had spoken to his disciples of the cup they shared as the blood of his covenant, "poured out for many" *(Mark 14:24; Matt. 26:28)*. This is the content or aim of his obedience to God, enacted in the events climaxing the Gospel story. To be obedient to God was to pour out his blood in behalf of men. Who, then, was Jesus? He was what he did, the man completely obedient to God in enacting the good of men on their behalf.

JESUS POWER AND POWERLESSNESS

The obedience of Jesus must be seen at once in the *coexsistence* of his power with his powerlessness and in the *transition* from the one to the other.

About the coexistence of his power and powerlessness, we shall not say much, important though it is. Were it not there at all, it would be difficult to see wherein the actual saving efficacy of his helplessness lies. Moreover, it would be difficult to get any glimpse at all of the complex and yet positive interrelation between God's action and Jesus' action at the climactic stage of the Gospel story.

We may note the coexistence of Jesus' power and helplessness when he stands silently before the accusations of the Roman governor. The silence is broken only at the moment of Jesus' own choice, when the governor asks him if he is the king of the Jews. "You have said so," is Jesus' reply, and thereby he actively turns the governor's question into unwitting testimony to himself, the Christ *(Mark 15:2; Matt. 27:11; Luke 23:3)*. Again, in Luke's account of the crucifixion, we have several sayings that testify to Jesus' abiding initiative in and even over the circumstances that hold him in thrall, so that they come to be, by a subtle reversal, at *his* service. His promise to the thief that he should be with him in paradise; his active placing of his spirit in the hands of God *(Luke 23:43, 46)* are instances of this sort.

The writer of the Fourth Gospel took this stress and made it one of the main themes of his interpretive account, to the point of the elimination of Jesus' passive, helpless suffering. He portrays Jesus as actively laying down his life for his sheep; he is not robbed of it: "I lay down my life, that I may take it again. No one takes it from me, but I lay it down of my own accord" *(John 10:17-18)*. Likewise, in John's account, the last word spoken on the cross is neither the pathetic cry concerning God's forsaking him, not even the commendation of his Spirit into the hands of God, but the announcement that this is the completion and fulfillment of his own activity *(John 19:30)*. Thus, Pilate's proclamatory superscription of Jesus' kingship which he had placed over the cross (vv. *19-22)* loses almost every vestige of ironic quality in the seriousness of Jesus' own claim in John's Gospel.

So Jesus is and remains powerful to the end, constraining all acts and words, even those of his opponents, to testify to him. Hence, our earlier statement that Jesus' helplessness is a theme in the Synoptic Gospels must be drastically modified, if not eliminated, when one looks at the Fourth Gospel. Yet even in the Synoptic Gospels, the coexistence of powerlessness with saving efficacy is one of closest contact, though they are united in complex fashion and never directly merged. The rulers' words, "He saved others; he cannot save himself," are perhaps the most striking instance of the complex relation of efficacy and helplessness and of ironic reversal between them. In summarizing and articulating his complete helplessness, the rulers are witnesses to his saving power.

Having spoken of the coexistence of the power and powerlessness of Jesus, we now turn to what is involved in the transition from one to the other. Though Jesus in his helplessness is still the Savior with power, he is nonetheless genuinely helpless. The Gospel writers show us a picture of the actual *transition* from power to helplessness, a transition held together through the experience of the one undergoing it. To this end the terrible story of Jesus in the Garden of Gethsemane is a vivid example. The transition in the story is from a certain liberty of action to an equally certain elimination of it. This transition is effected through his own decision, as well as through the action of the authorities. The process in the story is irreversible. Once Jesus gives himself over to the authorities, his liberty of action will be at an end, and the result will be almost certain death for him. In his agony he remains obedient to his mission and consents to powerlessness, even unto death.

We have already mentioned that the story of the temptation in the Garden of Gethsemane is one of the crucial turning points of the Gospel narrative. There, as perhaps nowhere else, Jesus' intention is depicted as that of being obedient to God. What we are given in this narrative, then, is access to the storied Jesus' intention at a crucial point.

We are not unprepared for what comes to pass after this agonizing scene in the Garden. The web of circumstances had already given ominous signs of tightening around Jesus. The atmosphere of the story had become fraught with heavy foreboding from the moment he announced to his disciples that he was going with them to Jerusalem *(Luke 18:31-34;* cf. *Mark 10:32; Matt. 20:17).* The scenes of controversy in the Temple in Jerusalem are particularly sharp and seem almost bound to provoke with tragic finality the insight that clarifies the meaning of the whole story of Jesus *(Mark 11:18,* 27-33). But it is the scene in the Garden of Gethsemane that pinpoints the transition between what went before and what comes afterward. Up to this point Jesus had had freedom and scope of movement. He had been portrayed as a figure of authority and power, but now in the Garden, with circumstances narrowed to the decisive point, it became part of his own free agency to enact the coincidence between his own decision and the developing events. From that coincidence would develop the crucial pattern of events in which his identity would be enacted.

Earlier we said that the identity of an individual is described in part by the answer to the question, "What is he like?" This kind of identity description we called intention-action description. It locates the identity of an individual at the point at which his inward life, coming to outward expression, is linked with or meshes into the train of public circumstances. Such a description of Jesus' identity comes at the crucial point of his transition from authoritative power to helplessness. It is in the sequence in the Garden of Gethsemane that we begin to discover the identity of Jesus through an intention-action description that reaches its climax in the crucifixion and resurrection. The intention of Jesus is nothing without that sequence in the Garden, in which it is enacted. The inner intention never comes into direct view again with such intimacy as it does in this sequence. More and more thereafter we are forced to behold him from the distance of outward events—from enactment and circumstance rather than from inner life—except for the isolated and sudden, yet fitting, bereft cry on the cross, "My God, my God, why hast thou forsaken me?" *(Mark 15:34)*

The pattern of significance embedded in this intention-action sequence is startlingly illumined by the words of Jesus near the beginning ("Yet not what I will, but what thou wilt") and by the rulers' words at its consummation ("He saved others; he cannot save himself"). In these two sayings and in the events they circumscribe, we see the transition of Jesus from power to powerlessness, a transition made in the full consistency of the same identity carried from intention into action: Jesus was what he did and suffered, the one whose identity was enacted in his passion and death.

Chapter 11

JESUS AND GOD

In our attempt to describe the pattern of intention and action in the Gospel story, we spoke of the continuing coexistence of power and powerlessness in Jesus, and also of the transition from one to the other in the portrayal of the obedient redeemer in need of redemption. Now we turn to a further element in this complex pattern—the coherence and interaction of the intention-action of Jesus with that of God.

Having observed Jesus' transition from power to powerlessness, we may now ask, "To whom does the power to initiate action pass, once Jesus submits to arrest?" The immediate answer is that it passes to his accusers and judges, together with all the complicated vested interests they represent, and back of them to a vast mass of humanity. Together they all constitute a wide span of what may be called "historical forces."[15] The phrase points to the forces of world history that the Gospel writers discern as acting powerfully upon Jesus at the moment of his powerlessness. Now, there is in the New Testament, of course, a sharp distinction between these "forces" and the ultimate, divine origin from which all action derives. God and the world (or God and daemonic powers) are never confused in either the Old or the New Testaments. Still, there is a mysterious and fascinating coincidence or "mergence" between divine action and the "historical forces" at their common point of impact—Jesus' judgment and death.

---

15. The phrase is used by Erich Auerbach in Chapter 2 of his remarkable book, *Mimesis: The Representation of Reality in Western Culture* (Garden City: Doubleday Anchor Book, 1957).

THE INTERRELATION OF DIVINE AND HUMAN ACTIONS

The power of God and that of Pilate, though retaining their separate points of origin, nevertheless had a concurrent existence. Pilate clearly had the power to do what he would with Jesus. This is plainly expressed in John's Gospel, where, on the one hand, the unbridgeable distinction between the power of God and that of the world is depicted. On the other hand, this account depicts the "mergence" of both forms of power into a common impact, as is illustrated by the dialogue between Pilate and Jesus: "Pilate therefore said to him, 'You will not speak to me? Do you not know that I have power to release you, and power to crucify you?' Jesus answered him, 'You would have no power over me unless it had been given you from above; therefore he who delivered me to you has the greater sin'" *(John 19:10-11)*. The enigmatic last clause, which has the effect of lightening the load of guilt on the governor, actually emphasizes the power of Pilate and that of God at their common point of impact. It is at this point that Pilate's power and the power of God cohere. Pilate clearly has the power to do what he will with Jesus, but coexistent with that fact is another: he has no power at all apart from that which God gives him. By contrast, we note that in the case of Judas the power of God is either absent or related differently to the disciple's treacherous act from the way it is related to Pilate's act. Something of the same theme is indicated in Luke's reference to the fact that Christ "should" have suffered "these things" and then have entered his glory *(Luke 24.26)*. Indeed, all the Gospels and the book of The Acts stress again and again that these events were appropriate, for the "scripture must be fulfilled." On the whole, there is clear indication of the will of God in the rising tide of events.

We are beginning to describe the interrelation between the divine and human actions in the Gospel story. But this interrelation is more complex than we have indicated so far. There is, as we have said, a distinction between the rising initiative of the "historical forces" that destroy Jesus and the initiative of God. But this distinction becomes less and less clear as the two forms of initiative combine to bring Jesus to his death. Indeed, both forms seem to increase in proportion to the *decrease* of initiative on the part of Jesus. Nevertheless, Jesus' intentions and actions become increasingly identified with those of the very God who governs the actions of the opponents of Jesus who destroy him. Yet, despite this fact, a distinction between the agency of God and that of Jesus remains, as the cry of the cross clearly indicates, "My God, my God, why hast thou forsaken me?" *(Mark 15:34)*. Moreover, even though Jesus' intentions and actions are superseded by those of God, Jesus retains his own identity to the very end. He is not merged with

God so that no distinction remains between God and Jesus. Nor do we mean to say that Jesus' intentions and actions become subordinate to those of God or that they lose their personal force. Indeed, the very opposite is true. Despite the decrease of initiative in Jesus, his intentions and actions, as well as his identity, retain their personal quality and weight. It is he who commends his Spirit into the hands of God and gives up the ghost, as Luke's Gospel climactically indicates *(Luke 23:46)*. On the cross the intention and action of Jesus are fully superseded by God's, and what emerges is a motif of supplantation and yet identification. This motif is unlike a simple subordination of Jesus to God, for in such a case Jesus' intentions and actions, and hence identity, would bear no weight of their own. Instead, we see in the story a crucified human savior, who is obedient to God's intention and to his action.

This motif of supplantation and yet identification is one of the main themes of the liturgical hymn found in Philippians 2:6-11. In this passage, Jesus, though in the form of God, humbled himself, took upon himself the form of a servant, and was made in the likeness of men. "He humbled himself and became obedient unto death, even death on a cross." By virtue of this action God bestowed on him the name that identifies him above every name, Jesus Christ the Lord. Thus Paul, following an earlier tradition, depicts God's supplantation of Jesus' initiative in passion and death in terms of Jesus' obedience, in virtue of which he made God's intention and action his own, consenting to the divine initiative that willed his death.

But nowhere is the complexity of this pattern set forth more fully than in the Fourth Gospel. John stresses the dominance of the Father's will over that of the Son *(5:19, 30; 6:37-40; 12:49-50; 14:28)*. He speaks of the Father's initiative over the Son in sending him *(7:16, 28; 8:42; 13:16)* and says that the Father alone has power to testify effectively to the Son. This claim of the Father's priority, however, is presented in such a way that the Son and the Father are nevertheless one *(10:30)*. Hence both are glorified together in the Son's glorification *(13:31-32; 17:1, 4-5)*. And though he who believes in the Son believes not in him but in the Father *(12:44)*, nonetheless to believe in God is to believe in the Son *(14:1);* and to see the Son is to see the Father *(12:45; 14:9)*.

Now, we should, for the sake of accuracy, say that in John's Gospel the balance between the dominance of the Father over the Son, on the one hand, and their unity, on the other, is delicate. There is, we may note, a tendency in the earlier part of the account (though we dare not push it too far) to underline the Father's dominance, in which it is the Father's witness to the Son that makes the latter's testimony true. The other aspect, their unity, tends to come to the fore gradually after its first outright mention in Chapter 10:30. It gathers strength after the enunciation of the Son's hour of glorification *(13:32)* and rises to a climax in the great prayer in Chapter 17 for the unity of the believers through the unity of Father and Son (especially vv. *21-26).*

The theme we are talking about, supplantation or super-session in unity or identity rather than subordination, though articulated in greatest detail in the Fourth Gospel, is deeply embedded in the events of the story as told by the Synoptic writers. In a sense their increasing stress on the rising curve or dominance of God's activity over that of Jesus reaches its apex, not in the account of Jesus' death, but in that of his resurrection. In fact, it is by virtue of this theme that one may and even must speak of a literary unity between the accounts of Jesus' death and those of his resurrection. That is to say, the authors' increasing stress on the dominance of God's activity over that of Jesus, starting with Gethsemane and Jesus' arrest, reaches its climax, not in the account of Jesus' death, but in that of his resurrection. It is here—even more than in the crucifixion—that God and God alone is active. Up to this point his efficacy had come increasingly to the fore in the steadily decreasing scope and activity of Jesus and the increasing tempo of the authorities' acts. Now, as the story comes to a climax, the stress is on God's increasingly direct and exclusive activity. But it is so in a peculiar fashion. For the hand of God, though obviously dominant and alone efficacious and directly present in the raising of Jesus, remains completely veiled at this point in the story.

The unanimous testimony of the earliest Christian commentaries on the events, such as Peter's sermons in the Acts, insists that it was indeed *God* who raised him from the dead, and that is, of course, the logic of both the situation and the story. As for the situation, could a person who is said to have raised himself really be said to have died? The logic of the story is similar. It presents us with a rising tide in which the will of God supersedes increasingly that of Jesus, moving by means of the "historical forces" that take charge. At the very crest of this tide we should expect God's will to supersede even that of the "historical forces" hitherto at work. And so it does, in its own manner, in the raising of Jesus. No other agency can possibly play any significant initiatory or even instrumental role here. Hence the earliest Christian preaching insists over and over again that *"God* raised him on the third day and made him manifest" *(Acts 10:40;* cf. *2:32; 3:15; 4:10)* and that "we testified of *God* that he raised Christ" (I *Cor. 15:15).*

But when we turn to the actual accounts of the resurrection, the hand of God is scarcely in evidence at this point in the story. In fact, the word "God" is hardly mentioned at all here.

To some extent, this is due to the fact that the actual raising is nowhere described in the Gospels, and hence there is no direct appeal in the story to the agent of the act. Nonetheless, it is surprising that the absolute and direct initiative of God, reaching its climax at this point and stressed in the early preaching of the church, is completely unmentioned in the narrative itself. It is *Jesus,* and Jesus alone, who appears just at this point, when God's supplantation of him is complete. To summarize what we have said in a somewhat exaggerated form: In his passion and death the initiative of Jesus disappears more and more into that of God; but in the resurrection, where the initiative of God is finally and decisively climaxed and he alone is and can be active, the sole identity to mark the presence of that activity is Jesus. God remains hidden, and even reference to him is almost altogether lacking. Jesus of Nazareth, he and none other, marks the presence of the action of God.

In the narrative of the Gospels and the preaching commentary on it, Jesus is thus not simply in need of redemption but is, in fact, redeemed *(Acts 2:24-32, 36; 13:35-37).* The resurrection is the vindication in act of his own intention and God's. Moreover, in the unity and transition between his need for redemption and his being in fact redeemed, Jesus' identity is focused, and the complex relation and distinction between his identity and that of God is manifested. We have to add immediately, however, that there is no simple and direct coherence of the identity of the crucified and risen Jesus by means of one rhythmic or cyclical movement. The Gospels' accounts tell us quite clearly that the abiding identity of Jesus in the crucifixion and resurrection is held together by the unitary identity of him who is the same person whether crucified or resurrected.

The point is that we misunderstand the narrative if we regard the risen Lord as a phantom of the crucified Jesus or, conversely, if we regard the crucified Jesus as the earthly shadow or perpetual death stage of an eternally rising savior figure. Each of these stages has its own indelible uniqueness unexpunged, even though both are held together in the transition by which we move from one to the other. We may put the same point quite simply and in almost banal fashion: It was the crucified Jesus who was raised from the dead. The identity of Jesus who preached and died and that of the risen Lord are one and the same. As a result, the crucifixion remains indelibly a part of his identity, an event or act that is an intrinsic part of him. Thus, though the New Testament claims that Christ is genuinely present to believers as the *risen* Lord, its testimony is that it is the *crucified* Jesus who rose and is present. We can, we are told, no longer regard Christ, now risen, "from a human point of view" *(II Cor. 4:16);* nevertheless, the one who is now present is no "spirit" *(Luke 24:36-43),* but the one bearing the wounds of his mortal body *(John 20:27-29).* He is none other than Jesus of Nazareth (Cf. *Acts 9:5; 22:8; 26:15).* Thus Paul's experience on the Damascus road is clearly set forth in the Acts as an occasion for the self-manifestation of the risen Lord as totally identical with Jesus of Nazareth. The "I am" of the self-identifying remark, "I am Jesus," in that account has an almost Johannine force.

DID JESUS ENACT HIS OWN RESURRECTION?

In itself what we have just said may not appear to be a very startling claim, but let us say the same thing in a different way by proceeding from a parallel that has already appeared several times. We have said that Jesus' obedience to God and his steadfast intention to enact the good of men on their behalf hold together those personal qualities that would otherwise appear as unrelieved and abstract paradoxes. It is Jesus who holds power and powerlessness together, not they him, both in their simultaneity and in the transition from one to the other. It is likewise he whose intention is vindicated. He is, both in their simultaneity and in transition from one to the other, the Savior in need of redemption and the Savior in fact redeemed and redeeming. But this is really a very hard thing to comprehend, for it amounts to saying that he holds together his own identity in the transition from death to resurrection. Now, we have already suggested that Jesus' identity was what he enacted it to be in the crucial events leading from Gethsemane to his death. He was what he did. Are we then implying that he enacted his resurrection also? If not, how are we to understand the relation of God's and Jesus' intention and action in the structure of the New Testament narrative?

Whatever our answer to this difficult question is, we must stand by our affirmation that the unity and continuity of the narrative's structure is such—especially in Luke's account—that to leave out the climax furnished by the story of the resurrection (and even that of the ascension) would mean doing irreparable violence to the literary unity and integrity of the whole account. It would violate the story at its integrating climax. It would violate the story also to take this climax to be the "meaning" integrating the previous "events." Instead, we must insist that the story, as a connected sequence of events (with patterns of meaning embedded in it), comes to a climax in the story of the events of the resurrection and the ascension. Hence, the difficult question is inescapable: Since Jesus enacted his identity in what he did and underwent, and since his identity is the same—that of Jesus of Nazareth—in crucifixion and resurrection, does the story suggest that he raised himself from the dead?

To deal with this question we must stress again the fourth pattern in the Gospel story, that of an irreducibly complex pattern of interrelation between God's action and that of Jesus. We have already described it as one of supplantation by identification rather than subordination. The interesting fact about this pattern with regard to our present question is that, although God and God alone is the agent of the resurrection, it is not God but Jesus who appears.

THE RESURRECTION AS MANIFESTATION OF GOD'S HIDDEN ACTION

We spoke earlier (Chapter 9) of two types of identity description, intention-action and self-manifestation description. In the resurrection accounts, the two descriptions become intermingled. There, where God enacts his intention most directly (though veiledly), it becomes most clearly evident *who* Jesus is. Contrariwise, when Jesus' own intention-action sequence reaches its climax, in his passion and death, the question of his subject identity—who he is—is left most severely in doubt. The upshot of this subtle and puzzling issue is that the Gospel narrative presents us with neither a simple unification nor a simple distinction between Jesus and God, either in terms of intention-action or of self-manifestation identification. The pattern of their interrelation remains irreducibly complex.

To a degree, a pattern of unification prevails, in which Jesus is set forth in his resurrection as the manifestation of the action of God. This is in itself an odd way of speaking, for ordinarily the correlate of "action" is not "manifestation," but "enactment in public occurrence." "Manifestation," in turn, is the correlate of "presence" or "subject" rather than "enactment." Yet there is little doubt that exegesis of the Gospel story will indicate that in the resurrection Jesus is set forth as the presence or manifestation of God's hidden action. In this respect, then, God's deed in raising Jesus is actually a deed in which the identity of Jesus is *manifested,* rather than being the achievement of a historical *occurrence.*

Yet this particular emphasis meets a firm limit because the logic of the story and of the situation as well as the claim of the sermons in Acts all suggest that the resurrection of Jesus as an *enacted event,* and not merely as the *manifestation* of his *identity, is* the climax of the Gospel narrative. In this respect there is a clear distinction between God and Jesus, and there is an identification of Jesus through an intention-action sequence and not merely by means of self-manifestation.

More than this we cannot say in response to the strange but inevitable question, posed by reading the Synoptic accounts, Did Jesus raise himself? Obviously, he did not. And yet the complex pattern of unity in differentiation between God and him was not broken in the transition from crucifixion to resurrection. On the contrary, it reached its climactic fulfillment in the resurrection. We cannot simply say that the narrative pattern points us to the conclusion that where God is active, Jesus is not, and vice versa, or that where Jesus' identity is manifest, God's is not. Yet certain themes of this sort do appear in the story. Whatever further comment we may make on the identification of Jesus in relation to God, it is unlikely that we shall get beyond the pattern of unity in differentiation and increasing identification by supplantation.

The nature of the narrative therefore imposes a limit on theological comment. It is not likely that we shall be able to get beyond the descriptive accounts presented to us in the Gospels concerning the resurrection and the relation of God's and Jesus' actions. And if we do go beyond them in explanatory endeavors, we are clearly on our own and in speculative territory, just as we have suggested that we are in speculative realms when we look beyond the narrative for the writers' and Jesus' own inner intentions. In that instance, our speculation would be historical; in the present, metaphysical. But it is never easy and usually not desirable to transform a literary description, such as a narrative sequence, into an *explanatory* scheme using abstract concepts and categories. What is perfectly fitting in a narrative may be banal or absurd in an explanatory scheme drawn from our general experience of occurrences in the world. The task of transforming a narrative into such a scheme may be hardest of all in the case of the Gospels.

It is doubtless true that, since the narrative involves truth claims concerning facts and salvation as well as some lifelike and also some stylized religious elements, its eventual transformation into *conceptual* schemes was not only inevitable but even welcome. Descriptive schemes about such things as resurrection of the spiritual body were bound to come in its wake—and so, in the long run, were dogmas about the relation of the Father to the Son. However, necessary as such *descriptive* schemes may be, they cannot provide *explanatory* theories for the narrative's claims and for the various patterns of meaning inherent in it, and inherent in it in such a manner that meaning cannot be detached from the narrative form.

Chapter 12

JESUS AS SELF-MANIFESTED

In our endeavor to understand the narrative of the Synoptic Gospels, we have so far stressed four patterns of meaning embedded in the narrative itself: (1) Jesus' obedience, (2) the coexistence of power and powerlessness, (3) the transition from one to the other, and (4) the interrelation of Jesus' and God's intention and action. In the course of commenting on all of these, but especially the third, the transition of Jesus' power to his powerlessness (Chapter 10), we began to see the identity of Jesus in terms of his *intention-action* description. His specific identity was what he did and underwent, the Savior in need of redemption, the crucified human savior identified as the one, unsubstitutable individual, Jesus of Nazareth. Further, in the course of comment on the fourth pattern, that of the interrelation of Jesus and God in the story of the events, we began to touch upon the complex question of the identity of Jesus in terms of what we have called *self-manifestation* analysis.

Though self-manifestation and intention-action description are ultimately inseparable in the understanding of identity, they may, nevertheless, represent stresses in differing accounts (or strands of the same account) of any person. We have, so far, quite naturally—in line with our four patterns or themes—stressed the Gospels' intention-action description of Jesus. Now, however, we shall turn to the second way of examining the Gospel narrative.

What is meant by self-manifestation description here is, as we indicated before (Chapter 9), the structuring of the Gospel story as a whole into a single developing series of stages in the identification of its persisting subject, Jesus of Nazareth. Unlike the patterns of which we spoke earlier, involving certain specific and limited sequences of actions and events, the structure of which we now speak is concerned with the transitions in the sequence of the one whole narrative and their cumulative identification of who Jesus is.

Just what this means may be grasped if we draw the distinction once again between the two kinds of identity description. *Intention-action* description deals with a specific, enacted project of a person—a specific sequence in the perfection of its enactment from initial inception to completed execution. The sequence of Jesus' last days—beginning with his announced intention at the Last Supper to enact the good of all men on their behalf, through his inner resolve at Gethsemane and the outward implementation of his resolve when arrested, to its full and public enactment on the cross—is best seen in this kind of description.

Self-manifestation description, on the other hand, tries to point to the continuity of a person's identity throughout the transitions brought about by his acts and life's events. Hence, there is about the person, at any given stage in this description, a certain elusive and unfinished, but also persistent, quality. This form of identity description deals with nothing less than the whole scope or stretch of a person's life, in vigorous contrast to the other type of description, which deals only with a specific sequence of events. It is evident, then, that self-manifestation description of Jesus involves the full scope of the Gospel story.

Now, it is no doubt true that the task of writing a life of Jesus by reconstructing the events is at best difficult and at worst impossible. Nevertheless, the Gospel accounts, regarded as a story and taken as one self-contained whole, do provide us with a kind of order-in-sequence, consisting of a series of distinct transitions from stage to stage. Each of these stages is marked off from the preceding by providing a further insight into the identification of who Jesus is. But we must add that in any piece of literature, the Gospels included, it may be possible to find a variety of such formal ordering schemes, some of which may be in conflict with others.[16]

JESUS MANIFEST IN HIS NATIVITY

The first stage includes the birth and infancy stories. In Matthew and Luke this first phase comes to an end with the transition to the next—Jesus' baptism at the hands of John the Baptist. (In Mark's Gospel, the baptism is, of course, the beginning of the whole story.) The striking fact about this first phase is that both in the prose story (or stories) and in its liturgical and poetic forms, as, for example, in the canticles in the first two chapters of Luke, the person of Jesus is identified wholly in terms of the identity of the people of Israel. He is not the indi-

---

16. For one such scheme for the whole story, profoundly perceptive and quite different from that set forth in this chapter, see Karl Barth, *Church Dogmatics* (New York: Scribner, 1956), IV, 1, pp. 224 ff.

vidual person Jesus, not even "of Nazareth." He is not even really an individual Israelite, but Israel under the representative form of the infant king figure called Jesus. He is a representative, stylized figure in the form of an individual.

In his being and in the events surrounding him that also focus on him, we get a cross section of the whole history of events that together make up the people of Israel. He is, in effect, a climactic summing-up of that whole story. The crucial events that happened to Israel at large and constituted Israel as a people happen on a small scale to Jesus, but in such a way that there is now a completion or fulfillment of what was left incomplete in Israel's life. Jesus' identity in Matthew is determined by references to Abraham, the single progenitor of the seed of Israel, to Jacob, the figure from whom the nation Israel first took its name, to Judah, the father of a particular tribe in Israel, and to David, Israel's great king whose name was to be lent to the future reclamation of Israel's heritage. In Luke, Jesus' identity is signified in terms of Adam, in whom Israel, mankind, and God are all directly connected. Luke's procedure is reminiscent of Paul's bringing together the first with the second Adam, who is Christ *(Rom. 5:14,19; 1 Cor. 15:21-22);* this theme, in turn, is reminiscent of certain Gnostic and Jewish themes with which early Christianity was mixed. This is who Jesus is, not an individual in his own right, but Israel and (to some extent) mankind. They lend their identity to him; they bestow it on him. But the emphasis at this stage of the story is much more on their identity than on his and on him in terms of them. He, the infant king, is little more than a symbol of Israel.

In Matthew, this identification is reinforced by the character of the early events befalling Jesus. For example, Jesus, like ancient Israel, is called out of Egypt, his parents having taken him there in fear of persecution at the hands of Herod. "This was to fulfill what the Lord had spoken by the prophet, 'Out of Egypt have I called my son'" *(Matt. 2:15).* The identification of Jesus in terms of Israel is made by paralleling two events that have Egypt as their center and by means of the subtle blending of the identity of the subjects, Israel and Jesus, to whom these events happen. That is to say, the prophecy as fulfilled is claimed to refer to the one person Jesus, God's Son, though the original Old Testament reference is to all Israel, "When Israel was a child, I loved him, and out of Egypt I called my son" *(Hos. 11:1).* In this way Jesus and Israel become identified, establishing Jesus' identity more in terms of Israel and what has happened to her than the other way around.

The turn of events following hard upon Jesus' departure for Egypt illustrates the same motif. In a rage, Herod killed all the male infants in the Bethlehem region. It is a stylized little account, with its moral, or rather prophetic, clue immediately attached:

Then was fulfilled what was spoken by the prophet Jeremiah:

"A voice was heard in Ramah
wailing and loud lamentation,
Rachel weeping for her children;
she refused to be consoled
because they were no more."

(Matt. 2:17-18)

Not only the deliverance but also the agony and destruction of Israel are embodied in the events focusing around Jesus' birth. The story, moreover, has a certain ambivalence in its overtones. Explicitly it refers us to the events surrounding the fall of Jerusalem and the exile. But quite automatically, even if the author says nothing about it, we are also put in mind of Pharaoh's destruction of the Israelites' infant sons and Moses' escape from this fate. So Jesus, together with the events focusing about him, is identified by means of the crucial turns in the people's past, several of them, as it were, converging on him at once and signifying who he is because of all that he embodies.

THE BAPTISM AS A POINT OF TRANSITION

With the account of Jesus' baptism, the story undergoes a break, or rather a decisive transition. Though he still is the one who fulfills the prophecies concerning Israel, he now, far more than in the first stage, appears in a limited way as an individual in his own right. Certainly he is no longer simply a representative of the people as a whole or of Israel's history. He now performs mighty deeds that are signs of the imminent Kingdom of God. He proclaims its advent and teaches the manner of life in it. Nonetheless, he retains something of the symbolic quality that he had in the first part of the accounts. Now, however, it is not so much the summation of Israel's past that he represents, but the direct and immediately pending rule of God, newly present or about to come. Thus, he begins to emerge as an individual figure in his own right, and yet it is as the witness to and embodiment of the Kingdom of God that he does so.

Though it is somewhat precarious to say so, it seems that in this stage of the accounts his identity is largely defined in terms of the Kingdom of God. Even the titles with which the authors dignify him—Son of Man, Son of God, Christ, Holy One of God, Lord—serve to indicate his representation of the Kingdom of God and his identification by means of that Kingdom. The very offense to which his preaching and bearing give rise is caused by the fact that his hearers are confronted with his claim to authority in representing this kingly power and with the need for choice for or against it.

The frequent questions concerning the *true* identity of this apparently familiar man ("Is not this Joseph's son?" *Luke* 4:22; cf. v. 34) point us in the same direction. He is now, far more than in the infancy stories, identified in his own right as the son of Joseph of Nazareth, whom everyone knows. However, it is also true that *who* he is is defined by his proclamation of the fulfillment of the promise of deliverance to the captives, i.e., by the coming of God's Kingdom. It is a fulfillment to which he witnesses by preaching and by the signs of his mighty works; it is also a fulfillment that takes place in his preaching and deeds. "Today this scripture has been fulfilled in your hearing" *(Luke* 4:21). Thus his witness to and embodiment of the Kingdom of God define who he is, but he is now, much more than in the infancy narratives, the specific, unsubstitutable man called Jesus, who hails from Nazareth and is uniquely himself.

Luke places this emphasis right at the point at which he has Jesus begin his public ministry, just after his baptism and temptation in the wilderness. It is worth noting that Luke places the first instance of this bold and thematic announcement, which identifies Jesus wholly by reference to his theme and its embodiment, in Jesus' hometown, lending to his particular identity a thoroughly bedrock and unsubstitutable quality. We find something of the same double emphasis in the reply to the question from John through his disciples concerning Jesus' identity, "Are you he who is to come, or shall we look for another?" *(Luke* 7:19-23) In his answer, Jesus points to the signs of the Kingdom of God effected in him, to his mighty deeds and proclamation of the good news to the poor. It is in terms of these signs of the Kingdom that he is to be identified. Yet it is equally obvious in this episode that this identification of God's Kingdom among men is to be focused on a specific man, the specific, unsubstitutable person of Jesus.

We could multiply examples to illustrate this same point. At this stage, past the childhood stories and commencing with his baptism, Jesus becomes more nearly an individual in his own right, and yet his identity is established by reference to the Kingdom of God. It has frequently and rightly been noted that in the earlier stage we find so obvious a proliferation of legend and stylized tales that historicity—understood either as lifelike representation or as events that actually took place—is not appropriate as a category to be applied in understanding the reports, although there is "history" here as the climactic fulfillment of patterns of meaning summing up the past life of Israel. In the second stage, on the other hand, the lifelike or history-like represen-

tation of the specific individual in specific situations raises the question
of historical veracity in acute fashion. About certain events reported in
the Gospels we are almost bound to ask, Did they actually take place?
With regard to certain teachings we ask, Were they actually those of
Jesus himself? Nonetheless, the specific individual's identity and the situations in which it is enacted are at this stage so often tied to their referent—the Kingdom of God—that it is quite speculative (in the absence
of external, corroborative evidence) to ask, in many instances, how
much actually happened, what he actually said, and how much is stylized
account, illustrative of his representational character and the author's
beliefs. Moreover, the meaning of these texts would remain the same,
partially stylized and representative and partially focused on the
history-like individual, whether or not they are historical.

THE LAST STAGE OF JESUS' LIFE

It is worth emphasizing these matters in order to stress the contrasting situation in the third and last stage in the story's structure. In the
first place, this part is most generally agreed to reflect actual events with
considerable (though not absolute) accuracy. But even more important,
it is the part of the story most clearly history-like in the sense that it
describes an individual and a series of events in connection with him
that, whether fictional or real, are what they are in their own right. He
and his actions and the events converging on him are not simply representative or symbolical. They are what they are quite unsubstitutably
and gain all their significance from being this specific series of linked circumstances and no other. He alone is at their center and lends them
their character, so that they can focus neither on any other hero, human
or divine, nor on that "everyman" for whom he might mistakenly be
thought to be a symbol. Even a saying such as, "Daughters of Jerusalem, do not weep for me, but weep for yourselves and for your children"
(Luke 23:28), is no exception to this fact. It does indeed bespeak an
identification of others with his own fate; but it does so in terms of the
specific events that may befall them, as these events are foreshadowed or
perhaps even triggered by his particular fate. His specific identity is such
that others cannot merge into a common indistinguishable identity with
him; instead they find that their own specific and unsubstitutable identity becomes sharply accentuated by relation to Jesus' own unique identity.

The transition to the third stage in the identification of Jesus comes,
it appears, with Jesus' brief announcement to his disciples that he and
they would now go to Jerusalem and with his prediction of what his fate
would be there. The atmosphere now becomes heavy with foreboding.

The troubled anticipation is all the more effectively conveyed for its cryptic nature, "And they were amazed, and those who followed were afraid" *(Mark 10:32)*.

We are still at a point at which Jesus is characterized by means of the Kingdom of God. Nonetheless, that very identification now becomes increasingly problematical and tenuous. The connection between Jesus and the Kingdom of God becomes loose, and the figure of Jesus emerges more and more as one whose mission it is to enact his own singular destiny—while the Kingdom of God and the Son of Man who embodies it and its authority fade into the background. There is an increasing tendency to utilize the titles of that authority—Christ, Son of Man, Son of God, King, etc.—with an ironic and pathetic twist in their application to Jesus, indicating the seeming utter incongruity between them as well as the Kingdom they represent and the figure supposedly embodying them (See *Mark 15:17-19, 26-32*).

By means of this pathetic or ironic ambiguity or detachment between Jesus and the Kingdom, the focus of the story's last part falls more and more on him in his unadorned singularity. He is simply himself in his circumstances. Everything else about him, by virtue of which he is a representative figure or symbol of something more than himself—everything with which he had hitherto been identified—now becomes ambiguous, questionable, and, in a way, detachable from him.

Something of that ambiguity and detachment between Jesus and his titles is indicated in Luke's account of the turning toward Jerusalem. All three Synoptic Gospels speak of Jesus as saying, *"We are going up to Jerusalem."* Jesus goes on to prophesy the Son of Man's passion, death, and resurrection. However, Luke alone adds, "But they understood none of these things; this saying was hid from them, and they did not grasp what was said" *(Luke 18:34)*. In other words, the disciples did not at this point really understand what turning to Jerusalem meant. They could not, at this vital juncture, make an unambiguous connection between Jesus, one of "us" going to Jerusalem, and the Son of Man and his Kingdom. Only Jesus himself, and he only after he was resurrected, could effectively provide for them "in their hearts" the connection between Jesus and the Christ.

The question is not whether the Gospel writer himself was ambiguous in his own mind concerning the identity of Jesus. Obviously, he was not. A more significant question might be, Did the writer think Jesus had become identical with the Son of Man at some climactic point (e.g., the resurrection), whereas earlier he had not been? But even this question is not for us to adjudicate. Nor can we here raise the question as to whether Jesus applied the title "Son of Man" or other messianic titles to himself. Again, that is a speculative matter that takes us beyond the pattern and structure of the narrative.

For us the issue is rather to understand that the ambiguity of the connection between Jesus and the Son of Man, which begins to be particularly tense at this point, is real *within the narrative*. At this stage of the unfolding events of the narrative, there is uncertainty on this issue. And now the story, beginning with Jesus' arrest, starts to accelerate into an increasingly terse and spare climactic telling, proceeding virtually unimpeded by any didactic material in its final stages. The focus of the story remains on the action by which Jesus' destiny is accomplished, and on Jesus himself as the unsubstitutable person he is. He is shown as an unsubstitutable individual in his own right, his unadorned singularity focused on both his passion and his resurrection.

THE FOCUS ON JESUS' SINGULARITY

We recall here the last of the patterns or themes we discerned earlier in this story: the increasingly close interaction between Jesus and God, an interaction in which Jesus' action is superseded by that of God. A fascinating feature of the narrative is that this increasing action of God does not detract in the slightest from the increasingly sharp focusing on Jesus' singularity. Further, it is in this interaction that Jesus' identity is clarified as the one unsubstitutable Jesus of Nazareth. Indeed, at the climactic point of the divine action, the resurrection, where God alone is active, it is Jesus alone who is manifest.

With this in mind, we note that, in the passion narrative, Jesus' *enactment* of his identity comes to a climax in one sense in the crucifixion and in another sense in the resurrection. But, in another way yet, it is true to say that this sequence, beginning either with the turn to Jerusalem or with the events after the Last Supper, *manifests* Jesus' identity in his own right. This manifestation is expressed by a focus on Jesus alone in the passion account and the simultaneous fading out of the Kingdom of God and its titles. But in another sense it comes to concrete expression in the resurrection appearances, where Jesus identifies himself most fully as Jesus who is the Son of Man, the promised one of Israel, the Christ. Here he re-establishes the connection that had become so ambiguous when the spotlight first fell on him in his unsubstitutable identity at the beginning of this stage. But now, as the one who has been resurrected, he re-establishes that connection, the identity between his singular person and the Kingdom and its titles, by "demythologizing" the savior myth. He, the unsubstitutable Jesus, now makes the stylized titles his own. He claims them for himself in his very identity as Jesus of Nazareth. Hence, the resurrection story, as a narrative description, is anything but mythical, no matter what one may think of its factuality.

Unsubstitutable identity is simply not the stuff of mythological tales. Jesus identifies the titles rather than they him. Thus, walking with two disciples after the resurrection, he informs them, "Was it not necessary that the Christ should suffer these things and enter into his glory?" But now, the earlier ambiguity having been resolved, the author can add, "He interpreted to them in all the scriptures the things concerning himself" *(Luke 24:26-27)*.

Here, then, he was most of all himself, and here most fully manifest as the individual, Jesus of Nazareth. Concerning the resurrection in particular, this is a hard saying. The structure of the narrative is such that the entire focusing of Jesus as a full human being in manifest identity, rather than as a mythical savior, comes to its climax here. In the first stage, we recall, he was described merely as a representative figure and not as an individual at all. In the second stage, he was much more nearly manifest as an individual in his own right, and yet he was more nearly identified in terms of the Kingdom of God than it in terms of him. In the third stage, he emerged fully as the one unsubstitutable Jesus of Nazareth—and this as much in the resurrection as in the passion. In focusing his identity, i.e., who he is, the full sequence as such, passion, death and resurrection, is one stage. Who is this man? He is Jesus of Nazareth who, as this man and no other, is truly manifest as the Savior, the presence of God.

Taken one way, the direction of the process of identification is unilinear—from no singularity to the fullest singular identity Both intention-action analysis and subject-manifestation analysis find their full and climactic application in the strange and supple narrative that identifies Jesus in the passion-resurrection sequence. In another way, this same narrative identification process brings us, at its conclusion, full circle—though with a difference. At the end of the story, as at its beginning, there is full identity between Jesus and Israel. But whereas at the beginning it was the community that served to identify him, the reverse is now the case. He, Jesus, provides the community, as well as God's Kingdom and the stylized savior figure, with his identity. He is the Christ of Israel who, in his own singular identity and unsubstitutable history, sums up and identifies the history of the whole people.[17]

We have tried to describe the identity of Jesus in his story by means of a formal scheme for identity description. We asked, "What was he like?" and answered with an intention-action description provided by the narrative, pointing us to the crucified savior, the obedient Jesus who enacted the good that God intended for men. The enactment of this

---

17. For a similar interpretation of Jesus as the sum and climax of the history of God's "covenant" with Israel, see Karl Barth, *Church Dogmatics*, IV, 1, par. 57.

intention came to a climax in the crucifixion-resurrection sequence. We also asked, "Who is he?" and answered with an identification description provided by the whole Gospel in its transitions pointing us to the unsubstitutable Jesus of Nazareth who, as that one man, is the Christ and the presence of God. And again, his identity is most transparent in the crucifixion-resurrection sequence.

Whatever else may be evident from the results of this analysis, surely it is obvious that a descriptive scheme less formal than this would endanger the integrity of the story. This would be especially true if we were to go "back" of what is given in the story and infer the character of Jesus, his policy for action, and his significance for mankind by means of preconceptions of human nature, human existence, or the human condition derived from elsewhere, especially from our psychological or cultural experience. For the upshot of our investigation is that, in order to understand the function of Jesus in the story, we do not need—indeed, we must not use—more heavily freighted identity descriptions, such as that of "alienation." On the contrary! We must neither look for his identity in back of the story nor supply it from extraneous analytical schemes. It is evident that in the story Jesus' true being is not mysteriously hidden behind the action or within a supposedly distorted, "objectified," or "mythological" self-manifestation. No. He is what he appeared to be—the Savior Jesus from Nazareth, who underwent "all these things" and who is truly manifest as Jesus, the risen Christ. Such, it appears, is the story of Jesus in the Gospels.

It follows, concerning the identity of the others for whose sakes he was obedient, that they also—in the context of this story—cannot be said to be identified as "alienated" or "estranged" or in "self-contradiction." In contrast to the Gnostics with their savior myths and to the similar traditions of modern idealist and existentialist philosophy, the story of Jesus represents at its very core an insistence that because there is at least one man, Jesus, who has an identity others have identities also; for he, as the first of many brothers, gained that possibility for them in dying and rising in their behalf. Hence, although they are sinners in need of his redemptive power, they cannot be characterized as alienated from their own identity. Whatever sin may be, it must not be confused with this clutch of cultural and philosophical notions. Not only the substance of the claim that human beings are self-alienated in this world, but even the idea applied as a formal scheme for the description of human identity is inapplicable in connection with the Gospel story.

Chapter 13

JESUS IDENTIFIED IN HIS RESURRECTION

The story of Jesus' resurrection, we have said, does not function like a myth in the Gospel narrative. Unsubstitutable identity gained in unsubstitutable circumstances is simply not the stuff of mythological tales. To bring this point into focus, let us return to an assessment of myth.

Myths are stories in which character and action are not irreducibly themselves. Instead they are representations of broader and not directly representable psychic or cosmic states—states transcending the scene of finite and particular events subject to causal explanation. The deepest levels of human existence, the origin and destiny of the universe, including humanity, are the themes that myths evoke through storytelling. Myths are convincing or true by virtue of their embodiment or echoing of universal experience. "Universal" may be too strong a term, but it is not too much to say that a particular myth is the external and expressed mirroring of an internal experience that is both elemental within the consciousness and yet shared by a whole group.

Given this setting for a myth, it is frequently (and doubtless rightly) asserted that, if the meaning of an account can be discovered by mythological interpretation, the question of its factuality need not arise. The explanation of its origin as myth is enough. Myth thus becomes the unconscious poetizing of a folk consciousness.

We should ask, then, if the Gospel account of the resurrection can be understood to be a myth. At the very least a positive answer to this question would have to be heavily qualified.

In fact, we have argued precisely the opposite. The literary structure of the account, we have said, points in favor of the thesis that the resurrection account (or, better, the passionresurrection account as an unbroken unity) is a demythologization of the dying-rising savior myth. For, in contrast to the substance of myth, the passion-resurrection account concerns an unsubstitutable individual whose mysterious identity is not ineffably behind the story but is inseparable from the unsubstitutable events constituting it, with the resurrection as its climax.

A myth is convincing when it evokes inner experience that cannot be expressed directly because it does not belong to the order of experience of explicable events. "Did this happen?" or even, "Could this have happened?" are not questions to ask of a mythical account. We must ask, rather, "What elemental aspiration does it evoke and express?" or "To what transcendent dimension of truth does it unite us?" The truth of myth is *religious* rather than historical or factual. In contrast, then, the resurrection account, by virtue of its exclusive reference to Jesus, and by virtue of its claim that here he was most truly manifested in his human particularity, allows and even forces us to ask the question, "Did this actually take place?"

This one thing historians and novelists have in common: they deal with specific actions and specific human identities. If a novel-like account is about a person who is assumed to have lived, the question of factuality is virtually bound to arise, for psychological if no other reasons, either at specific points or over the whole stretch of the account. Now there may well be points in the story where the individual is depicted in such a manner that he becomes more nearly or directly accessible to us than he does at others (as I have argued in the case of the Gospel story), so that we are able to say, in terms of either kind of identification scheme or both, "this is the way he really is." However, one should not equate such accessibility through depiction, i.e., life-likeness to the point of intimate knowledge of the depicted individual, with probability or likelihood of reliable historical information about him. In the instance of Jesus, it may well be that certain of his sayings or specific, isolated episodes recounted from his brief ministry, which are quite enigmatic in character and tell little about him, such as his condemning a fig tree because it would not yield fruit out of season *(Mark 11:12-14)*, are much more nearly reliable historical reports than those in which his over-all personal intention is more clearly depicted.

It is not likely that successive generations of critics will agree on what is probable fact in the Gospel accounts. The criteria for historical reliability in regard to the Gospel story will—in the absence of external corroborations—always rest on shifting grounds. Speculations about Jesus' cultural milieu and its relation to him, the influence of the earliest church's setting on the Gospels, the shape and religious functions of the earliest oral traditions handed down by the first community of believers, the likely shape of the first written documents, and the interests or prejudices of the final editors—all these factors will keep on influencing and changing what is regarded as historical or historically likely about Jesus, to say nothing about the changing cultural influences playing on the generations of scholars doing the speculating.

In sum, though the question of historical likelihood is bound to arise in the case of the most history-like or sharply individualistic reports, both of the sayings and of the incidents of Jesus' life, the force or urgency of the *question* does not make a positive *answer* to it any more credible. However, *if* the story or text and history are to coincide directly at any point, *if* Jesus rendered directly accessible in depiction is to be joined to fact claims about what happened, then it will have to be in the sequence depicted in the last stage of the story, from the passion through the resurrection or ascension, not in his teachings. The upshot of this observation is very simply that *if* the Gospel story is to function religiously in a way that is at once historical and Christological, the central focus will have to be on the history-like narration of the final sequence, rather than on Jesus' sayings in the preaching pericopes.

It is in the final sequence in the story that his person as individual figure in a story is most clearly accessible, not in his sayings taken simply as sayings. The specific content of a man's preachings, even if we take it that we have direct access to them, does not by itself make the preacher accessible, who might be either quite unknowable or quite different from even full, to say nothing of fragmentary, reports of his sayings. If the depicted Jesus' (not even to mention the "historical" Jesus') sayings are to function Christologically, they will have to do so as expressions of the person who comes to be portrayed in the last stage of the story. One cannot with any confidence proceed in the reverse direction. A Soteriology or Christology involving assertion of the indispensable uniqueness of Jesus cannot possibly make good on any claim that the person of the depicted Jesus is directly known from his teachings and that his final personal bearing and destiny in the story are but functions of these words. The case is even less convincing if one appeals from a selection of the teachings, regarded as historically reliable, to a supposedly reliable knowledge of the "real" historical figure uttering them, and thence from the unique authoritativeness of the teachings to both the religious uniqueness and the historical accessibility of the teacher. The inference-series, at once religious and historical, leading to such a conclusion is extremely tenuous and speculative. In addition, the ontology which focuses the being of a person wholly in the personal functioning of his words, so that he turns into a "word event" through whom being-as-meaning communicates itself, or "language speaks," is not only philosophically questionable but of very doubtful value for connecting reported words and the person of the speaker to any ostensibly reliable historical claim about him. It is, in fact, a category confusion between philosophical and historical argument.

I have argued that Jesus' individual identity comes to focus directly in the passion-resurrection narrative rather than in the account of his person and teaching in his earlier ministry. It is in this final and climactic sequence that the storied Jesus is most of all himself, and there—unlike those earlier points at which we can get to his individual identity only ambiguously—we are confronted with him directly as the unsubstitutable individual who is what he does and undergoes and is manifested directly as who he is. Whether or not we know much or anything about the "historical" Jesus is probably a well nigh insoluble question; but once again, *if* the accounts rendering the storied Jesus are to be joined to fact claims about the "historical" Jesus in such a way as to make the depicted Jesus genuinely accessible and thus give the historical person significant history-like religious content, the union will have to be in the sequence where the crucified Jesus is raised from the dead as the Christ.

The realistic or history-like quality of the narrative, whether historical or not, prevents even the person who regards the account as implausible from regarding it as mere myth. Rather, it is to him a kind of hyperfiction claiming to be self-warranting fact. For the believer, on the other hand, the claim of the narrative concerning the resurrection is not surprising, but a direct and logical consequence of his belief in the presence of Christ and in the unity of his identity with his presence.

All of this is not to say that we are bound to ignore the story of Jesus' ministry in identifying him. It is simply to affirm that Jesus, in his unique identity, is not available to us directly or unambiguously—either as a character in a story or historically— in the portion of the Gospel accounts describing his ministry. And this is not surprising, not only on historical grounds, but in view of the type of writing that the Gospels represent. Even the most reliable historical or biographical account still leaves us in the situation of a certain amount of mystery, after all the thoughts and actions of an individual have been described. Indeed, the most searching biographies of great men point to the ambiguities in the possible interpretations of their subjects' thoughts, intentions, and reflections. In other words, our knowledge of the "private person" remains tantalizingly incomplete. That is what makes biographical history a fascinating quest that is never finished. We never fully know a person in his inmost being, as indeed in a related sense we never fully know ourselves. And historical or biographical knowledge is surely in part projected in analogy from our own self-knowledge. If we add that the account of Jesus' ministry prior to his last few days in Jerusalem is probably largely not biographical, it is evident that we cannot gain access to his identity as a historical or as a storied, history-like figure in the earlier portions of the Gospels.

The fiction writer's acquaintance with a subject's character is differ-ent from that of a biographer, though it has affinities with it. We are bound to judge the success of a piece of writing by the integrity or cred-ibility of the characters. Conversely, the manipulation of his characters spells the author's failure. Nonetheless, the novelist obviously has a direct or inside knowledge of his subjects, their intentions, and the direct bond leading from their intentions to their actions that the histo-rian or biographer cannot have. In a manner different from the histo-rian's or biographer's analogy of self-knowledge, the fiction writer also uses the analogy of self-discernment. But it is a surer kind of self-knowledge. All of us may know ourselves and others well in several ways, some ways more veiled and ambiguous, others less so, some more nearly inferential after the fashion of the biographer-historian, some more akin to the novelist's direct knowledge of his subject. Yet the dif-ference between fiction-writing and history-writing is obviously not absolute. As we mentioned earlier, they do have in common at least the fact of narration, the fact that character and circumstances cannot be abstracted from each other, but gain their specific qualities through each other.

With regard to the Gospels, we are actually in a fortunate position that so much of what we know about Jesus, beginning at the crucial ini-tiatory point of the climactic, unbroken sequence, is more nearly fic-tional than historical in narration. Yet the story is about an individual who lived; and, by common agreement, it is within the passion-resurrection sequence that we come closest to historical events in his life (specifically in the trial and crucifixion). But also, in that most nearly biographical sequence, the form of the narration is more nearly like that of fiction. The main example of that fact is the direct inside understanding of the person of Jesus provided by the scene in the Gar-den of Gethsemane. Surely one would not want to call this description biographical. It is not even pertinent to the story to ask how this sequence can be historical, if Jesus was alone there and his disciples were sleeping some distance away. It is precisely the fiction-like quality of the whole narrative, from upper room to resurrection appearances, that serves to bring the identity of Jesus sharply before us and to make him accessible to us.

But throughout the narrative, and most particularly at the crucial climax of the resurrection, fictional description, providing direct knowl-edge of his identity in, with, and through the circumstances, merges with factual claim, whether justified or not. The narration is at once intensely serious and historical in intent and fictional in form, the com-mon strand between them being the identification of the individual in his circumstances. To know *who* he is in connection with what took place is to know *that* he is. This is the climax of the story and its claim. What the accounts are saying, in effect, is that the being and identity of Jesus in the resurrection are such that his nonresurrection becomes inconceivable. This does not mean that we can take away the double negative in the preceding sentence and say that the resurrection is conceivable or that we can think our way through to an understanding of it. It is, rather, that, however impossible it may be to grasp the nature of the resurrection, it remains inconceivable that it should not have taken place.

To express the matter in a way totally uncongenial to the Synoptic writers, what they are saying is something like this: "Our argument is that to grasp what this identity, Jesus of Nazareth (which has been made directly accessible to us), is is to believe that he has been, in *fact,* raised from the dead. Someone may reply that in that case the most perfectly depicted character and most nearly lifelike fictional identity ought always in fact to have lived a factual historical life. We answer that the argument holds good only in this one and absolutely unique case, where the described entity (who or what he is, i.e., Jesus Christ, the presence of God) is totally identical with his factual existence. He is the resurrection and the life. How can he be conceived as not resurrected?"

Something like this argument seems to be present in the resurrection account. Putting it this way, and stressing the identity of the person of Jesus with his being resurrected, does, of course, leave out certain things. Corresponding to the uniqueness of the fact that his being and his identity cannot be thought apart, the apprehension or grasp of his presence is also unique. Of what other fact can we say that complete commitment is a way of taking note of it? But grateful love of God and neighbor is the proper manner of appropriating the presence, based on the resurrection of Jesus, who in perfect obedience to God enacted men's good in their behalf on the cross. That this act is the only manner of appropriating the resurrection we cannot doubt. In this instance— and in this instance alone—commitment in faith and assent by the mind constrained by the imagination are one and the same. But we cannot dwell here on the manner of appropriation. (In any case, that the description of our appropriation of Jesus' resurrection might serve to make the resurrection more credible or intelligible does not seem to be the Synoptic authors' point.)

The passion-resurrection account tends to force the question of factuality because the claim is involved as part of the very identity that is described as enacted and manifest in the story-event sequence. One can obviously understand this as a literary feature of part of the account, and therefore either leave the question of facticity suspended or else answer it (independently from the narrative) in the negative. But one cannot deny that in the accounts themselves the fact question was bound to be answered the way they did answer it. As we said earlier, this is not mythological description but a piece of hyperfiction, if one chooses to regard it as fictional. It seems difficult, further, to deny that the question of fact *tends* to be raised beyond the literary analysis of the account.

How, then, might one answer the question in the affirmative? Presumably by a kind of thought movement similar to and reiterative of that of the original authors, in which grateful discipleship and factual acknowledgment seem to have been—mysteriously—one and the same act. But we have gone afield in this last remark; for it constitutes a reflection concerning the possibility of making the transition from a literary description to historical and religious affirmation. However, explaining how this transition becomes possible—to say nothing of demonstrating its actual occurrence—is what we claimed from the beginning to be impossible, certainly in the context of our analysis of the unity of Christ's presence and identity, if indeed at all.

Let us therefore return to the account and its description. Its claim, we said, is that, in the instance of this singular individual, his identity and its manifestation involve his actual living presence. Who and what he was, did, and underwent are all inseparable from the fact that he is. (The reverse is obviously equally true: That he is brings with it the manifestation of who he is and what he did. The affirmation some theologians make of the importance of Jesus' historical factuality, coupled with their denial of any significant content given with this factuality, seems to be completely artificial. A human fact, significantly apprehended, cannot be separated in this way, except in the most artificial philosophical dogmas.) Once again, if in the resurrection he was most clearly manifest as Jesus of Nazareth the Savior, then it was here also that the accounts could say that he lives.

Something like this seems to be the significance of the words spoken by the "two men" to the women at the empty tomb, even before Jesus himself was manifest. "Why do you seek the living among the dead?" *(Luke 24:5)* they ask, as though it were evident that he is living, as though it were startling to think of him who is "one who lives" as not living but dead. The Fourth Gospel, as if in comment on this perspective, extends Luke's identification of Jesus' being alive to an all-embracing generalization, "I am the resurrection and the life" *(John 11:25)*. Jesus defines life, he is life: How can he who constitutes the very definition of life be conceived of as the opposite of what he defines? To think him dead is the equivalent of not thinking of him at all.

In explanation of what they have just said, the "two men" add immediately: "Remember how he told you, while he was still in Galilee, that the Son of Man must be delivered into the hands of sinful men, and be crucified, and on the third day rise" *(Luke 24:6-7)*. The reiteration of this prophecy appears in all the Gospels like a steady refrain. It is the primary content of what little we have in the way of description of the sequence of Jesus' life in the earliest preaching of Christians. In the present context the saying is obviously designed to serve as commentary for the question, "Why do you seek the living among the dead?" Had Jesus not foretold what would come to pass? But the saying is also designed to focus his identity as one who lives, who is life and not death. Jesus lives as the one who cannot *not* live, for whom to be what he is is to be. But who or what he thus is is unambiguously Jesus of Nazareth; and as Jesus he is the Son of Man. He is the one who was delivered into the hands of sinful men, to be crucified and to rise again. The prophecy (here taken as fulfilled) is the content of his identity as the one who lives.

The content of the prophecy does not add anything new to the question, "Why do you seek the living among the dead?" The relation between Luke 24:5 and the following two verses, the prophecy fulfilled, is not that of giving more and new information. Rather, the prophecy provides the content for the assertion made in the preceding verse: *That* he is ("the living") is one and the same with *who* and *what* he is, what he did, and underwent ("The Son of Man must be delivered...."). The relation between these verses is similar to that between the two parts of Exodus 3:14-15. In response to Moses' query about his name, God tells Moses to convey to the Children of Israel that "I AM" had sent him unto them. Immediately, as though in an explanation that says the same thing over again, God adds: "Say this to the people of Israel, 'The Lord, the God of your fathers, the God of Abraham, the God of Isaac, and the God of Jacob, has sent me to you.'" The reference to God as the God of Israel's fathers does not add something new to his being "I AM." For him to be and to be this specific one are the same. Similarly, for Jesus to be and to be Jesus the Son of Man and Israel's redeemer are one and the same thing. The ambiguity is over. He, the Christ, can now interpret to them "in all the scriptures the things concerning himself." *That* he is and *who* he is—Jesus of Nazareth who, as that one man, is the redeemer undergoing in obedience all that constitutes the climax and summation of Israel's history—are one and the same thing. His identity is so unsubstitutable now through the event of resurrection that he can bring it to bear as the identifying clue for the community that becomes climactically focused through him. Indeed, the New Testament will ask just this of all men: To identify themselves by relation, not to a universal hero or savior figure, but to Jesus of Nazareth, who has identified himself with them and for them.

This, then, is the identity of Jesus Christ. He is the man from Naza-

reth who redeemed men by his helplessness, in perfect obedience enacting their good in their behalf. As that same one, he was raised from the
dead and manifested to be the redeemer. As that same one, Jesus the
redeemer, he cannot *not* live, and to conceive of him as not living is to
misunderstand who he is.

To know who he is is to believe in his self-focused presence. This, it
appears, is the testimony of the New Testament and, hence, the understanding of believers. His identity and his presence are given together in
indissoluble unity. But the proper order for understanding this fact is to
begin with his identity, which cannot be dissolved into our identity or
presence—the danger we found so acute when we started by asking
directly concerning his presence.

WHAT IS INVOLVED IN BELIEF
IN THE RESURRECTION?

What shall we now say about the manner of his presence? Before
trying to answer that question, let us finish these reflections on his identity, as focused in his resurrection, by asking, What kinds of affirmation
would be involved if one were to believe in Jesus' resurrection? Note
that we do not ask: Is it possible? Is it demonstrable? How can we
become persuaded of this difficult belief? Just these are the kinds of
questions that would call for the dubious kind of bridging of the gap
which we have avoided, between the believer with his formal question
affirming and seeking to describe the presence of Christ and the unbeliever with his inability to presuppose or grasp that presence.

Having directed attention all along to the descriptive structure of
the accounts and not the factual historicity of their contents, we must
say that belief in Jesus' resurrection is more nearly a belief in something
like the inspired quality of the accounts than in the theory that they
reflect what "actually took place." But at one point a judgment of faith
concerning the inspiration of the descriptive contents and a judgment of
faith affirming their central factual claim would have to coincide for the
believer. He would have to affirm that the New Testament authors were
right in insisting that it is more nearly correct to think of Jesus as factually raised, bodily if you will, than not to think of him in this manner.
(But the qualification "more nearly... than not" is important in order to
guard against speculative explanations of the resurrection from theories
of immortality, possibilities of visionary or auditory experiences, possibilities of resuscitating dead bodies, miracles in general, etc.) This judgment that they were right has to do with a particular understanding of
what identity means and of where the identity of Jesus is to be found
most directly in the Gospel accounts, i.e., in the crucifixion-resurrection

sequence. It also has to do with the issue of where to make the transition from literary description to factual, historical, and theological judgment, i.e., precisely in the sequence of passion and resurrection.

If what is said to have happened here is true, there is no evidence in its favor other than that which we have already adduced. It is clear that no matter what the authors' intentions—if indeed they can be made the subject of independent historical investigation—the accounts are not mythological in literary character. But that fact, surely, is only negative evidence—negative in the sense that the accounts cannot simply be explained away as belonging to the Gnostic savior myth variety, for the origin of which factual plausibility is not even an appropriate criterion. Such negative evidence, however, is certainly not enough to evoke positive belief in the resurrection of Jesus. Although the endeavor has frequently been undertaken, there appears to be no independent historical or other evidence that lends strong or conclusive support to the likelihood that this event took place or that it belongs to a credible type of occurrence. To what historical or natural occurrence would we be able to compare the resurrection—the absolute unity of factuality and identity? None. There appears to be no argument from factual evidence or rational possibility to smooth the transition from literary to faith judgment. But this is really not surprising, for faith is not based on factual evidence or inherent historical likelihood.

On the other hand, because it is more nearly factlike than not, reliable historical evidence *against* the resurrection would be decisive. In other words, if the resurrection is true, it is unique, but if false, it is like any other purported fact that has been proved false: there is nothing unique about it in that case. Until such evidence comes along, however, it seems proper to say that there is a kind of logic in a Christian's faith that forces him to say that disbelief in the resurrection of Jesus is rationally impossible.

But whether one actually *believes* the resurrection is, of course, a wholly different matter. "God raised him on the third day and made him manifest; not to all the people but to us who were chosen by God as witnesses...." (Acts *10:40-41*). We may not wish to cast this thought into the mold of election or predestination, but may want to speak of faith instead. In either case, it is necessary to say, with this passage from Acts, that, no matter what the logic of the Christian faith, actual belief in the resurrection is a matter of faith and not of arguments from possibility or evidence. Why some believe and others do not is impossible for the Christian to explain. Like many a pilgrim, he may find himself strangely on both sides at the same time. All he can do then is to recall that the logic of his faith makes it rationally impossible for him not to believe.

PART V

THE PRESENCE OF
CHRIST

Chapter 14

THE PATTERN OF CHRIST'S PRESENCE

To say that Jesus Christ cannot not be, that who he is constrains the imagination to acknowledge him as present, that in him identity and presence are given together completely as one—to say all these things is not yet to say anything specifically about his presence. Indeed, we have stressed from the very beginning that, even though identity and presence are one in him, the direct quest for his presence—including the endeavor to grasp his identity in or by means of his presence risks grave failure. What we come across at the end of that quest is not his own self-focused presence, but a diffused presence that seems strangely elusive and haunting as well as difficult to describe: It is that of ourselves, individually or collectively, seeking to grasp identity from the fear of nonidentity, presence in the midst of the fact and conviction of fleetingness.

The self-focused identity of Jesus Christ, which is his self-focused presence, cannot be abstracted from that of God. The whole Gospel pushes in the direction of that claim. The climax of the Gospel story is the full unity of the unsubstitutable individuality of Jesus with the presence of God. That same climax, the passion-crucifixion-resurrection sequence, involves also the supersession of Jesus' intention and action by that of God. In short, to speak of the identity of *Jesus*, in which he is affirmed by the believer to be present, is also to speak of the presence of *God*. The identity of Jesus in the accounts before that last and final stage is a matter of ambiguity: but in and after the final sequence it is, as a storied identity, accessible to us. And in that final sequence his identity is declared to be the complex unity of the unsubstitutable Jesus from Nazareth with the presence and action of God.

THE HOLY SPIRIT AS CHRIST'S IDENTITY AND PRESENCE

When Christian believers speak of the presence of Jesus Christ now—in contrast to his presence at the time of his earthly life, death, and resurrection, as well as in contrast to his final presence in the future mode—they use the term "Spirit" or "Holy Spirit." What they mean by this term is described, first of all, by the complex unity of which we have just spoken—that the unsubstitutably human figure, Jesus of Nazareth, and the presence and action of the God who superseded him are given together indissolubly from the climax of the Gospel story onward. This claim will concern us again when we speak of the presence of God as the determining impulse of the providential course of history. At the moment it is enough for us to affirm that the climax of the Gospel story involves an insistence that from now on we can no longer think of God except as we think of Jesus at the same time, nor of Jesus except by reference to God.

Secondly, reference to the Spirit means that the presence of this complex unity, Jesus of Nazareth as the presence of God *now*, is *indirect*. His presence has, as we said in Chapter 2, a spatial and temporal *basis*. He must be conceived of in analogy to the only manner in which we know presence: Presence means something like physical proximity and verbal communication; and it also involves self-presence, without which there cannot be presence to others. It is only insofar as he is self-focused that he can be present now. Although Christian believers assert his self-presence now as a literal fact, they do not know how to imagine or conceive it (Chapter 2); all they can say is that it must have a spatial and temporal basis without itself being subject to these confinements in such a way as to be trammeled in its freedom. The first assertion about the presence of Christ must be cast in negative terms. It is the presence of one whose identity is such that he cannot be conceived as not present. This, however, does not mean that his presence can be directly grasped or conceived. In the New Testament, this indirectness both of Christ's presence and of our grasp of it as a mysterious, self-focused presence is expressed in the stress (particularly in John, Luke, and Acts) on the fact that Jesus had to withdraw from men before the Spirit would be bestowed on the community of believers. Yet that bestowal, after his withdrawal, is nonetheless no other presence than that of Jesus Christ, a fact that believers find confirmed in the gifts of Word and Sacrament— the spatial and temporal bases of the presence of Jesus Christ.

Thirdly, in their reference to the Spirit, Christian believers affirm the strange unity of factual affirmation with commitment and love as the appropriate response to the unique unity of presence and identity that is Jesus Christ. In every other instance a fact is simply noted; trust and love are moral and attitudinal perspectives appropriate for other than merely factual occasions. They are reserved for the affective life and personal relations. But in this unique instance the distinction will not work. For the believer to know who Jesus Christ is, to affirm his presence, and to adore him are one and the same thing. The believer does not choose between them or claim that one has priority over the other. Just as Christ's presence and identity cannot be conceived apart, factual affirmation of him and commitment to him cannot be conceived apart either, no matter how far short a person may fall in practice in respect to the one or the other or both.

On the one hand, in their imperfection and temptation, believers will often seek refuge in dogmatic affirmation, escaping selfishly from the works of love and the risks of nonconformity involved in committing oneself to the presence of one who made his lot not with the righteous but with the rejected of this world. But they always know better, and their very lack of love of God and neighbor and their insistence that others agree with their own opinions, attitudes, and dispositions will indicate the uneasy and defensive way in which they hold their dogmatic affirmations.

On the other hand, believers will, in their doubt, seek to escape the burden of factual affirmation by identifying response to Christ's presence with making the causes of the disinherited their own (often quite automatically). But their conscience is almost always uneasy because commitment to one's neighbor may have many impulses, of which appeal to the presence of Christ in and to the neighbor is only one. Apart from the factual affirmation of Christ's presence, the association of his particular image with one's sensitivity to humanity in oneself or others will seem a halfhearted or forced undertaking.

But reference to the Spirit is the affirmation that the unique unity of Jesus Christ's identity and presence calls forth a similarly unique response. It is a response, the unity of which is rendered only by the effective gift to us of the unity of Christ's identity and presence. Reference to the Spirit or to the gift of the Spirit means that, concerning Jesus Christ and him alone, factual affirmation is completely one with faith and trust of the heart, with love of him, and love of the neighbors for whom he gave himself completely.

THE CHURCH AS CHRIST'S PRESENCE

Fourthly, when Christians speak of the Spirit as the indirect presence now of Jesus Christ and of the God who is one with him, they refer to the church. The church is both the witness to that presence and the public and communal form the indirect presence of Christ now takes, in contrast to his direct presence in his earthly days. Although we cannot even begin here to develop a "theology of the church," we should point to a certain parallel between the church and the appropriate response to Christ's presence of which we have just spoken. In the instance of the believer's response, we said that reference to the Spirit means the claim to the unity of the simultaneous gifts of factual affirmation with faith, hope, and love. In the instance of the church, reference to the Spirit means affirmation of the spatial, temporal bases of Christ's indirect presence in unity with his presence in and to the shape of public events of the world and of human history. The church is constituted by the one (his presence, which must be spatially and temporally based—even though these bases are not identical with his presence) as well as by the other (his presence to the course of human history) and by their unity.

Reference to the Spirit is the affirmation of Christ's indirect presence in this unity, which constitutes the very being of the church. But the two aspects of the church are almost always tenuously related, for it is a frail human instrument to whom Christ is only indirectly present. It is, for example, notorious that ecclesiastical bodies characterized by sacramental or Biblicist traditionalism have found passionate commitment to the fulfillment of human hopes and aspirations in history a difficult thing. On the other hand, Christian moral activists, trying hard to bestow significance on Sacraments and Biblical Word in the compass of a passionate concern for the world, have had equally great difficulty becoming convinced of—and doing justice to—the integrity of the Word and Sacrament—the two permanent or localized expressions of Christ's identity and presence. Unease in each instance is perfectly sound. It is only by reference to the Spirit, i.e., to the complete unity of Jesus Christ's identity and presence given to us now indirectly, that Word and Sacrament cohere with passionate Christian concern for the world in its mysterious passage from event to event. Of themselves and separately, the one (Sacrament or Word) is simply religious ritual and the other humane ideology, and the two have very little in common. The church is founded on and sets forth the unity of both only through the presence of Jesus Christ.

It is not easy, then, to describe the church. In one sense, it is the indirect, localized presence of Jesus Christ in and for the world. But even if we stress that he is in that community only because he is present for the whole world, the assertion still sounds so exclusive, if not arrogant, that it seems to come dangerously close to dissolving the mystery that is the presence of Christ. So it is best to go on and balance this statement by saying that the church is simply the witness to the fact that it is Jesus Christ and none other who is the ultimate presence in and to the world in its mysterious passage from event to event in public history.

This is indeed what believers must affirm, for Jesus Christ himself was declared (in the Fourth Gospel) to be a witness, and the disciples surely are not above the Master.

Nonetheless, this description also is insufficient. The relation between the church and Jesus Christ is somewhat like that between Israel and Jesus. To describe the people of Israel is to narrate its history. And to identify that people (as Christian believers are bound to do) with the identity of Jesus Christ is to narrate the history of Jesus—as we sought to do earlier—in such a way that it is seen as the individual and climactic summing up, incorporation, and identification of the whole people, by which the people receive their identification. The church likewise moves toward an as yet undisclosed historical summing up that must be narrated, though it cannot yet be because the story is unfinished and the new Israel's Kingdom of God not yet climaxed or visible in our midst.

What we are here saying is that the church has a history, indeed it is nothing other than its as yet unfinished history transpiring from event to event. The identity description that we applied to Jesus in the Gospels must, to a lesser extent and in merely analogous fashion, be applied also to the church as his people. We can only touch on what this means. The elusive, persistent, and continuous "subject" that is the church—and the indirect, abiding presence of Christ—is constituted by the Word and the Sacrament. It is therefore proper to say that they constitute the church rather than the church them. The given and instituted, spatial and temporal bases for the indirect presence of Christ allow the church that relatively permanent institutional structure without which no community can exist or be self-identical. But it is obvious that this understanding of the church as a "subject self" is analogous to rather than identical with the subject self that is Jesus. Even if we discount the complete uniqueness of Jesus, we have to say that no community or institution is a "subject" in the same way in which the term applies to an individual.

The other side of the identity description can also be applied to the church, indeed it can be applied much more directly or literally. Jesus' identity was the intention-action sequence in which he came to be who he was. His being had to be narrated, as historians and novelists must always narrate the matters they describe. He was constituted by the interaction of his character and circumstances. So also is the church. Like Jesus, like the people of Israel, the church is its history, its passage from event to event in a mysterious pattern that is dictated neither by a mechanical fate nor by an inner and necessary rhythm of the human psyche.

The intention-action pattern of the story that is the church differs from that of Jesus in at least two respects. First, the church must be a follower rather than a complete reiteration of its Lord. "To enact the good of men on their behalf" has already been done once for all. The church has no need to play the role of "Christ figure." Rather, it is called upon to be a collective disciple, to follow at a distance the pattern of exchange, serving rather than being served, and accepting (as the disciple, as differentiated from his Lord) the enrichment given to him by his neighbor. In the church's case, that neighbor is the human world at large, to which the church must be open in gratitude without forsaking its own mission and testimony. (It is surely difficult—seemingly impossible—to claim that the church is ever unambiguously true to this discipleship.)

Secondly, unlike that of Jesus, the church's intention-action pattern—evolved in the interaction of character and circumstance, of church with humanity at large through history—is obviously not finished. Reference to the presence of God in Jesus Christ in and to the church, therefore, involves an inevitable appeal to the undisclosed future and, hence, to the mysterious, distinctive future mode of that presence. Just as Jesus was at once an individual person and event and yet also the climactic summary and incorporation of that history which is the people of Israel, so the future mode of that presence will be a significant, incorporative summing up of history in a manner that we should be fools to try to imagine or forecast in literal fashion. But let us note that the history in which we try to discern pattern and movement toward summation is not a private history. History is not to be equated with a series of cultural perspectives, or with a moment of decision in which a self takes a stance of "openness" toward what will happen in any case in an unending series, regardless of what kind of action might be appropriate. Nor is history some specialized or hidden portent within public occurrences. History is public history—the intention-action pattern formed by the interaction of the church with mankind at large; and it is this history which forms the mysterious pattern of meaning to be disclosed by the presence of God in Jesus Christ in the future mode. We are saying that this presence to history means that history is neither chaotic nor fated, but providentially ordered in the life, death, and resurrection of Jesus Christ, who is Lord of the past, the present, and the future.

In this respect, as in so many others, we see in a glass darkly. But seeing darkly is not the same as discerning nothing at all. Abiding mystery is not identical with absolute unintelligibility. In our endeavor to narrate the as-yet-unfinished pattern of history, we reach for parables that might serve to set forth a kind of pattern, though not to confine history and the mysterious providence of God to these symbolic meanings. Sequences of events differ from each other sufficiently widely and always take place in a sufficiently unexpected manner so that we cannot claim that any set of images or parables can give us *the* clue to the pattern of history.

One such parable is the apostle Paul's sense of a mysterious fitness between God's choice of the Gentiles in and by his rejection of his own chosen people, Israel, and the salvation of this same people: "For the gifts and the call of God are irrevocable. Just as you were once disobedient to God but now have received mercy because of their disobedience, so they have now been disobedient in order that by the mercy shown you they also may receive mercy. For God has consigned all men to disobedience, that he may have mercy upon all" (*Rom. 11:29-32*). The interaction pattern here worked out may serve as a possible parable for the providential presence of God in Jesus Christ to the history that takes place in the interaction of the church with humanity at large. In a sense, that means that the really significant events may well transpire among the "Gentiles" from whom the church ("Israel") receives the enrichment of her own humanity. Humanity at large is the neighbor given to the church, through whom Christ is present to the church. It follows that, even though events in history, such as the imperative move toward church reunion, are important, there are other events in the history of mankind at large that may parabolically bespeak the presence of Christ in a far more significant and evident way.

This brings us to our second parable: Jesus Christ, precisely because he is not only an individual but an individual in a narrated story, serves as a parable. Hints of the pattern of union through the agonized exchange of radical opposites do break forth in history. In the story of Jesus itself this stage is not simply transcended by his resurrection. Unlike the dying and rising savior myth, Jesus' death remains a once-for-all and significant occasion that has its own final and ineradicable "thereness," after the fashion of all historical events. The same is true of all terrible sacrifices dimly setting forth the same pattern. The pattern itself looks toward reconciliation, redemption, and resurrection, but as yet there is no full realization of it for the creatures of history, though the hope is there.

Surely the pattern of this agony and hope may be discerned in such instances as a nation of brothers fighting a civil war to purge itself of the curse of slavery and so achieve concretely a union previously little more than a contractual arrangement. One may dimly discern the same pattern in the equally agonized and uncertain fight of the same nation to complete the unfinished task of reconciliation of those who have lived in estrangement from each other because of racial discrimination. Dare we hope that the terrible suffering inflicted on a small East Asian people by the defensive provinciality of a large power may someday in retrospect exhibit the same pattern of reconciliation of extreme opposites, instead of mere aimless and terrible futility?

We may hope that it will, but we cannot do more than that. The parabolic application of Christ's passion and resurrection is limited. It does not light up all history. (It is, in the first place, not a parable at all, but an event climactically summing up a long series of events.) This is the clue it provides: There will be a summing up of history, a summing up of the history of the church together with the world. It will be a summing up in which not only the events we find significant by the use of certain parables but *all* events will find their place: the technological revolution with its present hopes *and* fears, the marvelous secular integrity of the sciences, the fight against poverty and discrimination, the agony of the Vietnamese people, the reunion of the church, the gift of literature and the arts, the horror of overpopulation as well as the fight against it and the despoliation of nature, the search for humaneness and for the care of people's souls—in short, a summing up of the story of humanity within the vast world of nature. This is the Christian's hope in the future mode of the presence of Jesus Christ, of which the interaction of life in the church and the world is for him a token and a pledge.

The past cannot be an absolute clue to the future, if the future is a genuinely open one. Not even the event of Jesus Christ can be such an absolute clue. The providential action of God over and in his creation is not that of a mechanical fate to be read off of one occasion. God's work is mysteriously, abidingly mysteriously, coexistent with the contingency of events. The history of his providence is one that must be narrated. There is no scientific rule to describe it and eliminate the need for narration. Nor is there any historicist perspective or universal claim that can eliminate history's narrative form. That is why Christians, precisely because they believe in providence, know far less than certain ideological groups about the shape of the future, e.g., the Marxists. Christians can always engage in grateful colloquy with Marxists because, unlike certain others, such as existentialists, Christians and Marxists are both concerned with the future shape of public history; but agreement with Marxists will be difficult for Christian believers precisely because faith in the providential government of the world allows for far less knowledge of the future than the Marxists have in their ideological clue to what must happen.

To be consistent, then, the Christian believer must apply the reserve of not knowing even to his own faith in the future presence of Jesus Christ. The event that sums up cannot simply be assumed to be a repetition of the past event. For that reason, the believer must abide by the New Testament's complex rather than simple identification of God and Jesus—an identification that can only be narrated; to describe it in the abstract merely involves a reaffirmation at the conceptual level both of the unity and of the distinctness of God and Jesus in the resurrection appearances. The believer must affirm that the future summing up will be that of God with whom Jesus Christ is one, rather than simply a recapitulation in more enormous scope of the events of the story of Jesus. Beyond this confession the believer cannot go. Either to affirm that it is simply Jesus Christ as he was in past history, or to affirm that it is simply God manifest in Jesus rather than Jesus Christ himself, who will stand at the latter end, is an unwarranted short-cut of the New Testament's complexity and therefore an illegitimate dissolution of its mysteriousness.

THE MODE OF CHRIST'S PRESENCE NOW

What in the meantime of the spatial and temporal manner in which the present mode of Christ's presence is effectively there for the believer? John's Gospel in particular suggests a strange reversal of roles which it asks us to believe. The center of the Christian message is a mystery—the presence of God. To that center, to that message, Jesus Christ himself is a witness, so that he points away from himself to God. But the mysterious reversal is that the witness who points away from himself is the one who is witnessed to by the very God and the very Spirit to whom he witnesses. By analogy the feeble, often naive and simple word of written Scripture—and even its usually pathetic, clumsy interpretation in the spoken word—becomes a true witness, yet more than a witness. The Word does indeed witness to that which it is not, the presence of God in Jesus Christ. But far more important is the fact that indirectly (rather than directly, as in the case of Jesus Christ) God witnesses to it, that he makes himself present to it so that the Word may become the temporal basis of the Spirit who is the presence of God in Jesus Christ. The witness of Scripture to God is sure, not of itself, but because the witness of God to Scripture is faithful and constant.

Similarly, the spatial basis of the presence of God in Jesus Christ now in the Sacraments is, by the order and promise of Jesus Christ given in his word, the self-communication of his self-focused identity. The Sacrament is not identical with his physical presence—for he is not physically present now—but it is the self-communication in physical form of one who is self-focused to us who cannot know self-focused presence except in physical form.

To the believer, the verbal and spatial bases of Christ's presence are the compelling means by which God's presence in Jesus Christ comes to be identical with his effective act of self-presentation now. The one who so gives himself is the very presence of the God of providence, whose grateful and obedient sons and daughters we are called to be in the breadth of our private and public lives, in our prayers, in the church, and in the world. The name and identity of Jesus Christ, set forth in the narrative of the New Testament, call upon the believer for nothing less than this discipleship.

EPILOGUE

A MEDITATION FOR THE
WEEK OF GOOD FRIDAY AND EASTER

Let us reflect on how we dispose ourselves toward the story of this week, and then let us think about the story itself.

It is one thing to hear or read a story for the first time. It is quite another to have heard it many times before and to trace it through again. In the first case the sense of an ending is in the anticipation; in the second the sense of an ending is simply our agreement or disagreement that the end is right and proper.

We cannot act as if we did not know the Easter story's outcome. Try as we may to provide suspense, we cannot elicit surprise about the reversal from grim failure to sublime triumph. We can only recite the story in a way reminding us of what we all know: the road to Easter Sunday is by way of Good Friday, and Christians have always insisted that this is the sequence and the end, and that both sequence and end are fitting and right. But we must also remember that religious stories are not recited simply for their moral or artistic interest. As long as they have any hold on us at all, their *recital* represents a *reenactment*. The Jewish tradition knows this better than the Christian, and some other religions know it better yet. To tell it is to have it happen again. A bedside tale to a child gains rather than loses from being told over and over again. How much more so religious stories that are part of the effective ritual of a living community! Mircea Eliade (in many of his books) goes so far as to suggest that in archaic societies the function of certain common rituals, including certain stories, is to obliterate or annul time, that inflicter of unbearable pain and inward homelessness. Through ritual, communities return and stand at the beginning again, made regenerate by the touch or recital of the things that happened—as we say—"once upon a time," and happen now by reenactment and retelling.

In one way this is true of this week's story in the Christian calendar. In the sweep of this narrative we are bound together, able to identify with and recall afresh its sorrow, its sense of the innocent victim dying at the hands and in behalf of the guilty. We are even able to identify, to some extent at least, with the note of triumph at the end—even though many people take literally the portrayal of the sorrow but only symbolically the note of triumphant hope.

Two things bear mention here: first, the sense of recall, reenactment and identification in the retelling of this story gains from its association with ritual performance. The passion story and the Lord's Supper belong together. Together they render present the original; each is hobbled when it is separated from the other. Secondly, the relation between this story and its applications or illustrations is the reverse of many another instance. Other stories we bring to life by filling them with meaning and significance drawn from illustrations. Other instances of the so-called mighty acts of God in Scripture gain power over our imagination only as we ourselves supply illustrative instances for them. It is as yet true that *this* story on the contrary tends to supply meaning to other stories like it. Without it they would not make sense, or at least not the same sense. There are multitudes of crosses in the world. But it is because of *Jesus'* cross that we apply the term to all the others.

But I said that this is "as yet" the case. For the story's sense of present and vivid meaning cannot be taken for granted—and for good reason. One of the extraordinary things about this story is that, in the words of Romans 6:9-10, Christ died to sin once for all. He is never to die again. And therefore the event and the story, like all things in time, can and does recede—unlike other religious stories which annul the temporal distance again and again. There is no automatic possibility that present recall can annul the temporal distance between this story and us. It moves farther and farther back, and gets more and more pallid to our common cultural imagination.

Currently, and curiously enough, I suspect, both these contrary things are true for many people. The Easter story is present in recall for them, and yet the distance from it is great. To the extent that it is distant, it likewise tends no longer to bestow meaning on other, similar events. The reverse becomes a matter of necessity: Their vivid reality lends strength to it. In that case the original story may serve as no more than a symbolic form for gathering all these stories under a common type. Or else it simply recedes before the larger, more recent instances, and *they* then render whatever vividness is left to the cross. (In this connection I need only remind you of all that we sorrowfully feel in connection with the mention, especially on Good Friday, of the word "Auschwitz.") Again, I suspect that many people are at both ends of this contradictory situation: The central Christian story in its recited and performed reenactment is the bestower of meaning for other similar events, and yet these other events have to evoke the original and breathe life into it.

There is no single lesson to be drawn from these ambiguities or contradictory tendencies. Yet I hope that reflection on them will be of some use. If you happen to have the sort of religious imagination to which this story speaks directly, as it were in the present tense, well and good—and lucky are you. If not, it doesn't matter in the last analysis, although it may make believing a bit more trying, troubled, and lonely in our time. But in that case the important thing to remember is precisely that this story by its very nature *does* recede, it does not annul time. Ultimately therefore its capacity to be reenacted in your sensibility and your imagination cannot be the criterion of its significance for you. And surely, the followers of Jesus Christ have recognized this from the very beginning. For whomever it becomes the truth it does so not by imaginative obliteration of time but by hammering out a shape of life patterned after its own shape. That does not mean that we repeat the original events literally in our lives, and certainly not completely, but it means that our lives reflect the story as in a glass darkly. The shape of the story being mirrored in the shape of our life is the condition of its being meaningful for us.

Many of you will recall Schweitzer's perverse but great account of Jesus' ministry and hope in *The Quest of the Historical Jesus*. Its enigmatic final paragraph remains a true account of the way the Easter story becomes a truth for us, even though it may have receded in time and may not have recall power:

> He comes to us as One unknown, without a name, as of old, by the lake-side, He came to those men who knew him not. He speaks to us the same word: "Follow thou me!" and sets us to the tasks which He has to fulfil for our time. He commands. And to those who obey Him, whether they be wise or simple, He will reveal Himself in the toils, the conflicts, the sufferings which they shall pass through in His fellowship, and, as an ineffable mystery they shall learn in their own experience Who He is.[1]

"Follow thou me!" It would be frightening to preach on that text. I want simply to draw your attention to what this passage and that text in particular, have in common with the passage from Romans to which I referred earlier. It does not say there "follow him," but in 6:4 Paul tells us that whereas being baptized means being buried with Christ, Christ's being raised means that our feet are set on a new path of life. And again in verses 12-14 he suggests that the embodiment of the Easter story's

---

1. *The Quest of the Historical Jesus* (New York: Macmillan, 1956), p. 403.

pattern in our lives means no mysterious archetypal consciousness of it, but a new way of governing our bodies. That is how we are in touch with the story. A little humdrum perhaps, considering the dramatic quality of what happened at Easter. But the point is clear in these as in Schweitzer's words: To know this story is to adopt a way of life consequent upon hearing it and shaped by it. That is how we are to be disposed toward it

But I think we may learn something more from its receding in time: not only about the way to dispose ourselves toward the story, but about the story itself. Schweitzer said that "He comes to us as One unknown, without a name." The Apostle Paul said that having died once Christ is never to die again, but that living—having been raised—he "lives to God." What I understand both men to be saying is this: The distance between Jesus Christ and us is not *simply* that of lengthening time. Even if we could annul the time and have the story present, a distance would still be there. He would still be One unknown to us. Only Christ's dying, not his now living to God, is literally in the same time sequence in which we live and die. *Reenactment can no more make him present than the passage of time can bear him away.* Indeed, even our life shaped by his story is no final clue to his identity and presence, but only a mirror of his story. The crosses of Christ's many brothers and sisters are not identical with his cross, any more than the shape of our life is identical with the shape of the events of this week in the Gospels. Why not? Because he lives to God—not to time in which he recedes from us, nor to the obliteration or annulment of time, in which he would be present now in the representation of his story. He does not live in or by his distance from or his presence to us: He lives to God. That is his life, not ours, or rather ours only in him.

There is a veil between his life and ours which we can comprehend neither by time span, nor imagination, nor even the Christian life. The life he lives to God is not accessible to us, although it is mirrored in all life. Even his cross, though mirrored in the innumerable crosses of the sons of men, is his own and bids us keep our distance. He died alone, though in the company of others and on behalf of a multitude. He was raised alone, though as the first of a multitude. His cross and his resurrection are a secret place all his own, for they leave behind every common medium, every comparison by which we know things. Living to God he is the Lord of life: He is life. Dying for his brothers and his enemies, he was the Lord of pity. He *was* pity—pity for the weak, pity for the strong. He is life and pity; he is love. Such knowledge is too high for us, we cannot attain to it. We know pity and being pitied, and Nietzsche's sound warning against the weak's tyrannical use of pitifulness in their conquest of the strong. But neither Nietzsche nor any of us know what it is to be pitied by the strong—the Lord of life himself—whose pity of us, in which he himself becomes weak, is not weakness but his strength which he *perfects* and does not *abandon* in weakness. Such pity, such love, such life remain the secret of a disposition we do not know. Before this incomparable thing we must ultimately fall silent and be grateful. Here the scale of life, of love, and of pity is *perfected* and yet *breaks down* in excess. Our Christian forefathers knew this and, trying to express it in classical idiom, called this disposition a passionless love in contrast to our passionate love. No doubt we must change the idiom, but like them we shall still have to express the perfection of the scale and its being broken, exceeded infinitely. The everlasting veil remains between him and us, but the story we have heard again today is that of a Lordship, a life and a love embracing both sides of the veil.

George Herbert spoke most appropriately concerning the veil and the story's embrace of both sides of it, the perfection of the scale and its being exceeded—all parts of this story:

> Love is that liquor sweet and most divine
> Which my God feels as blood, and I as wine.